The Unremarkable Wordsworth

Theory and History of Literature
Edited by Wlad Godzich and Jochen Schulte-Sasse

For other books in the series, see p. 248

The Unremarkable Wordsworth

Geoffrey H. Hartman

Foreword by Donald G. Marshall

Theory and History of Literature, Volume 34

University of Minnesota Press, Minneapolis

Published by the University of Minnesota Press
2037 University Avenue Southeast, Minneapolis, MN 55414
Published simultaneously in Canada by
Fitzhenry & Whiteside Limited, Markham.
Printed in the United States of America.

Permission was granted by the publisher for reproducing the
following chapters:

Chapters 5 and 9: "Wordsworth and Goethe in Literary History," *New Literary History,*
vol. 6, No. 2, Winter 1975, pp. 393–413; "The Use and Abuse of Structural Analysis:
Riffaterre's Interpretation of Wordsworth's 'Yew-Trees'," *New Literary History,* vol. 7,
No. 1, Autumn 1975, pp. 165–89. Chapter 6: "Blessing the Torrent: On Wordsworth's Later
Style," *PMLA,* 93 (1978), pp. 196–204, reprinted by permission of the Modern Language
Association of America. Chapter 7: "Words, Wish, Worth: Wordsworth," by Geoffrey
Hartman; from *Deconstruction and Criticism* by Harold Bloom, et al.; reprinted by
permission of The Continuum Publishing Company. Chapter 8: "Diction and Defense,"
copyright © 1980 by the Forum on Psychiatry and the Humanities of the Washington School
of Psychiatry; reprinted by permission of Yale Univesity Press. Chapter 11: "The Poetics of
Prophecy" by Geoffrey Hartman, in *High Romantic Argument: Essays for M. H. Abrams,*
edited by Lawrence Lipking, pp. 15–40; copyright © 1981 by Cornell University Press.

The following chapters were published previously:

Chapter 1: "Wordsworth," *The Yale Review* LVII, No. 4, Summer 1969. Chapter 2: "A
Touching Compulsion. Wordsworth and the Problem of Literary Representation," *The
Georgia Review* XXI, No. 2, Summer 1977. Chapter 3: "Wordsworth, Inscriptions and
Romantic Nature Poetry," in *From Sensibility to Romanticism: Essays Presented to
Frederick A. Pottle,* edited by F. W. Hillis and H. Bloom, Oxford Univesity Press, 1965. Chapter
4: "False Themes and Gentle Minds," *Philological Quarterly,* vol. 47, No. 1, January 1968,
pp. 55–68, University of Iowa, Iowa City. Chapter 14: "The Unremarkable Wordsworth" in
On Signs by Marshall Blonsky, Johns Hopkins University Press, 1985.

Library of Congress Cataloging-in-Publication Data

Hartman, Geoffrey H.
    The unremarkable Wordsworth.

    (Theory and History of Literature; v. 34)
    Bibliography: p.
    Includes index.
    1. Wordsworth, William, 1770–1850—Criticism and Interpretations.
I. Title. II. Series.
PR5888.H368 1987   821'.7   86-24887
ISBN O-8166-1175-0
ISBN O-8166-1176-9 (pbk.)

The University of Minnesota is an equal-opportunity
educator and employer.

Contents

Foreword
Wordsworth and Post-Enlightenment Culture
Donald G. Marshall

The appearance twenty-five years ago of *Wordsworth's Poetry* marked an epoch in the study of that poet and of romanticism generally. It was perhaps the last moment at which a reputation in literary study could be made solely by commentary on a single canonical poet. Hartman's essays on Wordsworth written in the intervening quarter century and gathered here are once again revolutionary, though their character and importance are much less likely to be perceived and absorbed. This difference tells us a great deal about the evolution of criticism, about Hartman's own career, and perhaps something also about Wordsworth.

Above all, it was the conclusions of Hartman's earlier study which were thought to be innovative. According to the common view, in Wordsworth the synthetic, creative and sympathetic power of imagination, nourished on a popular tradition of ballad and romance with roots in the great poetry pre-dating the Enlightenment, asserted itself against an instrumentalist reason, which in poetry took the form of a masquerade in the robes of conscious and merely willed classicism. Wordsworth found the true source of imagination: in nature and particularly in the poet's experience of nature during childhood, when he was most open to its varied and spirited influence. The language in which this recollected experience was transformed into the guide of later life and feeling derived from the ordinary language of men, particularly rural men, whose lives preserved the great rhythms of pastoral and agricultural life, recorded in and mediated by the Bible, anonymous folk poetry, and related literary forms. Hartman demonstrated instead an antagonism or dialectic between nature and imagination in Wordsworth. Imagination's power to draw the self into an autonomous, "apocalyptic" transcendence terrified Wordsworth. Against its risks, he set the healing continuities and mediations of nature.

In this reception, the question of Hartman's method in reaching these conclusions was overlooked or assimilated to a familiar model. Despite a few references to continental thinkers, he appeared simply to have read Wordsworth more closely and carefully and thus by a power of attentive sympathy to have escaped the clichéd and overhasty interpretation which imposed on Wordsworth the categories of a general view of English romanticism drawn chiefly from the history of ideas. Close reading again proved its validity against "high priori" historicism. But Hartman's achievement was taken as a tribute to his critical gifts, to his sympathetic and intense attention to the poetry itself, not as the product of a self-conscious and philosophically grounded method. The intervening quarter century has dramatically changed the nature of literary study, and now nothing will be widely read that cannot claim a place in the spreading polemics of "literary theory." Hartman has been a leader in this ivory palace revolution, and these essays intervene in a wide range of contemporary theoretical approaches, from psychoanalysis to structuralism, from deconstruction to phenomenology. Yet Wordsworth remains so much the focus of the book that "critical method" is strangely transmuted. It is not that Hartman measures theory by its usefulness for interpretation, nor even that he "tests" it against poems. Rather, he opens an interchange between contemporary currents and Wordsworth which has the reciprocal and dialogical character of genuine thought. It is questionable whether either the experts on Wordsworth or the experts on theory are prepared to enter such a dialogue.

Hartman's watchword has always been "beyond formalism." A doctoral student at Yale in the early '50's, he stood at the confluence of the two great streams in modern literary study: German philology, incarnated in Erich Auerbach, and Anglo-American formalism, practiced by Cleanth Brooks, Robert Penn Warren, and W. K. Wimsatt. His earlier work—represented here by the essays on inscriptions and romantic nature poetry, on Wordsworth and Goethe, and on "False Themes and Gentle Minds"—brilliantly synthesized the two, anchoring formalist analysis in the poet's concrete situation in literary and general history and animating historical scholarship with an acute sensitivity to poetic values and possibilities. In the general cultural upheaval of the late '60's and after, many literary critics found formalism bankrupt or repressive and reached out for fresh ideas to other disciplines—psychoanalysis, anthropology, marxism, linguistics, structuralism, and the philosophical movement of deconstruction. But for Hartman, "beyond formalism" never meant, as it did for many others, abandoning the disciplines of close reading and rhetorical analysis or replacing them with the deconstructive art of tangling and untangling "textuality." His book *Criticism in the Wilderness* (1980) showed his acute sensitivity to this contemporary situa-tion, which he characteristically presents not simply as an abstract clash of critical positions, but as concretely woven into the fabric of American and academic cultural life. The more recent essays in this volume repeatedly position Hartman "beyond formalism" in the Nietzschean sense of "jenseits," where formalist reading encounters alien modes of thought, neither to repel nor submit to them, but to raise the voltage of reading by sustaining a polar tension. It is precisely from such confrontations that Hartman clarifies the autonomy of the poem and its language, not only as what escapes the terms of alien systems, but as a special quality those alien terms take on in the specific context of criticism. Through Wordsworth, we can read Hegel's *Aufhebung* as "elation," and perhaps even "English" Heidegger's strange German.

What characterizes Hartman's "method"—though it cannot really be called that—is that when he takes up his major concerns, like time in "Timely Utterance" or "the subject" in "A Touching Compulsion," he cannot be said to take them either as simply thematic or formal categories. They are qualities of a peculiar kind which inhabit the poetry like the power of thought itself. Instead of calling what Hartman does a "method," one simply wants to say he is *thinking* with and about the poem. Reading and thinking are here one and inseparable. Hartman's feeling for language, his uncanny ear for sounds, evident even in the title of "Words, Wish, Worth," provides the ground for connecting them, just as it does for a poet like Wordsworth. Such a ground has a perplex-ingly shadowy materiality, not due to any putative universal abstractness of language, but due rather to a strangely physical grasp of every utterance's open-ness to and resonance with other utterances, present and—above all—past. Hart-man's gift is the power to hear echoes and to write a criticism as echo-chamber. This is not quite what is called "intertextuality," for what is at stake is not the disseminated play of signifiers, but having "ears to hear." This is evident in Hart-man's repeated concern in these essays for the kind of *act* an utterance is, and his combination of a precise grammar for naming these acts and his skill at rooting them in human situations and feelings carry him far beyond speech-act theory on the one hand and psychoanalysis on the other. Hartman shows also that the integration of the sound and force of language into a poem is a work of form. In his critique of structuralism and elsewhere, he keeps alive the historical reality genre has for the composing poet. But at no level of formal analysis are we deal-ing with a "method," for any separation of the critic from the poet being read will interrupt and still the reverberations which animate the reading. Not that Hartman "becomes one" with the poet he is reading. Instead, he makes of his consciousness, paradoxically, a self-consciousness for another, and hence, a self-consciousness impossible to the poet studied. Self-consciousness is, of course, not a method, but an intensification of consciousness itself. Consequently, when Hartman feels obliged to reflect on his own approach, he suffers the elusiveness and "embarrassment" (in its etymological sense, an "obstacle" or "blockage") of his subject, instead of lapsing into the impersonality of a discourse on method.

The "speculative" relation between critic and poet I have suggested invites reflection on the particularity of Wordsworth for Hartman. One could say that for Hartman, Wordsworth is characteristically the poet of ghostly middles. His narrators are not quite personal, not quite impersonal: Wordsworth is a shadowy subject, neither the definite ego Keats complained about, nor the disappearing subjectivity of Mallarmé, and yet despite its shadowiness, we are in the poet's mind, the main region of his song. Referentiality in Wordsworth has the same ghostly quality. He does not quite refer definitely, so that his "descriptive" poetry peculiarly blends "the fallen sublimity of classicizing or poetic diction. . . with the naturalism of elemental speech-acts of wishing, blessing, naming." And yet any tendency to take leave of the real world for a transcendent or apocalyptic realm is chastized, and natural mediators are re-inserted. Temporality likewise is middle: we get stopping or fixation (and all the sound devices and rhetorical turns which arrest progress), and yet there is a struggling move forward, a sort of quasi- or emptied-out narrative gesture, the anticipation of a possible narrative. Wordsworth scrupulously tells stories about the dead, he fictionalizes very reluctantly; but the scruple and the reluctance testify to a hidden force or attraction. The style similarly works a borderland between ordinary language and extraordinary language. One cannot decide whether the characteristic "there is. . ." introduces unemphatic description or the aura of sacral attentiveness.

One reason to occupy and stress this borderland is not just its critique of positivism, which has few defenders anyway, but its more implicit critique of deconstruction or of what we might think of as its methodological definiteness. Hartman wants not to decide on all those separations—spoken/written; inside/outside; metaphorical/literal; and so on—which must be asserted to give deconstructive analysis its purchase. Hartman thinks about this issue not only in terms of consciousness and self-consciousness: for him the quest to limit self-consciousness has always been definitive of romanticism. Even more, it is an issue of the sacred and the secular. Is deconstruction a thoroughly secular mode of thinking? Derrida would not say so, but would, undoubtedly, undo the opposition of secular to sacred: certainly, the secular takes its meaning from its opposition to the sacred, so that "thoroughly secular" is a contradiction in terms. Derrida has entertained the possibility that deconstruction may turn out to be a sort of negative theology, and he has been willing to hear and even encourage the explorations of those who see in deconstruction a necessary cleansing of every idolatry. But even where negative theology devours not only metaphysical, but ecclesiastical and institutional presuppositions (as in Kierkegaard), it makes clear its maieutic or propaedeutic position. Derrida has not said what deconstruction in his view leads to. De Man is perhaps even more austere. It is true that we might speculate that for him deconstruction unsettles every possibility of fixing a legitimated claim in language, a claim that could be translated into political, social, or even intellectual coercion. Yet de Man never actually said so, and in his last essays, he was already rebuking skeptics who seemed quite certain of what they did not know. His real dedication was rather to the reading of particular texts—or, rather, corpuses of texts, oeuvres—that, as he with surprisingly cheerful naivete remarked, "interested" him. Deconstruction poses less a critique of the sacred from the perspective of the secular than the question of what the experience and understanding of the sacred could possibly be, or more accurately what experience and understanding of the sacred could become possible only in a "secularized" world.

For Hartman, as for Walter Benjamin, poetic forms emerge from the life-forms of human beings before the French and Industrial Revolutions. The whole burden of the Enlightenment and its ambiguous outcome—the triumph and catastrophe of the French Revolution; the economic advance coupled with the diurnal oppression of the Industrial Revolution—weighs on these forms, as it weighs on the life they bring to speech. One can scarcely ignore science and the new questionableness of all institutions. Jean-François Lyotard has spoken of the breakdown of the "grand narratives," and indeed narrative itself, as a way of understanding human life, has been brought into question by theorists, just as practitioners have exposed its devices and by obstructing its conventional forms resisted its thoughtless consumption. In positive terms, these new experiences of human existence, so corrosive to traditional modes of thought and representation, demand their own responsive expression. Did not Wordsworth himself imagine a poetry which would have fully assimilated science? One could exemplify the opposition by Freud's *Future of an Illusion* and Buber's *I and Thou*. The central question for Freud is whether science can become ethos, can organize the conduct of human life, providing us with the assurance and the collective power of decision which enable fruitful individual work. He wants to answer that it can, but his language is so traversed with irony, with litotic double negatives, with futures merely imagined, instead of grasped with firm concreteness, that one can scarcely avoid the impression of a liberalism rather nostalgic for Voltaire than ready confidently to seize its destined place in history. Buber, on the other hand, can lucidly denounce the dried-out hollowness of modern life, prolonging a critique which reaches back by way of Nietzsche to romanticism itself. Yet he suffers his own evasions before a contemporary world all too susceptible to religious revival, to appeals to the immediacy of transcendence. Buber must insist repeatedly on transcendence's "in-dwelling," on its presence only through a glittering shard of mica, a tree, the love of one's spouse. The relation of encountered object to ineffable meaning is not merely allegorical: we are to be impelled to action, not just contemplation. But can this encounter be made difficult enough, demanding enough to escape resourceful self-delusion? The question here is the renewal of the symbol. For Freud, symbols are the mere instruments of purposive communication: if relation contains moral insights, why cloak reasonable claims in the fantastic imagery of outmoded superstition? Buber seems to attribute to the symbol intrinsic value, but even if the incarnation of meaning can escape the corrosive critique of the I-it, is our relation to an I-thou encounter solely one of obedience devoid of critique?

In Wordsworth, the elusive interplay between the sacred and the secular takes some exemplary concrete forms. We may focus, for example, as Hartman does, on the "subject" or self. The Enlightenment apparently replaced a religious conception of the creation of the subject with a secular idea, *Bildung*. Gordon Craig quotes the novelist Berthold Auerbach: "formerly the religious spirit proceeded from revelation, the present starts with *Bildung*," which aims to bring the "inner liberation and deliverance of man, his true rebirth." The contrast is between an abrupt and decisive foundational experience according to a single, teleological model ("conversion," followed by an *imitatio Christi)* and the natural and steady formation of an open and unique character. But *Bildung* retained the sense of a mysterious and transcendent force in individual development, as in the rituals orchestrated by a hidden Masonic order in *The Magic Flute* and *Wilhelm Meister's Apprenticeship*. Yet this force was normally translated from a divine providence into the hovering presence of cultural tradition. The self's foundation is abrupt, as in Christian "conversion," but Wordsworth feels immensely the dangers of that abrupt and discontinuous self: its solipsism, its temptation to an arrogant belief that it is self-created, its emergence at the price of the loss of nurturing love-objects (perhaps the mother, perhaps whatever lies behind all sense of being "mothered"). In tension with this experience, Wordsworth does not so much describe as forge—in every sense—the development of his own mind. This is, paradoxically, Wordsworth's tribute to the Enlightenment: imagination is set against tradition or history, just, strangely, as "science" was, and in both cases the formal idea of "progress" endows critique with a positive shape.

We can certainly put this in terms closer to poetic issues. In the Enlightenment, we find a tension between acknowledging any of the fantastic and enthusiastic strains of earlier poetry and the severe demands of a rational standard which required that poetic meaning be discursive or presented in firmly limned allegories immediately translatable into familiar ideas. The chief poetic virtue was not metaphor or imagery, but the capacity to convey with utmost economy a meaning that was complex, yet clear and condensed. The "classical" assumed its chief value as a means to this shorthand communication, this poetry through abbreviation. To put it this way is to claim that "neo-classicism" is less a living tradition than an assumed part of the audience's socialization, a merely cultural fact, so that the audience is immediately limited and focused ("gentlemen"). Poetry's (and culture's) asserted claim to universality is exposed as a refusal to acknowledge any audience wider than a socially determinate class. Concomitantly, history itself is emptied out. It becomes absorbed into science, something with which it is ultimately profoundly at odds: history becomes a matter of fact, instead of a matter of meaning, namely, a great collection of stories we would not willingly let die. The echoes of tradition in eighteenth-century poetry are conscious devices of communication, that is, decorous conventions sustained by an act of will between poet and (narrow) audience, but surrounded by the steadily encroaching territory of immediate matter of scientific fact.

Wordsworth could see this much (as could some Enlightenment writers as well—Edward Young and William Collins, for example). And it is not quite true that his response was merely to reject all tradition. Scholars have stressed Wordsworth's consciousness of an underlying popular tradition, alive in the country far from London, and absorbing into its essential orality even such written works as the Bible and Milton. But it is the orality which matters most: Coleridge simply missed the point by claiming that whatever poetic merits can be found in ordinary rural language derive from the Bible read in church. Moreover, it is not just that this undergound "tradition" dwells only behind the poetry as a ghostly resonance, it is that even this tradition is forced to pass through the archimedean point of the poet's subjectivity. As a consequence, it is difficult to argue that one must attend to anything traditional in Wordsworth: was there ever a poet whose work was less illuminated by knowledge of any or all of the history of Western culture? Such a knowledge simply gives us no foothold on what seems actually important here. That so much poetic power could be achieved without any cultural "backing," so to speak, remains astonishing. Nor, despite and in fact because of its "subjectivity," does his poetry rest on his biography, or at least not on the researches of biographers. Even when they uncover a sensation like Wordsworth's affair with Annette Vallon and the illegitimate daughter she bore him; or the painful losses he suffered from the untimely deaths of family members or the madness of Dorothy: even on these matters, the muted discretion of his poetry forces a recognition that Wordsworth's subjectivity is not confessional, but a mythic or more accurately epic creation.

We can therefore recognize in Wordsworth something characteristic of culture since the Enlightenment: the liquidation of the public sphere, to invoke the terms of Hannah Arendt's *The Human Condition*. It is by now difficult even to imagine that sphere, still less to find a language that is plausible and concrete in which to speak of it. To say that the public sphere is the realm of politics is to invite the illusion of understanding, for the "political" here is something different from the particular and always transitory issues in which it presents itself to contemporary men and women. When politics and history return in the later Wordsworth, they are, as Hartman suggests, parochial—narrow and local, revealing a lack of reflection and experience in any wider cultural or public sphere. In the quite terrible *Ecclesiastical Sonnets* and *Sonnets on Capital Punishment*, but also in *The Excursion*, one sees Wordsworth struggling to break out of his older style, reaching for large cultural topoi, and failing, lapsing repeatedly back into his mere self. The learning in these poems is as frigid as anything eighteenth-century poetry has to offer, and the poet's mind keeps drifting from the topic at hand to worry over what it all means to a poet young or old.

This sort of direct political or pretentiously moralizing poetry is itself testimony to the loss of the public realm. The displacement of the public by the private is visible in the sense that subject matter is unimportant, that there need be no agreement within a culture about what ideas, what symbols, what stories matter in an enduring way (and I repeat my assertion that the "neo-classical" agreement about these matters was merely contingent and quite rightly invalidated by the French Revolution). Too much of the claim on public attention depends on the poet's mere personality. That the mythic form of that personality we know as *The Prelude* remained unpublished is not the issue: publishing it would not have helped, for insight into the public affairs of human beings cannot be authorized by recollections of childhood. For the first time in history, so far as I know, a poet actually thinks his best work will be done when he is young, instead of imagining a career that moves toward its climax in an intelligence and craft acquired through long experience. The prominence given to youth, to insights whose value is claimed to lie precisely in their lack of reflection and experience, which are thought not to validate, but to dim or block insight, marks decisively the loss of the public realm. To get a sense of what engagement with the largest possibilities of the human enterprise in an era might mean we have to recall how Aeschylus struggles with the full dimensions of justice, how Vergil wrestles with the idea of the Roman imperium, how even Catullus incarnates the displacement of the aristocrat from history into a new world of eroticism. After Wordsworth, poetry has persisted in obtruding private and arbitrary experiences into the place where it itself feels it ought to encounter a public discourse, which is nevertheless lacking. Even Orwell had the greatest difficulty re-opening that sphere, though I think in his essays he succeeded in doing so.

Unquestionably, the source of Wordsworth's power lies elsewhere, and I think the only way to characterize that source is to say that it is religious. I am of course thinking of Augustinian Christianity's challenge to the obviously decayed remains of Roman public life. In place of the rhetor, who takes control of a situation by powerfully deploying a freely-invented discourse, Augustine puts the preacher, whose task is to find a mediating exposition between an audience closed within historical contingency and a canonically fixed text to whose letter and spirit he is bound to remain faithful (consequently dissolving the criteria which relate hierarchies of subject matter and style). In place of the citizen or "legal person," Augustine puts the individual self before God. And so on. I do not mean to discount the persisting power of Rome as a sort of determining after image, not only in the very organization of the *ecclesia*, but even in the counterformulation of a "City of God." But the core of Augustine's *Confessions* is its relocation of what had been a public religiosity of observances at once cultic and civic into a problematic and dynamic self, seeking its relation to its transcendent source and to the world it inhabits.

Wordsworth's sense of his own situation is surprisingly parallel. While the *Prelude* traces imagination to its sources in childhood, it is the French Revolution which emerges as the focus of the poet's own spirit when he returns home even before that event. In Britain, he finds himself out of sympathy with his government and even with his fellow citizens—severed like an "alien" from the prayers for British victory offered up in rural churches. This experience, Wordsworth remarks, was the first "shock" to his moral nature "that might be named/A revolution":

> All else was progress on a self-same path
> On which with a diversity of pace
> I had been travelling; this, a stride at once
> Into another region.
>
> (*Prelude*, 1805, X,238-41)

Yet the division here introduced between an attachment to his country rooted in childhood and a present conviction of the Revolution's rightness does not produce blockage and despair. In fact, his political awareness rises above the immediate political circumstances, good or ill, and leads him to general reflections on the "management/Of Nations." It is in this mood that he breaks into the great lines, "Bliss was it in that dawn to be alive,/But to be young was very heaven!" (1805, X,692-93) Using a word of exceptional importance for him, "spots," Wordsworth connects this political consciousness with a newly universal appreciation of nature: "Not favored spots alone, but the whole earth, /The beauty wore of promise." (1805, X,701-02) The passage concludes with another great expression of an essentially political faith: dreamers nurtured in the sublimity and beauty of nature could now "exercise their skill" at schemes of reform not on utopian insubstantialities,

> But in the very world which is the world
> Of all of us, the place in which, in the end,
> We find our happiness, or not at all.
>
> (1805, X,725-27)

Wordsworth then looked at the earth, he says, as does an heir first visiting his estates, delighted at the prospect of improving and perfecting them. This fusion of an aroused political consciousness with his persisting feeling for nature is destroyed by Britain's declaration of war and France's launching of an ultimately imperialist and acquisitive counterattack against all Europe. Only in the wake of this political disappointment does Wordsworth elaborate a different frame for his experience, the opposition of "reason" to "imagination." And it is in the course of that elaboration that the fundamental element in his conception of personal development reaches self-conscious formulation:

> There are in our existence spots of time,
> Which with distinct preeminence retain
> A renovating virtue, whence, depressed
> By false opinion and contentious thought,
> Or aught of heavier or more deadly weight
> Of ordinary intercourse, our minds
> Are nourished and invisibly repaired—
> A virtue, by which pleasure is enhanced,
> That penetrates, enables us to mount
> When high, more high, and lifts us up when fallen.
> This efficacious spirit chiefly lurks
> Among those passages of life in which
> We have had deepest feeling that the mind
> Is lord and master, and that outward sense
> Is but the obedient servant of her will.
> Such moments, worthy of all gratitude,
> Are scattered everywhere, taking their date
> From our first childhood—in our childhood even
> Perhaps are most conspicuous. Life with me,
> As far as memory can look back, is full
> Of this beneficent influence.

(1805, XI, 257-78)

There follow two exceptionally bizarre episodes, that of stumbling at the age of six onto an ancient and long-disused place of execution and that of waiting on a hillside among a single sheep, a blasted tree, and a stone wall for the horses being brought to bear him home from school at Christmastime. These moments are so obviously endowed with a sacred aura that I think one can set in Wordsworth the lure of a self essentially founded in a late adolescent or adult awakening to public, political life against the final assertion of a self whose source and development, it is claimed retroactively, are rooted in deeply cryptic religious encounters, dating almost exclusively from childhood. This opposition between the political and the sacred, interpreted in personal dimensions as an opposition between reason and imagination, constitutes Wordsworth's response to the Enlightenment. Since the challenge of the Enlightenment remains the core of subsequent culture, Wordsworth's response also founds his claim to continuing exemplary status.

What needs to be registered is that at this point in his career Wordsworth is not simply rejecting the Enlightenment and reasserting religious orthodoxy in the reactionary way widespread after the Revolution and documented in H.J. Schenk's *The Mind of European Romanticism*. His real interest is that he entirely accepts the spirit of Enlightenment critique of all organized religion. Indeed, "Nature," it seems to me, is invoked precisely to relocate the "religious" outside any sphere of "culture." What Wordsworth lives through is that experience of the sacred which can only be laid bare and made available after not just sects, but virtually everything that goes under the name "religion," has been stripped away. (Consequently, his later poetry seems to betray not just the Enlightenment or the French Revolution, but Wordsworth's own profound earlier intuition of the sacred.) If anything remains after such a purgation, it will be almost literally unspeakable. At once primitive and sophisticated, pre- and post-Enlightenment, it will evade thematic or doctrinal presentation. These intense and ghostly experiences will emerge only to a consciousness whose "culture" is held scrupulously in check. A plain style, purged of everything "poetic" and assured in its referentiality, made up equally of ordinary and indefinite language, will inexplicably yield descriptions possessing uncanny and hallucinatory power. Such a poetry baffles the ordinary resources of scholarly reading. A learned historicism will assimilate it precisely to the cultural topics and traditions it scrupulously evades. "Close reading" will seek in vain the precisely concrete linguistic structures for whose analysis it is alone suited. What is needed is a wholly different approach, one capable of focusing on the structures of experience and on language insofar as it is both the medium and itself an intentional object of experience. It is Hartman's phenomenological approach, which has known so well how to profit from students of religion like Gerardus van der Leeuw and Mircea Eliade, that, in my view, is most adequate to the historical and cultural significance of Wordsworth.

To see the force of Hartman's approach, we can examine some readings of a perhaps overread poem:

> A slumber did my spirit seal;
>   I had no human fears:
> She seemed a thing that could not feel
>   The touch of earthly years.

No motion has she now, no force;
　She neither hears nor sees;
Rolled round in earth's diurnal course,
　With rocks, and stones, and trees.

In "Irony as a Principle of Structure," Cleanth Brooks approaches the poem with an explicit generalization about poetic language and an implicit generalization about human feelings. The "lover's agonized shock" at Lucy's death is focused in the word "thing," to which the course of events has given a bitterly ironic sense. Replying to Brooks, F.W. Bateson stresses rather the loose or vague character of Wordsworth's language, which simply never becomes sufficiently rigid to sustain irony. The poem presents not contrasting moods, but "a single mood mounting to a climax in the pantheistic magnificence of the last two lines." E.D. Hirsch comments, I think rightly, that Bateson asserts a historically more concrete interpretation of what Wordsworth would actually have felt in such a situation. Nevertheless, the very word "pantheism" seems to me to insert far too sophisticated a cultural mediation into a poem which is perplexing precisely because its plain descriptive language directs us to no explanatory context.

In his celebrated essay "The Rhetoric of Temporality," Paul de Man uses the same poem to illustrate a large contrast between the temporal structure of irony and allegory. Lucy's death has demystified a prior consciousness, which now appears as "a flight into the inauthenticity" of repressing or forgetting human temporality. But the word "thing" was not ironic within that earlier consciousness: on the contrary, it "could almost be a galant compliment" to the woman. Its transformation into literal truth occasions only a "very Wordsworthian 'shock of mild surprise.'" The emergent consciousness is not ironic either: we have a "unified self that fully recognizes a past condition as one of error and stands in a present that, however painful, sees things as they actually are." His "insight is no longer in doubt," his consciousness "no longer vulnerable to irony." What is important, however, is that this change is represented as a temporal sequence, an incipient narrative pivoting on the blank space between the stanzas in which Lucy's death is contained and unexpressed. This "spreading out along the axis of an imaginary time" aims to "give duration to what is, in fact, simultaneous within the subject." De Man's critique of an analysis of romantic poetry based on the categories of subject/object relations and focused on the symbol is coupled with an analysis based on more fundamental, that is, constitutive categories of consciousness, including temporality and "forgetting" (Heideggerian *Vergessenheit*), and it is focused on the rhetorical figures of irony and allegory. Consequently, it feels better grounded than interpretation which moves immediately to the sophisticated and debatable realm of the feelings with which human beings do and can respond even to fundamental experiences like death. Yet I think it is vulnerable to objections parallel to Bateson's, though correspondingly more complicated.

Hartman has commented on this poem a number of times. In *Wordsworth's Poetry*, he characterized its mode as "lying between ritual mourning and personal reminiscence." Lucy is a "boundary being," a human in whom we take a personal interest, and yet more, the harbinger of a realm of spirit. But she is seen so entirely "from within the poet," that she becomes "an intermediate modality of consciousness rather than an intermediate being": she is a muse-like figure closely associated with the movements of the poet's imagination. She hauntingly represents an "elision of the human as a mode of being." The illusion that she is a "thing" human time cannot touch is "rigorously betrayed" when death fulfills an anticipation which even retrospectively remains more incipient in this poem than a prophecy, a wish, or even a fear. Yet the poet expresses no shock: "The poem may have its structural irony, but the poet's mood is meditative beyond irony." We have instead "a new 'sealing' of the wounded consciousness," one which, for Wordsworth, has always "already taken place." In the title essay for the volume *Beyond Formalism*, Hartman takes up the exchange between Brooks and Bateson. He avoids Bateson's immediate leap to a category of systematic philosophy, but tries to give the stylistic and formal analysis of Brooks a concrete historical reorientation. He briefly sketches the history of the "pointed" style which infected even elegy and against which Wordsworth reacted strongly. It is again the poet's consciousness, but in this case his consciousness of poetic form and language within his historical situation which guides formal analysis. In the essay on Wordsworth and Hegel in this volume, Hartman uses the subtle relation between the first and second stanzas of the poem to elucidate the connection between "Aufhebung" and the "aesthetic" he captures in the term "elation." "A Touching Compulsion" finely names this same relation as one of "image to afterimage" rather than "illusion to the shock of disillusion." This perceptual and half-bodily category burrows beneath de Man's analysis of consciousness and its ruses. Once again, Hartman invokes the idea of a "seal" and of a "wound" which founds the self. What is new is the auditory speculation, if the synesthesis is allowable, in the suggestion that between the stanzas "an image of 'gravitation' elides the grave." This felicitously obtrusive verbal play certainly evokes the psychoanalytic criticism which is Hartman's subject in this essay and elsewhere in the volume. But while he remains in the orbit of Freud, even the categories of sexuality are treated phenomenologically, not biologically. Phenomenology here appropriates psychoanalysis for the sake of its power to liberate the ear and thus to free structures of language fully adequate to represent the structures of an incarnated self. Hartman's most comprehensive reading of the poem (in "The Interpreter's Freud," reprinted in *Easy Pieces* [1985] but not here) is also inspired by this complex relation to psychoanalysis. By "reading Freud through Wordsworth,'' Hartman again appropriates psychoanalysis for criticism proper but also arrives at ''a critique of Freud'' that sets poetry's sense of language as virtually alive against Freud's dream of a purified scientific language for interpreting dreams and neurotic symptoms.

Nevertheless, it may seem strange to say that the measure of adequacy of Hartman's approach is its capacity to lay bare in Wordsworth fundamentally religious phenomena. It is evident that Hartman directs his attention to categories which are at once those of language and of consciousness. In ''Words, Wish, Worth'' in this volume, Hartman aims to reveal the structure or phenomenology of the ''word-wish'' in the form of fiat, of blessing, of curse. We may be prepared to see in these simply psychological modes. Where we find in Wordsworth what can be described as an attempt to convert a divine or willful imperative into a responsive or timely utterance, this may seem, insofar as the word ''divine'' is unavoidable, to belong to what is merely historically contingent, dead and gone, in Wordsworth. Hartman's wager, however, is that, as he says, ''A reading which recovers the strange interplay of cultic feeling and modern self-consciousness will also recover the precarious subjectivity of the poet.'' This interplay circles around the pole of religion, but with a hesitancy and scrupulous diffidence that do not merely evade every lure of enthusiasm, ecstasy, and delusion of grandeur, but ultimately dislocate the temporality of human experience itself. It is difficult to know what to call this experience. As Hartman says, interpretation here tries to transcend the dichotomizing of religious and non-religious modes of understanding and of earlier (that is, prophetic) and later (that is, poetic-visionary) texts. Nevertheless, I want to insist on the claim that what we must call, lacking any less misleading word, the religious in the *text* of Wordsworth's poetry maintains an indefeasible legitimacy and autonomy vis-à-vis the political in all subsequent culture. To test this claim, I want to turn to a writer who knew nothing of Wordsworth, and yet shows in a central modernist text another version of the symptomatic interplay between politics (conceived at its most fundamental) and a religious mode of thought incapable of articulating itself in any of its traditional forms, precisely because it could emerge only in the wake of an Enlightenment critique of religion, which the writer himself has fully assimilated.

The text I have in mind is Hugo von Hofmannsthal's ''Letter of Lord Chandos'' (1902). To recall its well-known premise, Chandos is an Elizabethan aristocrat whose brilliant youthful works brought into language the whole of traditional culture by expressing his own self-conscious and unified sensibility. Yet he has ceased to write, having ''lost completely the ability to think or to speak of anything coherently.'' One might imagine that Divine Providence was thereby chastening the overweening ambition of his youthful projects, but he insists that all such religious ideas have no power over him. Chandos describes the gradual crumbling of language, beginning with abstract terms and ending with the most ordinary opinions. Incapable of achieving the unthinking simplification of experience into judgments, every atom of experience crowds closely and absolutely on him, and every word becomes a vertiginous whirlpool into the void. Nevertheless, he occasionally experiences "good moments," when some "flood of higher life" seems to fill him like a vessel. The instances are absurdly ordinary: "a pitcher, a harrow abandoned in a field, a dog in the sun, a neglected cemetery, a cripple, a peasant's hut." Such images fill with a "silent but suddenly rising flood of divine sensation," replacing temporality with the "fullest, most exalted Present." He finds in them "such an abundance, such a presence of love, that my enchanted eye can find nothing in sight void of life." Under their impulsion, he feels "as if we could enter into a new and hopeful relationship with the whole of existence if only we begin to think with the heart." His body suddenly seems the cipher or key to everything, yet he can no more put his experience into words or bring it to consciousness than he could "say anything precise about the inner movements of my intestines or a congestion of my blood." Yet this check to consciousness and its language impels to a different language: "What was it that made me want to break into words which, I know, were I to find them, would force to their knees those cherubim in whom I do not believe?" He feels as though he were "about to ferment, to effervesce, to foam and to sparkle," and this feeling is correlative with or perhaps even equivalent to a "feverish thinking, but thinking in a medium more immediate, more liquid, more glowing than words." He will, he concludes, never write another book, because he realizes that "the language in which I might be able not only to write but to think is neither Latin nor English, neither Italian nor Spanish, but a language none of whose words is known to me, a language in which inanimate things speak to me and wherein I may one day have to justify myself before an unknown judge."

Chandos consciously rejects traditional religious ideas and images: "To me the mysteries of faith have been condensed into a lofty allegory which arches itself over the fields of my life like a radiant rainbow, ever remote, ever prepared to recede should it occur to me to rush toward it and wrap myself into the folds of its mantle." Nevertheless, I have quoted somewhat tendentiously most, but by no means all, of the passages which make clear that Hofmannsthal is exploring a fundamentally religious experience—all the more fundamental in that it can be expressed only in a language which rejects at the very moment it invokes religion ("those cherubim in whom I do not believe"; "jusify myself before an unknown judge"). Hermann Broch did not hesitate to say that Chandos is seeking "some equivalent to the true humility of piety." His quest requires openness to images of terror, absurdity, in short, abjection: a mother rat, surrounded by her brood, dying of the poison he has had scattered in his milk cellars; a Roman senator who falls in love with a pet fish. The point of these images is that they impel him beyond every category and judgment of traditional culture, including religious culture, into a direct confrontation with the very grounds of existence.

Hofmannsthal imagines the "Letter" as a reply to an inquiry from Francis Bacon in order, I think, to suggest that it is science, the deliberate empiricism which arises out of common sense, which now speaks on behalf of culture and calls us to account. The Enlightenment critique of religion is understood as "secularization," a purgative isolation and appropriation of whatever in religion can fit into a new culture and ethos based on scientific method. The counterstrategy is to accept fully this process of critique and secularization because doing so uncovers a mode of experience more deeply integral to human existence than either the conventionally "sacred" or secular. This line of thought is given added force, I think, by the date Hofmannsthal assigns the letter: 22 August 1603, five months after James I was proclaimed King and one month after Bacon was knighted, beginning the rise to political power which is precisely coordinated with the emergence of his philosophical works from the *Advancement of Learning* in 1605 on. It is well known that Hofmannsthal found his way to drama as a very different vehicle for imagining the possibilities of political renewal, of a social coherence rooted in symbols and ritual actions whose grace integrated more of human being than could any rational, scientific, Enlightenment-inspired liberalism.

It would be easy to name many modern artists who face the same problem, with unique responses in each case, to be sure. My point is to underline that only Hartman's approach to Wordsworth has shown itself adequate to bring out in his poetry a fundamental concern that remains at the core of our culture. Wordsworth certainly has his limits. He knows little or nothing of a darker side of the religious impulse that runs from Coleridge through Poe and Baudelaire and whose manifestations in modern literature, full of troubling political implications, are brought out in Julia Kristeva's analysis of the "abject" and of Celine in *The Powers of Horror*. The central issue is not simply a choice between politics and religion. Beginning from Carlo Ginzburg's *The Cheese and the Worms*, we could ask whether Wordsworth gives voice to a persisting strain of "peasant radicalism" which links pre- or sub-Christian experiences of the sacred with certain forms of social and political protest (the same speculation could apply to Blake, with allowance for the difference between rural and urban populism). Karl Löwith and Eric Voegelin have shown how easily a superficial critique of religion can lead political thought to repress the continuing presence within itself of theology as its "secret passion" (Hartman's phrase in *Criticism in the Wilderness*). Hans Blumenberg in *The Legitimacy of the Modern Age* has most vigorously and extensively defended the contrary thesis that the secular is not best understood as transference or translation of sacred categories. But in *Work on*

Myth, he too stresses the complex interaction of the political, the secular, the scientific, with the realm of myth which remains after all traditional reliance on an accessible divine order has vanished. The central issue, therefore, is our willingness to face what both politics and religion have become in response to the Enlightenment and to face equally the enduring autonomy and legitimacy of each, the inevitability of their interaction, and the impossibility of a culture not founded on both.

Introduction

I have never been able to get away from Wordsworth for any length of time. The moment I was obliged to read him during high school in England, he reflected back my own sense of nature: rural nature, but more generally a world that felt as ancient and immemorial as "rocks, and stones, and trees," that encompassed, inanimate yet animating, the mind in its earth-walks. But the discovery prompting me to write about him was that he could brood about himself in a way that nurtured rather than violated a "culture of feeling." No one before him had so naturally brought perception and consciousness together, had charted the growth of the mind without over-objectifying it; and so not only anticipated developmental psychology but made us inherit unforgettably, after the Enlightenment, and in the dawn of the Industrial Revolution, a sense of "unknown modes of being."

Even if we discount Wordsworth's prophetic fear that nature was fading from the human mind, who before him conveys so succinctly the mutual dependence of nature and imagination? His own term, actually, is "mutual domination," which moves the issue beyond epistemological niceties. Each poem becomes a new test of imagination, or where the world fits in. Such testing, however, is inevitably comparative and temporal, and opens Wordsworth to latent memories of childhood and adolescence. This temporal complexity shapes a poetic instrument containing very subtle eddyings that cannot be fixed in the amber of neoclassical verse. The poem of this mind reacts on itself, composing even "blind thoughts" that usurp the attempt to write, and compel Wordsworth to revise his self-understanding.

In staying so close to his own mind Wordsworth seemed to me more remarkable than Rousseau, Schiller, even Hölderlin—and other writers of Continental Europe who played so crucial a role in "Romantic" and later thought. I have put "Romantic" in quotation marks because while the term was an important historical marker in the 1960s, I feel it fading now. The same could be said of "Modern." So startling yet undramatic is Wordsworth's originality that it is hard not to see him as an inaugural figure for both modern philosophy and poetry. Yet the newness may not be important, since he worked against violent change, things suddenly gone out of mind, or mind having to depend on disruptive and escalating stimuli. The causes for this dependence he laid on a convergence of factors: urbanization, a "degrading" thirst for news incited by the Napoleonic Wars, and the heady hopes of ideologists of the French Revolution, who parted the new order from the old "as by a gulph."

This perceptive conservatism produced a revolution in poetry; yet it may be that Wordsworth's fear about nature setting like the sun, but irreversibly, is only being realized now, after the "tragic euphoria" of such anti-evangelical ideas as Nietzsche's Eternal Return, or Adorno's negative dialectics (and similar critiques of the hope in absolute progress), or John Ashbery's crepuscular verse. In Ashbery's poems we are already beyond what Wallace Stevens calls "a great shadow's last embellishment": they are more like an electrotherapy relieving the stiff neck of the sublime, and helping our numbness to speak. "A knotted rope of guesswork looming out of storms / And darkness and proceeding on its way into nowhere / Barely muttering" (Ashbery, *A Wave*). Despite rare auroras, poetry as well as nature is going out. This meditation on the end of poetry in our climate (overcivilized, yet shaken by unspeakable violence) has darkly inspired English verse since William Collins.

It says something about our moment in criticism that we prefer the preacherly and excited writing of French culture-critics to the sober lights of Wordsworth and Ashbery, or even to Thoreau's *Walden* and passages in Emerson. How seriously are we taking our own tradition, especially its poetry? In England Wordsworth remains, for the most part, a cottage industry. On the Continent, he has not been received as more than a parochial nature-poet. In our own intellectual circles, despite more complex readings, his reputation remains fickle. He is appreciated for anticipations of how the unconscious works, for *The Prelude*'s eye-witness account of a phase of the French Revolution, for his type of autobiography (putting the subject in question), and for the rhetoric of a few sublime episodes. Wordsworth's style, unfortified by the interest that a philosopher of the order of Heidegger, Sartre, or Derrida might bring, does not survive (in translation especially) the forgivable extravagance of Blake, Byron, and Shelley. All of these, moreover, were more sustained ideologists of Revolution.

Yet Wordsworth recapitulates in his poetry, by a spontaneous phenomenology, feelings about nature that link up with both religion and politics. In his call to save nature he expresses not only a residual agrarian sensibility but a response to apocalyptic stirrings which institutionalized religions cannot always bind or subdue. He knew that religion, like poetry itself, arises from imaginative sensations that might be channeled into human-heartedness. Yet the transition from those early experiences (the fearful elations he describes so well in *The Prelude* and the great Ode) to social feelings, rather than self-isolating visionary fancies, is not assured. Wordsworth is preeminently the poet of "dark passages" that lead from immature ecstasy to socialization. His theme of the growth of a mind, capable of regenerating itself and perhaps society, includes a most faithful description of how, on the level of individual sensibility, we pass from nature as the unthinking object of desire to a haunting awareness of it as purposive and even alien, and from that concomitant nature-consciousness and self-consciousness to words that restore the world's body, without idolatry or the denial of something in either nature or imagination that breaks—violently or subtly—what is not inappropriately called their "marriage."

Where would I like the study of Wordsworth to go? Toward an understanding of the radicalism that shapes even his evasions or euphemisms. The peculiarity of his later style, its increasing, ambivalent attraction to Classical figures (including personification and prosopopeia) is not an "academic" topic but important to gauging the traumatic fundamentals of psychic, religious, and political development, and poetry's answerable style. But this sort of study would come of itself, if the intellectual scene shifted, and Wordsworth could be taken seriously by a philosopher. Yet one cannot even be sure about the results of such a shift, since Stanley Cavell's book on Thoreau, *The Senses of Walden*, remains more honored than effective.

Perhaps I am looking for an enlargement of our notion of commentary. Criticism (which continues to be the mode of these essays) is the secular aspect of commentary: it seeks to settle or unsettle values by recovering, through the comparative method, historically diverse forms and transformations, and it does not authorize itself by leaning on a sacred text. Yet it is not as progressive as it thinks. Do we still know what commentary is, or have we forgotten nine-tenths of its tradition from Philo and midrash on? The loss in doing criticism, the narrowing of our relations to the text, balances out the secular gain.

What if, in Derrida's *Glas*, the right-hand commentary had been on Wordsworth rather than Genet, to accompany the left-hand column on Hegel? Parallel texts set up a presumption that they are translations: that despite a linguistic or cultural difference there is translatability or some sort of equivalence. Having read *Glas*, we know how complex that correlation may be, and that the structural apposition breaks down in important ways. But one wager in this remains to haunt us: can "denken" (*noesis*) and "dichten" (*poesis*)—to adopt Heidegger's favorite terms—be joined again, though they have given rise to separate, often antagonistic disciplines? To restore a connection (a hope of German Romanticism, and perhaps of Coleridge) is the one move toward foundations I would not find regressive.

The English tradition, on the whole, blessed by a fruitful mixture of language-strains, and a remarkable array of idiosyncratic writers, has not been "religious" about anyone, with the possible exception of Shakespeare. To liven things up, an intellectual contest sometimes breaks out as to the place of Milton or Pope or Shelley or Yeats, but the sort of devotedness Heidegger brings to poems and even fragments of Hölderlin, or more questionably to great-enough lyrics by Trakl and Rilke, is just not evident. Moreover, it is disconcerting that Heidegger's fervor invests itself so exclusively in German and Greek, accompanied by an ideology with racial overtones concerning their superiority to other language-traditions. How can a philosophical mind of that order be so boorish?

Nearer to us, and more acceptable, is the dialogue between Wordsworth and Coleridge. It remained lacunary and was not continued within English criticism. It broke down because Coleridge could not really equate German idealism with the "philosophy" (thoughts sounding their way) of Wordsworth. I suspect Coleridge feared the solipsistic streak in both Wordsworth and the German philosophers, but trusted Wordsworth's more experiential account, which revealed both the autonomy of imagination and its chances of bonding with the world. Moreover, the place from which Wordsworth spoke, or which he addressed, his "England"—or the umbilical nature-refuge of Grasmere—was hardly comparable to Jena or Göttingen or the ideal Oriental campus to which Hölderlin's genius aspired.

Such remarks as William Carlos Williams's "The Classic is the local fully realized, words marked by a place," are more obviously true of English poetry that took its direction from Wordsworth. Coleridge, instead, *displaced* himself, most strikingly in the "Hymn Written before Sun-Rise in the Vale of Chamouny." His experiences on Scafell are transferred to Mont Blanc, and a convergence is sought of a sublime rhetoric derived from Milton and James Thomson, with a German tradition leading from Klopstock to Friederike Brun. The terrible abstractness—*bodenlosigkeit*—of Coleridge's fake composition of place does two things at once: (1) it honors the antithetical example of Wordsworth, who links word to original place almost superstitiously, as if not being in place was to be out of nature and out of spirit; (2) it evokes an archetypal scene or superground, a divine, sacred, fixating spot, whose cosmic weight (and power of blackness) must be transformed by the benightmared soul into a morning voluntary—a supreme test of the paralyzed voice. Yet Coleridge's "place" (in nature? in God's eye?) remains counterfeit: the hymn's landscape is so patently a sublime imitation, and there is nothing reminiscent of Wordsworth's ability to draw the logos-power of voice out of nature, as in his ascent of Snowdon in *Prelude* XIV.

This contrast of Coleridge and Wordsworth is not meant to devalue the former but to disclose a missed connection in England between philosophy and poetry, one that became a great divide. It is not philosophy that can be my concern; my solicitude for its health would seem, in any case, misplaced. The question is, rather: Can we take poetry as seriously as Coleridge took Wordsworth, expending a similar quality of intelligence? English poems, one scholar has declared, have little or nothing to say. The character of that "nothing" is then frittered away in local insights about Englishness. Instead, we should explore the negativities involved, for poetry may certainly undo thought and resist certain kinds of assertion. Whether we place poetry under the sign of the negative or the positive is less important than escaping false dichotomies or reversible oppositions, including that between "denken" and "dichten." So I remain hopeful that readers of this book will come away with a clearer picture not only of Wordsworth but of the difference poetry can make in our thinking.

The Unremarkable Wordsworth

1
Wordsworth Revisited

When Wordsworth was fourteen, the ordinary sight of boughs silhouetted against a bright evening sky left so vivid an impression on his mind that it marked the beginning of his career as poet. "I recollect distinctly," he writes as a man in his seventies, "the very spot where this first struck me. It was in the way between Hawkshead and Ambleside, and gave me extreme pleasure. The moment was important in my poetical history for I date from it my consciousness of the infinite variety of natural appearances which had been unnoticed by the poets of any age or country." Such nature-consciousness, joined to an answering self-consciousness, is the "incumbent mystery" from which Wordsworth's poetry springs. He begins with the weight of sense-experience through which, as two of his characteristic metaphors put it, the "foundations" of the mind are laid, or the soul is "seeded" by feelings and images capable of sustaining it throughout life. There is no vision in his poetry that is not a vision of natural appearances pressing upon child or adult in this way. Nature—for Wordsworth chiefly rural nature, the abiding presences of mountain, lake, and field under the influence of the changing seasons—is a haunted house through which we must pass before our spirit can be independent. Those separated too soon from this troubling and sensuous contact with Nature—the strongest passages in Wordsworth's autobiographical poem *The Prelude* are devoted to Nature's ministry of fear rather than her ministry of beauty—may grow up with an empty, if powerful, sense of self. They have skipped a necessary stage of development; and without a filial relation to Nature, to that animate earth and heaven which plays so crucial a role in ancient myth, they become unimaginative or require increasingly personal and violent stimuli. "The sun strengthens us no more, neither does the moon" (D.H. Lawrence). The result is that revolutionary or self-alienating, rather than creative, personality in which Wordsworth saw the great temptation of his epoch, and to which he himself almost succumbed. His poetry, with its emphasis on "the infinite variety of natural appearances" and on the way the simplest event can enrich mind, sets itself against "gross and violent stimulants" in the realm of the senses or of public action.

If Wordsworth seems prophetic in his concern with the revolutionary mentality, and with our alienation from Nature, it is because he lived at the beginning of our epoch. A country boy, born and raised in the English Lake District, he found himself at nineteen years of age in the midst of two great upheavals, the Industrial Revolution and the French Revolution. Between 1790, his first visit to France and the Alps on a walking tour (on partial truancy from his studies at Cambridge, which was little more than an "inter-world" to him), and 1800, when he settled down for good in the Lake District, Wordsworth lived these events as eyewitness and participant. He lived the French Revolution, in particular, so strongly that it shook his identity as poet and Englishman. He passed through the crisis, however; and the poems that ensued, of which *Lyrical Ballads* was the first collection (1798; 2nd edition, expanded by a new volume, 1800), are not naive nature lyrics but expressive of a mind that had returned to health after long sickness. While the response of Wordsworth's contemporaries was less than enthusiastic, later generations were struck by the prophetic and representative character of these poems. John Stuart Mill and Matthew Arnold felt that Wordsworth's sickness, or crisis, was also theirs; and they wished for his kind of strength in overcoming it. How much agony lay behind that strength was not revealed till *The Prelude* was published in 1850, the year of the poet's death.

The Industrial Revolution was, of course, only in its beginning in the 1780s and 1790s. A "lyrical ballad" has little in common with a ballad of protest like Thomas Hood's "Song of the Shirt." At first sight it appears to be as removed from politics as Jane Austen's novels. Wordsworth could still harbor the wish of treating the disease itself, as well as its symptoms. He diagnosed the disease as a disturbed relation between man and his environment. The pressures of city life were divorcing man's imagination from an organic connection to the earth even more than poverty had done, or supernaturalistic religion. His preface to the 1800 *Lyrical Ballads* notes a "craving for extraordinary excitement" created by the accelerating rhythm of modern history and by "deluges of idle and extravagant stories in verse." To offset this tendency he shows us men of an older and different order, touched by the new events yet un-uprootable, like oak and rock. The shepherd's strength of mind, in "Michael," belongs to nature as much as to mind: it is as "indestructible" as the "great and permanent objects that act upon it." Wordsworth knows, of course, that rural people like Michael are types rather than ideals: he is not proposing we become them. But through them he depicts qualities of mind that must be carried over into modern life, and he questions whether they can be fostered in an industrialized society. *Lyrical Ballads*, though not literature of protest, is engaged with the problems of its time: it is a reflective, not a naive, poetry, and draws its sustenance consciously from "the common sights of mother earth." It remains in touch with native ground, like the English ballads edited by Bishop Percy in the 1760s, but relies on ordinary, rather than extraordinary, incidents.

It was, however, the French Revolution that impinged decisively on Wordsworth's life. Wordsworth took a second trip to France in 1791 and stayed till obliged to return to England at the end of 1792. He spent his time in Paris, Blois, and Orleans; and he became increasingly involved in revolutionary circles. There was also some private turmoil: an affair with a French girl, Annette Vallon, which resulted in the birth of a daughter. (This is not revealed in *The Prelude* but was brought to light by dramatic scholarly sleuthing in 1916.) Yet his own inner life did not suffer a crisis until England formally went to war against France in 1793.

Wordsworth had considered the French Revolution an extension of British ideals of liberty and democracy. The war against France struck him, therefore, as unforgivable, a betrayal of England as well as France. No fewer than three times does he return in *The Prelude* to the shock he suffered in 1793. Betrayed by their own country, the whole of the younger generation seemed threatened with a deadly skepticism vis-à-vis national ideals. The deteriorating course of the Revolution itself (not only the massacre of the Girondists but also increasing French aggressiveness, which led to the Napoleonic Wars) then confirmed the young poet's conviction that the individual had henceforth to act alone. Social liberty, as he put it, had to be built on personal liberty. Without guidance except his will and individual reason, he saw himself as a man without a past, thrown entirely upon himself in the pursuit of the millennial future of which he still dreamed.

What Wordsworth suffered so acutely may lie in the destiny of all men: a betrayal into autonomy, into self-dependence. That is the story wherever the tragic sense of life is strong: in *Oedipus Rex*, in *King Lear*, in Albee's *Who's Afraid of Virginia Woolf*, and in Wordsworth's own drama, *The Borderers* (1796-1797). The wound inflicted is that of self-consciousness: "And they knew that they were naked." It is significant, however, that in Wordsworth's case the wound seemed to be caused by political events, and that since the time of the American Revolution it is *patricide* (murder of one's father*land*) as much as *parricide* which is the great trouble in the modern consciousness. On the part of the individual there is a sense that his country has betrayed him by crushing a War of Liberation which its own founding principles inspired; and on the part of society there is a fear of the alienated intellectual who is considered a potential enemy from within.

Wordsworth's inner turmoil lasted at least until 1795, the year in which he met several times with the social philosopher William Godwin. *The Prelude* does not mention Godwin by name, and it is difficult to say what part his theories of reform may have played in a mind "Sick, wearied out with contrarieties" (*Prelude* XI, 304). But we do know what brought Wordsworth to his "last and lowest ebb." It was his trust in the naked individual reason which Godwin's theories may have abetted. His loss of faith in England, that "ancient tower" on which he was "fast rooted," had meant abandoning his vocation of poet—giving England up was tantamount to giving his past up, to cutting off "all the sources of my former strength." In this state of spiritual poverty nothing but "Reason's naked self" remained. But reason, Blake's "idiot questioner," questioning every-thing and resolving nothing, finally began to question itself.

This proved to be the turning point of the crisis. The poet saw that reason was merely another kind of passion. It was an "idealistic" disorder all the more dangerous for claiming to be above disorder. Like Nietzsche, Ibsen, and many nineteenth-century thinkers, he understood that the obsession with analysis was a modern kind of fanaticism, insidiously solipsistic under the guise of promoting social reformation. Once reason was unmasked, the way was open for other in-fluences to reassert themselves. Wordsworth decided he could not ignore the past just because its action on him was mainly unconscious. His relation to childhood and country (a very concrete relation, as *The Prelude* would show) might not be denied any more than syllogistic reasonings might "unsoul" the "mysteries of being." He returned consciously and devotedly to Nature—to rediscovering his roots.

Wordsworth's recovery is therefore a rediscovery of inner continuities. A per-sonal sense of destiny is reestablished, and the past reintegrated in the stream of life. He returns to "sweet counsels between head and heart," and mends all kinds of dualisms. The famous "spots of time"—early experiences that, like Proust's involuntary memories, unexpectedly affect a present moment—reveal that we are less isolated than we think. We live in a large and beneficent sphere of influences. This sphere did not open itself to the poet at once: the period of recovery stretches from his return to the English countryside in 1794 to his stay in Germany in the winter of 1798-1799. But chronology is not helpful here, and *The Prelude* avoids it: while there was one intense period of crisis there seems to have been no one intense recovery, but rather a widening consciousness of the mind's power to renew itself, and of Nature's role in this. The poems written between 1797 and 1807 reflect the triumph of an outgoing sensibility over a brooding, self-centered mind: often they are that triumph itself.

It was, indeed, a whole sphere of influences rather than one event which re-stored Wordsworth. There was Dorothy, his sister, reunited with him in 1794, who maintained for him, even in the depth of his dejection, "a saving intercourse with my true self." There was, too, Coleridge's almost daily company at Alfoxden, where the *Lyrical Ballads* were planned as a joint venture. And Coleridge undoubtedly brought with him certain philosophical comforts. We know the two poets talked about Spinoza, for whom every true increase of intellectual power produced not only more intellect but more love; and there was Associationism, which had played so important a role in English empirical philosophy, and which Wordsworth used in his own way. He accepts the principle that ideas get attached to ideas, and people to places, by force of association, but denies that we can, through any sort of rational or methodical procedure, reform human nature by fostering true rather than false habits of mind. The associations that matter are too deeply and variously planted in us to be influenced by logic. In this Wordsworth is "necessitarian": he insists that the origins of our development lie beyond rememberable time, and that the process of maturation which *The Prelude* traces (its subtitle is "The Growth of a Poet's Mind") is significantly open to chance and accident. A child who had held "unconscious intercourse with beauty / Old as creation" cannot be pressed into a priori educational schemes. Wordsworth's optimism concerning a person's strength to renew himself is based on his belief in this generous multiplicity of developmental influences. His *credo* is that integration—or reintegration—will triumph. In fragments of poetry associated with "The Ruined Cottage" (c. 1797), his greatest verse-story about human hopes and their defeat, Wordsworth foresees a strengthening of the heart's contact with natural influences:

> All things shall live in us and we shall live
> In all things that surround us. This I deem
> Our tendency, and thus shall every day
> Enlarge our sphere of pleasure and of pain.

The idea of such a tendency, and even of a providential "compact" between imagination and the things of this world, is strengthened in Wordsworth by Edmund Burke's view of the social principle as a "great primeval contract...connecting the visible and invisible world"—a view which stresses political continuity and which the younger Wordsworth had explicitly denounced in his "Letter to Bishop Landaff" (1793).

I have spoken of a *credo*, and *Lyrical Ballads* had at least this in common with a new religion, that it proved to be a stumbling block for its generation. It was not, as recent scholarship has shown, Wordsworth's humble subject matter that caused the trouble. The magazines of the time (equivalents of our *Ladies' Home Journal* and *Saturday Evening Post*) were full of Christian sentiment about Crazy Kate or the fate of the common soldier or the starving robin. They were true to their age, the age of sensibility, and reflected the taste of a growing class of bourgeois readers. What mostly scandalized the latter were Wordsworth's strange moods of exaltation: the way he inflated a trite or private happening as if it contained a truth never before perceived. He sinned against that ironclad law of literary and social decorum which limited the poet's role to putting before his public "What e'er was thought, but ne'er so well express'd." For, in Wordsworth, the novelty seemed to lie in the quality of thought rather than the quality of its expression. The expression, indeed, was obviously flat; and whereas in the ordinary run of magazine verse the manner helped to raise the matter, here was a poet who overtly disdained this yeasty virtue of style.

Anna Seward, a not unintelligent bluestocking, failed to restrain her "disgust" on reading that now harmless anthology piece on the daffodils, "I wandered lonely as a cloud." She berates Wordsworth as an "egotistic manufacturer of metaphysic importance on trivial themes." Even Coleridge accused him of "thoughts and images too great for the subject." Keats too would be disturbed by the "egotistical sublime" in Wordsworth. We cannot dismiss contemporary opinion out of hand, or reduce its relevance to that part of his poetry in which an inflated commonplace expressed in a deflated style yielded a bathos easy to parody:

> Behind a cloud his mystic sense,
> Deep hidden, who can spy?
> Bright as the night, when not a star
> Is shining in the sky.
>
> (Hartley Coleridge)

The only way to respond to the forceful criticism of Wordsworth's time is to face the question it raised: is there anything radically new in his thinking?

Let us take the idea which dominates his poetry. His view of Nature as "the nurse, / The guide, the guardian of my heart, and soul / Of all my moral being" helped his recovery and inspired his greatest decade (1797-1807). Now this return to Nature involves a return to the idea of a cosmos: of the world and man as interdependent powers. Each is fitted to the other; each lives the other's life. The *credo* already quoted, and the great "Recluse" fragment published in 1814 as part of the preface to *The Excursion*, are direct and eloquent statements of the idea. Yet the shadow-side of such reciprocity, a view of Nature as parasitic, which we find in Milton's vision of Hell, or in the third section of Shelley's *The Sensitive Plant*, and above all in Shakespeare's darkest moments, seems hardly to arise. The "ennobling interchange," the "mutual domination," the "blending" of which Wordsworth speaks rhapsodically, is based on love rather than on need: the mind may be insatiable, but the world is inexhaustible; they are of matching dignity and power. If this concept of Nature, then, has little moral complexity, it has even less originality. The concept can be attached to pantheistic as well as Christian thought (cf. St. Paul's vision of a divine environment "in which we live and move and have our being"); in the seventeenth and eighteenth centuries, moreover, as J.W. Beach has shown, concepts of a "sympathetic" universe remained commonplace.

Wordsworth's originality does not lie in his ideas as such. It has to do with the way they emerge from the depth of felt experience. They are organic thoughts: we see them growing on him, we watch him struggling with his own—often unexpected—imaginings. "A shy spirit in my heart — That comes and goes / will sometimes leap / From hiding-places ten years deep"(*The Waggoner*). A new attitude toward consciousness—a radical consciousness of consciousness—is brought to light: Wordsworth is truly a subjective thinker. He is the first to establish a vulgate for the imagination, to use words which are our words and feelings which move in a natural rather than fictionally condensed time. Today, when every poet "walks naked" (Yeats), it may be hard to appreciate the courage Wordsworth showed and the advance in sensibility he made possible. All the more so because, having cleansed the doors of perception, and made a supremer fiction possible, he drew back from releasing his imagination toward that end. His poetry may renounce too much and be too self-involved in its struggle against fictional or visionary devices. Many of his contemporaries did not value the stripped nature of his poetry, the characteristic Wordsworthian bareness: what they saw was poverty of imagination and the scandal of subjectivity.

A *subjective thinker*: the phrase comes from Kierkegaard. But what exactly does subjectivity, that most abused word, mean? Especially when qualified by "Romantic" it conjures up a world in schism: here objects, there subjects, here idiosyncrasy (calculated oddities, unpredictable sublimities), there normative behavior. This understanding of subjectivity is in error. Subjectivity means that the starting point for authentic reflection is placed in the individual consciousness. Not, necessarily, the empirical starting point, but the ontological, or what might also be called the Archimedean point. Archimedes said he could move the world had he a point whereon to rest his machine. "Who has not felt," Wordsworth says, alluding to the story, "the same aspiration as regards the world of his own mind?" If this Archimedean point is genuinely within the personal consciousness, dualism is overcome, for the source of inspiration (the empirical starting point) can be anything and anywhere.

The expansion of sensibility characteristic of the modern period is certainly related to this free and eccentric placement of the empirical starting point. The modern mind can start ("turn on") anywhere because it has a surer homing instinct, or because it accepts what Hölderlin called "die ekzentrische Bahn": the necessity of passing through self-alienation to self-fulfillment. Wordsworth finds his inspiration virtually anywhere: he recalls us to the simplest incidents, to words or events that would pass us by. "Behold," he says, as in "The Solitary Reaper," "Stop here, or gently pass." Gently, because we are on mysterious ground; and if we do not wish to stop and think further, we should allow the impression to develop in its time. The horizontal extension of the scope of the poet's subject matter is only an aspect of something more important: its vertical extension, its inward resonance.

There is always a reserve in the experiences Wordsworth depicts. It may suddenly develop in the poet or profoundly displace his initial thought. "The Solitary Reaper," for instance, did not fructify in him till two years after his sister had seen an analogous sight (Wordsworth often "borrowed" her eyes and ears), and it moves in an excursive yet natural arc from the girl through reflections covering past, present, and future. In "Tintern Abbey," this remarkable turning of the mind also makes us aware of the virtues of the vernacular, which Wordsworth brings back to dignity. Only the "subtle intercourse" of spoken language, its submerged metaphors, its quietly syntactic power, can really respect this expansion of the mind beyond its first impressions.

Let us sample this open and natural style, which can be so plain as to be anti-literary. In the first two books of *The Prelude* Wordsworth describes the education—mainly by natural influences—of a young boy. From the age of about five to thirteen consciousness of self is still merged with nature-consciousness, though there are intimations of real separateness, of genuine selfhood. Wordsworth recalls an incident which helped him to see nature as Nature: not only as a part of him but also as apart from him, as a presence enjoyed consciously rather than unconsciously, and so leading to firmer self-awareness:

> Our steeds remounted and the summons given,
> With whip and spur we through the chauntry flew
> In uncouth race, and left the cross-legged knight,
> And the stone-abbot, and that single wren
> Which one day sang so sweetly in the nave
> Of the old church, that—though from recent showers
> The earth was comfortless, and, touched by faint
> Internal breezes, sobbings of the place
> And respirations, from the roofless walls
> The shuddering ivy dripped large drops—yet still
> So sweetly 'mid the gloom the invisible bird
> Sang to herself, that there I could have made
> My dwelling-place, and lived for ever there
> To hear such music. Through the walls we flew
> And down the valley, and, a circuit made
> In wantonness of heart, through rough and smooth
> We scampered homewards. Oh, ye rocks and streams,
> And that still spirit shed from evening air!
> Even in this joyous time I sometimes felt
> Your presence, when with slackened step we breathed
> Along the sides of the steep hills, or when
> Lighted by gleams of moonlight from the sea
> We beat with thundering hoofs the level sand.

(Prelude II, 115-37)*

*All references to *The Prelude* are to the version of 1850, unless otherwise noted.

An aspect of inner life is vividly rendered here without the artifice of a fictional or displaced perspective: without allegory or personification or atomism. There is complete respect for ordinary experience as well as for its extraordinary potential. The theme of the episode is the emergence of Nature as a distinct presence, and the relation of this to the child's growing sense of "thereness"—of real, if still uncertain, identity. Yet a dimension is added which is hard to define because it is not purely the illustration of that theme. During the act of recall the poet's consciousness becomes, to adopt words of Wallace Stevens, "part of the *res* itself, and not about it." The memory Wordsworth set out to record yields as if spontaneously to a second memory (118-28) continuous with the first but more inward. The poet's initial memory still embraces it, but he is tempted to rest with the supervening memory as with a symbol. When he comes on that second, more internal image (on the "single wren," deceptively enumerated along with the cross-legged knight and stone abbot, though lifting the whole out of historical into human time), he is forced to stop, to enter the solitude he then intuited, the "I" rather than the "we." He dwells on that event to the point of slowing the narrative movement to a halt that parallels even now (some thirty years later) a moment in the past which prepared him for selfhood.

Wordsworth's "open" style—the displacement of a first memory by a second—shows that memory is creative rather than nostalgic: still sensitive to a past that can modify and even reverse a present state of mind. What is peculiarly Wordsworthian, however, is that the displacement of which we have spoken is continuous, that the supervening memory remains within the frame of its matrix. Belated intuitions, which arise "from the structure of [the poet's] own mind . . . without immediate external excitement" (though with the incitement, as here, of a prior, internalized image) are not allowed to break but merely to extend the matrix. Analogously, looking to Wordsworth's poetry as a whole, there are no sharp breaks or ritual passings between one state of mind and another: vision is always continuous with sensation. Even such licensed rapture as Keats's "Already with thee!" is avoided.

Wordsworth's "underconsciousness" of the past, or his sense for renovative continuities, is to be understood as aiming for greater stakes than mental health. It has a millennial as well as a therapeutic dimension. Wordsworth shares the myth of progress characteristic of the eighteenth century, though radically modifying it. Like contemporary demythologizers he believed that the mind of man could be "enlightened" or progressively purified of myth and superstition. What Shakespeare or Milton did by the liberal use of visionary devices he would do by truth to nature alone. However, instead of clearly breaking with the past, he conceives progress as the individual's greater participation in that past—his repossession of imaginative energies denied by reason but only displaced by myth and fable. The latter are imperfect expressions of that "fear and awe" (and sense of beauty) which befall us when we are nature-haunted. When myth or fable interpose too early between us and experience they alienate the growing spirit from its universal patrimony of "Nature":

> How awful is the might of souls,
> And what they do within themselves while yet
> The yoke of earth is new to them, the world
> Nothing but a wild field where they were sown.

(Prelude III, 180-83)

To that ground, then, which is in the form of memory or past experience only because of a false theory of nurture that dispossesses imagination while pretending to civilize it, Wordsworth returned. The imagination which has no past can have no future. It becomes blank or black, empty or apocalyptic. The episode from *Prelude* II roots us, therefore, in the past, and moves from the feeling of personal continuity to a vision of the chain of being. The immemorial nature of the earth evoked in the lines between dashes (120-24) adds itself to the historical past suggested by the ruined chapel and completes in this way the visionary resonance of one fugitive, personal event.

It was at Grasmere, a village nestling among the lakes of northern England, that Wordsworth became fully, prophetically conscious of his special role among the great English poets. He settled there with Dorothy in the winter of 1799 after his visit to Germany. Coleridge moved to the nearby village of Keswick. In 1802 the poet married Mary Hutchinson, a childhood friend; while her sister, Sarah, who came to live with the Wordsworths, was intended by them for the poet's brother John after he should have made his fortune as a merchant captain.

The Wordsworth household at Grasmere—the poet, three women, and Coleridge nearby—was not just a family but a utopian community: the Susquehanna scheme revived on the banks of Windermere. It does not last long: Coleridge, ill in health and disaffected from his wife, leaves for Malta in 1804 (*The Prelude* becomes an oversize verse letter to him); John Wordsworth is drowned in 1805, a shock from which the community never recovered; and there are many financial, as well as personal, worries. But those five years, from late 1799 to 1805, were essential. We know a great deal about them through Coleridge's recently published *Notebooks* and through Dorothy's Journals.

When Wordsworth said of Dorothy, "She gave me eyes, she gave me ears," it was no vain compliment. In her *Journals* we read, for example, of their meeting the poor old man who became the Leechgatherer of "Resolution and Independence" or that description of the daffodils which Wordsworth transformed into "I wandered lonely as a cloud." The members of the community exchanged feelings and observations, noted the slightest stirrings in nature and the simplest human excitements. Wordsworth's poetry becomes, even more than at Alfoxden, a "living calendar" which records the imaginative pleasures provided by the countryside, but also some contrary "fears and fancies...dim sadness...blind thoughts" ("Resolution and Independence"). These disturbances are often caused, paradoxically, by poetry itself: by the labor of composition which could make the poet physically ill. Wordsworth had an intense consciousness of what great poetry was before him, and a constant need to reaffirm his own genius and difference. Thus the mystery of vocation kept moving to the center and made an autobiographical poem inevitable.

Composing *The Prelude* Wordsworth discovers—not abstractly, but in the very act of reflective writing—how vulnerable the ego is, but also how many chances there are for self-renewal. Aided only by the action of the mind on itself, and the small, affectionate community he has built up, he describes the corporate nature of selfhood, the interpenetration of past and present selves, and the quiet yet infinite ties between man and man, or man and nature, without which we could not exist. Conscious of these ties, and reinforcing the most elemental as well as the most subtle of them, his poetry emanates a healing power celebrated by Victorian readers and still recognized by critics of our era from Walter Raleigh to F.R. Leavis and Lionel Trilling. In the famous preface, which was written at Grasmere, to *Lyrical Ballads*, Wordsworth announces clearly that link between poetry and the sympathetic imagination which the younger Romantics (Hazlitt, Keats, and Shelley) will espouse more militantly:

> What then does the Poet? He considers man and the objects that surround him as acting and reacting upon each other, so as to produce an infinite complexity of pain and pleasure; he considers man in his own nature and in his ordinary life as contemplating this...as looking upon this complex scene of ideas and sensations, and finding everywhere objects that immediately excite in him sympathies...He is the rock of defence of human nature; an upholder and preserver, carrying everywhere with him relationship and love. In spite of difference of soil and climate, of language and manners, of laws and customs, in spite of things silently gone out of mind and things violently destroyed, the Poet binds together by passion and knowledge the vast empire of human society, as it is spread over the whole earth, and over all time.

He considers man in his own nature and in his ordinary life. Milton did not, and Shakespeare generally did not. Only Chaucer, perhaps, comes close to being a master of ordinary life in poetry. But Chaucer's realism is accompanied, and ironically blended, with romance modes of narration. Nothing could be more realistic than his portrait of the Wife of Bath, or the psychology of the tale she tells, yet this tale is full of supernatural and romance motifs. This difference between Chaucer and Wordsworth is more than a difference between narrative and lyrical. Wordsworth teaches imagination to rejoice in itself in a new way: what was expressed, prior to him, in the displaced though magnanimous form of male

Vision or female Romance is now confronted humanely and directly:

> Not Chaos, not
> The darkest pit of lowest Erebus,
> Nor aught of blinder vacancy, scooped out
> By help of dreams—can breed such fear and awe
> As fall upon us often when we look
> Into our Minds, into the Mind of Man—
> My haunt, and the main region of my song.
>
> ("Prospectus" [written between 1798-1800]
> to *The Excursion* [1814])

Out of this farewell to myth contemporary poetry is born. Although the farewell proves somewhat premature (Wallace Stevens's "Phoebus is dead, ephebe," is still part of it) this example of a man resisting tradition in favor of imagination, then resisting his own imagination, dominates modern poetry. Rejecting all visionary aids, and all rhetorical inflation, Wordsworth had hoped for a progress of the sympathetic imagination anticipated by this change in the form of poetry: a progress that would humanize our feelings and expand them till they sympathized even with "mute, insensate things." Yet *The Excursion*, the later sonnets, and almost all poetry written after 1806 fail to show that progress. What went wrong?

There are many theories concerning Wordsworth's decline. Before we add to them it should be said that his later poetry is not uninteresting: its individual pathos, its awkward mixture of inwardness and unction, give it a character of its own. It is hard to imagine another poet writing those heavy odes, those crammed—and cramped—sonnets with their wish to "awe the lightness of humanity." This line stems from a poem composed in 1818: put it against that famous passage from "Tintern Abbey," written twenty years before, and celebrating the "blessed mood" in which "the burthen of the mystery...Is lightened," and you get a sense of development as well as change.

A falling-off is painfully obvious, however. The later poetry is without genuine form of its own, a stream of prosy reminiscence in sonnet, ode, or conversation piece. Though iconic form (the masterful impositions of a Milton or Yeats) is not everyone's forte, poetry must lead or purify ideas in some way. Wordsworth, however, not only fails to condense his thought into a clear structure or dialectic but begins to use poetry purely as a defensive reaction to strange sympathies and apocalyptic stirrings. He constantly betrays something in himself, and calmly writes about it: "That glimpse of glory, why renewed?" He protests the glory, and asks his imagination to let him alone. In 1827 Crabb Robinson is so alarmed at Wordsworth's change that he foresees the remark of a future critic: "This great poet survived to the fifth decade of the nineteenth century, but he appears to have died in the year 1814 [the year of *The Excursion*] as far as life consisted in an active sympathy with the temporal welfare of his fellow creatures."

If Wordsworth, as Keats recognized, bore "the burthen of the mystery" more intensely than previous poets, it is not surprising that there should have been emotional exhaustion or desire for stability. But this explanation does not fit all the facts. Miss Fenwick, a confidante of the aging poet, writes of him as he approaches seventy: "How fearfully strong are all his feelings and affections! If his intellect had been less powerful they must have destroyed him long ago." The trouble is that Wordsworth never really renounced his younger self: he secretly canonized it, and much of his later poetry is written in bad faith. For it is impossible to guess the content of *The Prelude* from reading, in a typical later sonnet,

> Earth prompts—Heaven urges; let us seek the light
> Studious of that pure intercourse begun
> When first our infant brows their lustre won.
>
> *(Ecclesiastical Sonnets)*

The sublime or public diction to which he returns conceals the fact that he relies for the vigor of this thought on the authority of his greatest poem, which remains unpublished, and as scripture to himself undermines the necessity of reconception. Whether publishing *The Prelude* in its time would have made a difference to his later development is impossible to say, but it would have reduced the number of poems reflecting earlier insights at second or third remove. The older Wordsworth is standing on ground already beaten; the brilliant quarry has been dislodged; the hiding-places will not yield more.

Wordsworth's real danger was always the "sublime"—the public and preacherly dimension—rather than the "egotistical." He hankers increasingly after vision old-style, after the explicit prophetic dimension of a poetry like Milton's. *The Excursion*, the only long poem published in his lifetime, is, like Cowper's *The Task*, a consciously public poem. When Matthew Arnold said that in Wordsworth "philosophy is the illusion, poetry. . . the reality," he must have meant by "philosophy" Wordsworth's desire to harmonize his experience with received ideas, and particularly with the sublime philosophy of the Anglo-Catholic Church. The *Ecclesiastical Sonnets* (1822) still describe a Progress of the Mind, but it is virtually equated with the emergence of the English Church in the Reformation.

We turn back to the young Wordsworth. His vision of that Progress was not parochial but universal. *The Prelude* implies a new and original model for human development. Its realism clarifies the mystery of identity. Like Freud, Wordsworth begins at a point far removed from the humanistic axiom, "Nothing human is alien to me." On the contrary: everything human is alien to us initially. The sense for the human is achieved, painfully won, not given. The quasi-mythical scheme underlying *The Prelude's* theory of development is similar to that sketched in the *Intimations Ode*: we are born aliens into a world which is at most a foster home, or substitute heaven. Our destiny, therefore, is to accept a world which is less than our hopes conceive, though great enough. Nature, with lesser glory than the mythical heaven from which the child fell, attracts our imagination until it becomes this-worldly. It sows its images in the child's mind, it blends with our imagination: the river Derwent, Wordsworth writes, "sent a voice / That flowed along my dreams." The first two books of *The Prelude* describe this naturalization of the child, its weaning from the milk of paradise, from inchoate dreams and apocalyptic stirrings. The sentimentalists who hold that for Wordsworth childhood is all could not be further from the truth. Yes, childhood is closest to divinity, but also to narcissistic self-absorption. The question is how to humanize one's soul without losing it, how to bind the child's imagination without binding it down. A man's sense of the light that was can be his greatest obstacle. Wordsworth describes some of the trials of the soul that we undergo to become civilized persons.

If Nature fails, the child's development is either arrested, and he becomes an idiot whose "life is with God," or a premature adult, doomed to cynicism or alienation. If Nature succeeds, the child is organically ready to be humanized, and humanization is the second developmental step covered by *The Prelude*. The two steps are, of course, interrelated: and the road from "love of nature" to "love of man," even though built, in Wordsworth's case, on a strong and sensuous foundation, is so precarious that its charting occupies the greater part of his secular poem. Thus *The Prelude* is a *Bildungsroman* that takes the child from solipsism to society and from his unconsciously apocalyptic mind, dreaming of an utterly different world, to a sense of realities. It is the epic of civilization, the epic of the emergence of an individual consciousness out of a field of forces that includes imagination, nature, and society. "How then are Souls to be made?" asks Keats. "How then are these sparks which are God to have identity given them—so as ever to possess a bliss peculiar to each one's individual existence? How but by the medium of a world like this?" That, after Wordsworth, is the unforgettable theme.

Wordsworth, together with Blake, is the last of a giant race of poets to whom the moderns are as indebted as the neoclassical poets to their Renaissance predecessors. Sometimes, with the pressures of contemporary life what they are, Wordsworth's poetry may seem too reflective or low-powered. Yet we rarely cease to feel the agony or urgency from which it sprang. It mediates between the modern world and a desperate imagination, one that sees itself deprived of genuine relations with that world. The tempo of industrialization seemed to Wordsworth to encourage a rootless and abstract kind of existence, a man-made nature alienating us from Nature. Love, or the sympathetic imagination, could not flourish long in that artificial environment: imagination, indeed, could not even grow to become love in that soil. It needed a slower birth and a more generous nurture, for the imaginative spirit in us is wild, and only gradually humanized. Wordsworth's sense of apocalypse is simply his pre-vision of the failure of that process of humanization. The modern imagination, stronger than ever, but also more homeless than ever, falls back into itself, or endlessly outward. It becomes solipsistic or seeming-mad. We understand Wordsworth best when we are too near ourselves, too naked in our self-consciousness. Then his poetry, its strange spiritual calculus, its balancing of imaginative failure with elemental gratitudes, can still infuse a modest and rocky strength: "O joy! That in our embers / Is something that doth live" (*Intimations Ode*).

2
A Touching Compulsion

In recent years psychoanalytically oriented criticism has become increasingly harder to do. Yet more and more people are doing it.

The reason interest has grown lies perhaps in the heightened difficulty of the venture. As the psychoanalytic study of art has become problematic, it has also become more worthwhile. Today no one can line up writers or their books according to clinical categories or an applied science model. Nor are we intrigued by how many sexual images lie behind the screen of words.

What, then, can psychoanalysis tell us about literature? Even if we overcome methodological and moral scruples, it is not at all clear that the light thrown on the literary text by psychoanalytic investigation does more than make a darkness visible. By darkness I do not mean only the "excrementitious" base which the work of art seems to refine into a curious and complex structure. In the "riddle of the sphincter," as Kenneth Burke calls it, the riddle interests us more than the sphincter. We all in a sense build on hell; and it is not merely a literary problem to what use, clinically or humanly, that knowledge may be put.

The *other* darkness is that of the elusive psyche, or the supposed subject of psychoanalytic investigation. The closer we get to that subject the less of a subject it is: the ego, personal center, *sujet* or signified, dissolves into a field of forces and is depicted by unstable diagrams, "with cycles and epicycles scribbled o'er."

The very language of psychoanalysis has become heavily aggressive, as traces of older models retard sentences laboring toward yet another revision. There comes a point when the question arises about what the subject of psychoanalysis may be. Is it still the psyche? Or how can we distinguish the psyche from 1) the involution of those sentences, more particularly of the Freudian corpus of texts which keeps revising itself, and 2) the involution of Freud's original *Project for a Scientific Psychology*, with its coil of neurological and topographical complexities? The speculation that the psyche is "like" a text corresponds to a state of affairs in which the psyche is burdened by texts explanatory of what the psyche is like.

Perhaps we have entered a period of constitutive doubt vis-à-vis speculative psychoanalysis. That there is need for a therapy along psychoanalytic lines I myself do not question. But the shape and rationale of that therapy keep shifting, and to the point where the presumptive *authority* which medical science cannot give up without becoming another ex-theology is in danger of being lost.

I offer the following pages as an attempt to lessen our dependence on the applied science model of psychoanalytic inquiry. Yet they could not have been written without Freud's exemplary formalizations that encompass such basic experiences as imagining, wishing, sensing, writing and mourning. Since my treatment of these issues arises as much from art as from Freud's science of mind, it may be best to call it *psychoesthetic* rather than *psychoanalytic*.

I

> Think, we had mothers...
> *Troilus and Cressida*, V, v

The created world, according to Blake, was a divine act of mercy to keep us from falling, endlessly, into a void. Even Satan's fall, in *Paradise Lost*, is bottomed—by Hell. Blake's imaginative axiom does not intend so much to honor nature as to indicate its limited providential function. But how do we understand this void, or voiding, of which the familiar world is the "lower" limit?

On reading Wordsworth's "Prospectus" to the 1814 *Excursion*, especially the lines,

> Jehovah—with his thunder, and the choir
> Of shouting Angels, and the empyreal thrones—
> I pass them unalarmed...

Blake complained that it gave him a bowel complaint that almost killed him. Henry Crabb Robinson reports, "I had the pleasure of reading to Blake in my best style (& you know I am vain on that point & think I read W[ordsworth]'s poems peculiarly well) the Ode on Immortality. I never witnessed greater delight in any listener & in general Blake loves the poems. What appears to have disturbed his mind, on the other hand, is the preface to the Excursion. He told me six months ago that it caused him a bowel complaint which nearly killed him." Blake has a figurative way of expressing himself which the bourgeois observer (a Crabb Robinson, for example) might take too literally. Perhaps Wordsworth's exaltation of

Nature in the Prospectus, and his vaunted "passing by" of the visionary realms, did literally make Blake sick. Or perhaps the comment is Blake's way of saying "Shit!"

Blake's reaction to another bard, Klopstock, was not dissimilar: "If Blake could do this when he rose up from shite / What might he not do if he sat down to write?" The imagery of purging (not necessarily anal purging) is very strong in Blake's poetry. Sometimes indeed one has the impression Blake wants to purge or void nature altogether. How different this seems to be from Wordsworth's honoring and reenforcing of "earth's materials." The "Prospectus" that so upset Blake goes on to declare:

> . . . . Paradise, and groves
> Elysian, Fortunate Fields—like those of old
> Sought in the Atlantic Main—why should they be
> A history only of departed things,
> Or a mere fiction of what never was?
> For the discerning intellect of Man,
> When wedded to this goodly universe
> In love and holy passion, shall find these
> A simple produce of the common day.

Yet there is something strange, too, about Wordsworth's relation to Nature. He tells us that when young he had to touch things to convince himself they were there. "I used to brood over the stories of Enoch and Elijah, and almost to persuade myself that, whatever might become of others, I should be translated in something of the same way to heaven. With a feeling congenial to this, I was often unable to think of external things as having external existence, and I communed with all that I saw as something not apart from, but inherent in, my own immaterial nature. Many times while going to school have I grasped a wall or tree to recall myself from this abyss of idealism to the reality" (Fenwick note to "Intimations of Immortality").

The difference between Wordsworth and Blake is not absolute, then. Nature, touched, also kept Wordsworth from falling into a void. What the poet calls "brooding" seems to have made his sight less real: if seeing is believing, here touching is believing. It is interesting that Wordsworth describes our earthly progress, our sensuous and psychic development, as moving subtly from a *drinking touch* to a *drinking via the eyes*:

> . . . blest the Babe,
> Nursed in his Mothers' arms, who sinks to sleep
> Rocked on his Mother's breast; who with his soul
> Drinks in the feelings of his Mother's eye!
> For him, in one dear Presence, there exists

> A virtue which irradiates and exalts
> Objects through widest intercourse of sense.[1]

This passage anticipates a central argument of the entire *Prelude*: our ability to make a transition from the first (and lost) love object to object love. There is a tendency, as in contemporary American psychoanalysis, to understand "object relations" as "love relationships taken in their broadest sense." Yet *The Prelude* is mainly, of course, about the hazards of that broadening. Loss of an earlier relation, or of the primary love object (the mother, "heaven"), is not easily compensated. When Wordsworth was eight years old, his mother died, and he was consciously troubled by the very "Nature" that comforted him:

> ...now a trouble came into my mind
> From unknown causes. I was left alone
> Seeking the visible world, nor knowing why.
> The props of my affections were removed,
> And yet the building stood, as if sustained
> By its own spirit!
>
> (*Prelude* II, 276-81)

How are we to interpret this? On the surface it states a perplexity. The mother dies, the world remains, and as an object of quest or desire. Why should the fact perplex Wordsworth who has just argued in the "blest babe" passage that the mother's function is to effect precisely this bonding: "along his infant veins are interfused / The gravitation and the filial bond / Of nature that connect him to the world" (*Prelude* II, 234ff)? You may say that the child did not know what the adult knows; that the child's ignorant wonder is what is expressed by the poet in a movement of sympathetic recollection. The child is astonished and troubled, not the mature poet. The child has to face the fact of survival, and particularly the evidence of a "spirit" independent of mother and child—to which the grown man can give the name of "Nature."

But is the child's wonder so simple an emotion? Or is it not the "trouble" itself? Wordsworth's phrasing is difficult; yet clearly the child knows the mother has died, so that the "unknown causes" must refer either to the spirit in Nature now manifest or to a psychic, if blind, reaction to that event. The mature poet seems to know two things rather than one, and the exclamation point suggests that his knowledge does not lessen the original emotion. He knows why the world survives the mother as an object of affection, and what made the child's astonishment a "trouble." The first kind of knowledge harmonizes with Freud's understanding of how the lost object becomes by internalization a constitutive part of the self that has lost it—how it helps to build the identity of the person or, as Richard Onorato has argued in Wordsworth's case, even the very notion of *poet* as a human type. But the second kind of knowledge is regressive rather than progressive and qualifies Wordsworth's optimistic theory about the growth of the mind. The troubled astonishment of the child may have expressed a defeated expectation, even perhaps a frustrated death-wish. Nature should not have survived! The reality-bond of motherly affection, being dissolved, should have meant the collapse of everything! Potentially there is here as deep an ambivalence as in Blake about Nature being a substitute love-object.

We are now in a better position to understand the young poet's touching compulsion. It is incited by a ghostliness in nature deriving from two related sources. (I omit his fascinating reference to brooding on visionary stories from the Bible.) The fixated or literally animistic mind feels that if nature remains alive when what gave it life (the mother) is dead, then the mother is not dead but invisibly contained in nature. On the other hand, if the mother *is* dead, then the affective presence of nature is but a phantom-reality that must dissolve just like the illusion it has replaced—the illusion of a permanent *dasein* (the mother's). Wordsworth's touching, then, is a kind of reality testing: it wants to undo the spell, or make contact with the "one dear Presence" in hiding.[2]

Let me try, somewhat quickly and aggressively, to generalize. Is not artistic representation (understood as a re-presencing) a similar kind of touching, or reality testing? There is, first of all, something inevitably regressive, animistic, or overcompensatory about all modes of mimetic representation; and if there were no other justification for critics we would need them to free the work of art from the potentially regressive understanding it elicits.

Second, art restores the sense of touch, for the artist at least. This is clearest in arts that involve more tactility than the passage of pen over paper. "When I draw I have a feeling of tactile communication as if every line and stroke palpitated under my hand and through this process only I learn to understand the essence of the model, in taking it into myself." Ernst Kris records this remark of a patient in his *Psychoanalytic Explorations in Art*, but of course it raises other issues too: that of sexual or libidinal feelings, and of incorporation. It serves to suggest that music, poetry, painting, even writing, involve touch through material composition or related psychic impressions. We "touch back" to move forward.

Last, the reality testing of art verges on reality challenging: the desire not to be mastered by, but rather to master, that phantom presence. Art is craftiness as well as craft. Its maneuvering of words or feelings can be as complex as that attributed to the ego in Anna Freud's *The Ego and its Mechanisms of Defense*—a veritable war-game manual. For the act of writing is deeply associated with feelings of trespass, theft, forgery, self-exposure. These are not merely private to the artist, and extricated by depth psychology; they are, as recurrent theme and subject, matters of public record. Our great myths display confidence men or thieves: cunning liars like Odysseus, amorous gangsters like Don Juan, robin hoods like Satan or Prometheus.

By means of representation the artist steals something from God (or Nature) or steals it back; and so it is almost inevitable that the representation, *qua* substitute object, invest itself as an autonomous, if alienated, source of value. "To counterfeit is death," we read on old American paper money. The game of art may run that risk: its reality testing wants reality to manifest itself, or let its mock be.

II

An esperance so obstinately strong
That doth invert th' attest of eyes and ears.
Troilus and Cressida, V, v

Art's restorative *touch* must be acknowledged, yet we should not forget the role of *sight*. It is the eyes which, naturally ghostly, suggest the possibility of "action at a distance." Yet they are unable to accept this negative touching and so are always questioning themselves. Though ears too are ghostly, sight, contrasted with hearing, seems to need more purification: always as full as it is empty ("O dark, dark, dark, amid the blaze of noon")[3] it must be purged of mere images, of the dead weight of *visibilia*, or "questionable shapes" possessing uncanny affectivity.

Wordsworth's "I wandered lonely as a cloud" moves with grace in this area of dreamy traumatism where sights or sounds "halt" the poet with "a gentle shock of mild surprise" (*Prelude* V, 382). One hardly feels the voracity of the poet's visual desire because it is so finely, gradually revealed through his casual encounter with the "golden daffodils." Yet what we are given here, and in many other poems, is a strange moment of bliss, a mild seizure or ecstasy that betrays the internal pressure—one that climaxes when the poet's "vacant" or "pensive" mood "fills" with the image of the daffodils. When Wordsworth writes: "I gazed—and gazed—but little thought / What wealth the show to me had brought," our ear may be justified in adding "I grazed—and grazed." Touch, or materiality, returns to the phantom of sight. The ear develops the image in its own way.

Wordsworth, of course, often singles out the ear as an "organ of vision," or a sense both intensely pure yet deeply in touch with earthliness:

> . . . I would walk alone,
> Under the quiet stars, and at that time
> Have felt whate'er there is of power in sound
> To breathe an elevated mood, by form
> Or image unprofaned; and I would stand,
> If the night blackened with a coming storm,

> Beneath some rock, listening to notes that are
> The ghostly language of the ancient earth,
> Or make their dim abode in distant winds.
> Thence did I drink the visionary power.
>
> (*Prelude* II, 302-11)

Where other poets might have invoked a heavenly music, he evokes a music of the earthly sphere.

The dialectic of the senses in Wordsworth is psychagogic and can be analyzed even if we are not sure where it leads. Interestingly enough, he rarely uses synaesthesia: his typical intensities are those in which he is "now all eye and now / All ear" (*Prelude* XII, 93-100 and XIV, 38ff.). The senses counteract the tyranny of the eye *and* themselves (*Prelude* XII, 127-39). An intrapsychic sensory process is said to free the poet from quasi-epiphanic fixations, from overinvested ideas or images. Nature functions here like Plato's dialectic (*Republic*, 523ff.) and encourages a *via negativa*.

Such natural transcendence remains, however, quite problematic. Indeed, it generally perplexes rather than purifies eye and ear. We get more a feeling of impasse than facilitation. When the limits of perceptibility are reached, through that process of

> . . . obstinate questionings
> Of sense and outward things,
> Fallings from us, vanishings;
> Blank misgivings of a Creature
> Moving about in worlds not realized
>
> ("Intimations of Immortality")

—when the light of sense goes out, and intimations of the death or the blankness of nature arise, there is a resistance, a counter-obstinacy. The line leading to vision or methodical hallucination is not crossed. Hence a poetry that fixes so constantly, retentively, on bare markers, totems or natural steles—"But there's a Tree, of many, one, / A single Field which I have looked upon" ("Intimations Ode").

Such markers, that still seem to point to what has departed, are strangely individuated. The "single" tree is not a prophetic and lamentable prop (a Dodonian oak) that has survived the stage set of more visionary epochs: it is part of an earth-writing, an undeciphered geography or geometry. One may call these markers boundary images or omphaloi (navel-points of the cosmos), a term Mircea Eliade adapts from Homer, and they link poetic to geometric absoluteness:

> On poetry and geometric truth,
> And their high privilege of lasting life,

> From all internal injury exempt,
> I mused.
>
> (*Prelude* V, 65-69)

Geometry/Geomatry: mother nature, or the mother-in-nature, is the guardian of something invulnerable, which is either the mother-child relation itself or an ideal of psychic development.

Yet every child is "untimely ripped from the womb," according to Freud's understanding of human prematurity. Later too there are no timely separations. The wound of birth, that primary separation from nature, is but the prelude to a psychic development subject to related wounds or traumas. Things always happen untimely, prematurely—Matthew, at seventy-two, still sings "witty rimes / About the crazy old church-clock / And the bewildered chimes" ("The Fountain," *Lyrical Ballads* of 1800). The wound supposedly overcome by the strangely consorted disciplines of poetry and geometry lies in the very necessity of growing up, of maturation.

Let me return a moment to the dialectic of the senses and specify the role it plays in psychic development. How do ears counteract eyes? There is, for example, a "gravitation" (*Prelude* II, 243) induced by music, or by periods of silence. It makes the sights of nature—when too still, and thus seemingly dead—rotate, or sink down into the mind (*Prelude* II, 169-74). These pauses, as in "The Boy of Winander" episode, may be untimely, yet that seems to allow something to penetrate so "far" into the mind that it is lodged as deeply as the dead mother, the "one dear Presence" in hiding:

> . . . in that silence while he hung
> Listening, a gentle shock of mild surprise
> Has carried far into his heart the voice
> Of mountain torrents; or the visible scene
> Would enter unawares into his mind,
> With all it solemn imagery, its rocks,
> Its woods, and that uncertain heaven, received
> Into the bosom of the steady lake.
>
> (*Prelude* V, 381-88)

The embosoming effect is unmistakable. Hearing seems to mediate touch.

In other poets too the ears can be a "trembling" medium that restores touch to visible things by picking up vibrations:

> I caught this morning morning's minion, king-
>   dom of daylight's dauphin, dapple-dawn-drawn Falcon, in his riding

> Of the rolling level underneath him steady air, and striding
> High there...

In this eye-catching bird-catching the sense of distance is qualified by the contagious touch of the elliptical metaphor ("I caught"). It renders both a far-striking image and the attempted grasping of it by the poet's appetitive eye. The air has waves.[4]

Yet here we approach the notion of what always defeats as well as exalts art. Eyeing is to become a kind of touching, but touching only augments the desire for ocular proof. Glittering eyes turn therefore into glittering hands. Like those of Midas they compulsively gild everything—make it accountable, touchable, money for sight. Art's attempt to "materialize" or "fix" a "presence" betrays paradoxically an "idealizing ("eye-dealizing") motive that ends in fixation. Whether it is Othello assaying Desdemona or the believer searching for evidence of the Divine—this quest for ocular proof culminates in desolation rather than consolation: in a deepened awareness of loss. What Freud named *Schau-Lust* (scoptophilia) verges on *Schau-Verlust* because of (1) what the eyes actually discover (cf. what Troilus sees in Shakespeare's *Troilus and Cressida* V, iii-v), and (2) what they can never discover, since there is no complete compensation for the first love object. Indeed, the very idea of a "first" love may be a fiction to anchor and so limit our sense of betrayal. We blame a particular experience or person rather than life itself. It is better, as Kierkegaard suggests in the "Prelude" to *Fear and Trembling*, to blacken the mother's breast. If we overcome that first "death," as Dylan Thomas writes, "there is no other."

III

> My negation hath no taste of madness.
> *Troilus and Cressida* V, v

Homer sings the wrath of Achilles. But what is inspiring about that teen-age tantrum? The hero who accepts no substitutes challenges more than the ethos of compromise and accommodation that preserves the social order. He challenges life—nature—itself, with its supposedly progressive sacrifice of love objects. To have a divine mother, like Achilles, is hazardous: for how can you lose her? Achilles has no human fears. His wrath is not a human but a divine tantrum.

Art displays an anger, a *furor poeticus*, similar to that of Achilles. But its anger includes itself, for art remains as ambivalent about its own status as about the comfort or complicity of all compensatory substitutions. In its cunning protest against life, art now sets nature against art, now art against nature.

Consider once more those apparent opposites, Wordsworth and Blake. Wordsworth tends to sacrifice art to nature, because the latter, as the first love-substitute, is the basis of all further sublimation in growing up. Blake, however, wishes to sacrifice nature, precisely because it exacts the "sacrifice" of substitution. His rage against the "Religion of Nature" and its artificial code is clearly against something that diminishes our imaginative energies and fosters instead an unreal or compensatory god-symbolism.

Yet there may be a resentment of nature even in Wordsworth. He says, in "Tintern Abbey," that nature never betrayed the heart that loved her; but that is already a betrayed person speaking. Nature is second best, a substitute heaven; and the object of Wordsworth's nature poems is not nature but the "one dear Presence" lost yet perhaps recoverable—like Eurydice. His moving beyond the eye (toward touch) is therefore tantamount to making nature disappear: collapsing it into the cache he is seeking. And often, rather than be deceived again—by "mother" Nature this time— he cultivates an ideal blindness not unlike that of the abstract sciences. He brings together, as in *Prelude* V, 65ff., poetry and geometric truth. They identify the *precious* as the *constant* object and anticipate a psyche "from all internal injury exempt."

No wonder, then, a "quiet" or "listening" eye determines the kind of poetry Wordsworth writes. His stately but static figures barely differentiate themselves from their landscape. It is hard to *see* them: they move in a blind or hypnotic trance as if they too did not need sight, theirs or ours. They are so stripped, so elemental, that little remains of them except the constancy of blind faith. At times, therefore, Wordsworth's poetry almost transcends representation, and thus reality testing. It gives up not only the eyes but also touch—tangible words. It seems to exist then without the material density of poetic texture—without imagistic or narrative detail. The presence it continues to evoke becomes "untouchable"; and the impossibility of being wounded through eye or ear adds to this untouchableness and intensifies the human invulnerability, as in the famous short lyric:

> A slumber did my spirit seal;
> I had no human fears;
> She seemed a thing that could not feel
> The touch of earthly years.
>
> No motion has she now, no force;
> She neither hears nor sees;
> Rolled round in earth's diurnal course,
> With rocks, and stones, and trees.

Sudden death does not wound either the loved person or the lover. The relation of the ecstatic consciousness (first stanza) to the mortal consciousness (second stanza) is more like image to afterimage than illusion to the shock of disillusion. Each of the stanzas shows a spirit sealed up and something that remains untouchable. The loved person, called a "thing" by proleptic or intensely understated phrasing, passes from life to death as if in fulfillment of the immutability attributed to her. There is no melancholy fit or cry of surprise: an image of "gravitation" elides the grave and suggests that poetry is a work of mourning that lies "too deep for tears." Mourning becomes Wordsworth.

IV

Your passion draws ears hither.
Troilus and Cressida, V, v

If what Wordsworth represents in his poetry is an absence, does not the term "representation" become questionable? The beloved is never present in the Lucy poems except as the absent one. The hypothesis, moreover, that the absence is the mother's cannot be verified. The psychic role of the lost mother could be, as I have said, a fiction to ground a sense of betrayal arising with consciousness, or self-consciousness. It is, in any case, the interpreter's hypothesis, since Wordsworth nowhere explicitly makes the connection.

A related difficulty is that the loss of the mother need not determine the feeling of loss. When the mother is around there may still be a sense that she is absent, that she is not the real mother. Freud discussed this feeling common to many children under the concept of Family Romance. The father, moreover, is not excluded from being the subject of the romance. For all we know the absent mother may be a screen for a sense that the father is absent—that *his* nurturance is lacking or inadequate. It is unlikely that the interpreter can come to a firm conclusion on the nature of the felt absence.

What, then, is the value of psychoesthetic inquiries? Perhaps that they lead us to this indeterminacy. They make us less sure, less dogmatic, about the referent of art, and without denying a mimetic principle they show the distance between mimetic and symbolic representation. Instead of taking as our starting point a presence that is lost, and viewing representation as a represencing of what is lost, we might alternatively begin with absence. As conscious beings we are always at a distance from the origin. Yet to begin with absence is still an epochal or grounding maneuver. It may also be a contemporary and formalistic *memento mori* acknowledging unsentimentally that what individuates us is at once ineffable *and* mortal. The stronger our consciousness of individuality, the stronger our sense of the betrayal that might befall it. Only the individual can be "betrayed" by death, mutability, or the awareness that he is not individual enough: in short, reproducible. Hence a temptation to re-ground him on nothing; more precisely, on his power continually to negate nothing. A quest for the Story of Nothing arises.

Wordsworth's role in this Story of Nothing is clear. Despite *expressions* that intimate a striving for absolute knowledge ("Praise to the End," "How shall I

trace the history, where seek / The origin. . . ?'') he *depicts* the lost object not literally but symbolically, that is, as a limiting or boundary term without which the
mind might lose itself in the hallucinating void of visionary images. Wordsworth
does not make absence present in the manner of gothic, ghostly, or surrealist fantasies, or animated spectres. The absent one remains absent in his representations. What is depicted is, as it were, the legacy of this absence, which he circumscribes with periphrastic inventions that have the strength of a breaking wave:
"And something evermore about to be" (*Prelude* VI, 608). ". . . the
soul, / Remembering how she felt, but what she felt / Remembering not, retains
an obscure sense / Of possible sublimity, whereto / With growing faculties she
doth aspire / With faculties still growing, feeling still / That whatsoever point
they gain, they yet / Have something to pursue" (*Prelude* II, 315-22). This kind
of periphrasis is not indebted to school rhetoric or precious diction. It does not
assume there is a proper term that could be expressed yet is avoided. Rather, the
gerundive evokes something "to be continued" and borders on the infinitive.
Things remembered or imagined are viewed as absent not because they are lost
(though they may be) but because their "trace" is difficult to substantialize as
a noun or a name.

So in poetry we often sense a word under the words. This *paragrammatic
doubling*[5], which may induce a *doubting* of the literal or referential meaning, can
be compared to what happens when the boundary between living and dead
becomes uncertain in the mind of the mourner. The poet feels that what is lost
is in language, perhaps even a lost language; under the words are ghostlier words,
half-perceived figures or fragments that seem to be at once part of the lost object
yet more living than what is present.

The ideal of psychic health deems it better, of course, to declare the absent one
as dead—absolutely lost to present experience. It asks the mourner to separate
himself from the dead by public rituals of a well-defined and terminal kind.
Mourning may last seven or thirty days: specific words of lament or consolation
are enjoined. The dead person is laid to rest in language and in time, and the living
find that they can and must continue as the living. But some situations are less
determinable. When Wordsworth opens "Tintern Abbey" with "Five years have
past; five summers with the length / Of five long winters! and again I hear. . . ,"
the drawn-out words express a mind that remains "in somewhat of a sad perplexity," a mind that tries to locate in time what is lost, but cannot do so with therapeutic precision. Or to adduce a more dramatic instance: Margaret's husband in
"The Ruined Cottage" is absent rather than dead and leaves her in a mental state
uncomfortably close to that of believers who know Christ is absent, not dead,
and await his return. In the passion of Margaret the period of mourning extends
itself until it is coterminous with time. Christ, of course, is not a "lost object"
(like Margaret's husband or Wordsworth's parents) but an object of faith—the

evidence of things not seen. Yet Wordsworth generally hovers between one passion and the other: his Christianity, such as it is, is not a congealed myth but keeps growing out of a secular understanding.

"The sounding cataract haunted me like a passion" is part of this understanding. And it reminds us of something evaded in the present essay: that laying the absent one to rest means silencing a voice as well as an image. The memorial poetry Wordsworth writes ("and again I hear...") at once expresses and represses a "ghostly language." The identity of this language remains uncertain: is it the mother's voice that, like Derwent's (*Prelude* I, 269 ff.), flowed along the child's dreams, or the lost sublime of Miltonic and Biblical figuration ("I used to brood over the stories of Enoch and Elijah...")? Biblical and balladic harmonize uneasily in Wordsworth's lyric experiments: both seem like the inland murmur of ancient tongues. Veritable ghost-meanings thus undermine the simple words he uses. "Strange fits of passion have I known"—how do we interpret "fits" and "passion"? Could the line mean, "I have been subject to the fitful (hallucinatory) hearing of an affecting voice"? Is the cry, "If Lucy should be dead!," which he voices only at the end of the poem, heard internally from the beginning? In "A slumber did my spirit seal" voice is completely internalized; there is no cry-ing.

"Sei allem Abschied voran," Rilke declares in one of his sonnets to Orpheus: "Outpace all separation." So Wordsworth's "fit" is also a quasi-heroic "feat" which fails to outrun an infinite misgiving. Even the most present gift of Nature—Lucy or the beloved in the prime of love—is subject to this misgiving: "Blank misgivings of a Creature / Moving about in worlds unrealized." A remark in Wordsworth's "Essay on Epitaphs" can serve to conclude my analysis; it reminds us of Wordsworth as a schoolboy grasping wall or tree to save himself from intimations of unreality: "I confess, with me the conviction is absolute, that if the impression and sense of death were not thus counterbalanced [by internal evidences of love and immortality anterior to memory], such a hollowness would pervade the whole system of things, such a want of correspondence and consistency, a disproportion so astounding betwixt means and ends, that there could be no motions of the life of love; and infinitely less could we have any wish to be remembered after we had passed away from a world in which each man had moved about like a shadow." In Wordsworth's poetry mourning and memory converge as an infinite task, a "work."

3
Inscriptions and Romantic Nature Poetry

The earliest genuinely lyrical poem by Wordsworth bears an elaborate title: "Lines left upon a Seat in a Yew-Tree, which stands near the Lake of Esthwaite, on a desolate part of the shore, yet commanding a beautiful prospect." The poem reached its final form between 1795 and 1797 and appears as the first of Words-worth's productions in the *Lyrical Ballads* of 1798. Its structure is simple: an apostrophe to the passing traveler commends a solitary spot in nature; this is followed by a moral and biographical epitome of the recluse who so loved this spot and its view that he built the seat ("his only monument") mentioned in the title; the conclusion admonishes once more the passer-by, asking him to heed the story just told and the moral now drawn from it. The poem is in the mature blank verse of Wordsworth's meditative poetry, and it reflects his strong eye for nature and his general moral sensitivity.

It may seem irrelevant to ask what kind of lyric this is. Coleridge, in the verses that follow it in *Lyrical Ballads*, invents a genre of his own, calling "The Night-ingale" a "conversation poem"; and Wordsworth's lyric challenges the same apparent freedom of designation. Its value, to us at least, does not seem to depend in any way on the recognition of the species to which it may belong. This is true, of course, of many of the best Romantic lyrics: consider "Tintern Abbey" or "Old Man Travelling," to stay only with *Lyrical Ballads*. There is a pleasure in not knowing, or not being able to discern, the traditional form; the lack becomes a positive virtue, and we begin to seek, not quite earnestly, for the proper formal description. Are the "Lines left upon a Seat in a Yew-Tree" a fragment of meditative-didactic verse, a chunk freed from some longer topographical poem, a disguised anecdote, an extended epitaph? To the naïve yet careful reader the form may appear, above all, as an effective way to sweeten a moral by human interest and immediacy of situation.

It is certain, however, that Wordsworth's first characteristic lyric belongs to a special genre. Charles Lamb recognized it instinctively. He heard the poem while visiting Coleridge at Nether Stowey in July 1797—the famous visit during which "dear Sara" accidentally emptied a skillet of boiling milk on her poet-husband's foot and set the stage for another of his great conversation poems: "This Lime-Tree Bower my Prison." During that visit, Wordsworth read the "Lines left upon a Seat in a Yew-Tree," and Lamb could not get them out of his mind. Shortly after returning home he wrote Coleridge about the poem. "You would make me very happy, if you think W. has no objection, by transcribing for me that inscription of his." And later in the same letter, "But above all *that Inscription!*"[1]

The term Lamb uses twice, and the second time in a generic sense, identifies a lyrical mode that has not attracted attention, perhaps because it is such a normal, accepted, even archaic feature of the eighteenth-century literary scene. The inscription, as Lamb calls it, was more genus than species, being the primitive form of the epigram, and was connected therefore with most of the briefer forms of lyric in the eighteenth century. It was in theory, and often in fact, a dependent form of poetry, in the same sense in which the statues of churches are dependent on their architectural setting or partly conceived in function of it. The inscription was any verse conscious of the place on which it was written, and this could be tree, rock, statue, gravestone, sand, window, album, sundial, dog's collar, back of fan, back of painting. It ranged in scope and seriousness from Pope's inscription on the collar of the Prince of Wales's dog: "I am his Highness' dog at Kew / Pray tell me sir, whose dog are you?" to Thomas Warton's "Verses on Sir Joshua's Painted Window at New College."[2] This general form of the inscription was accompanied by a special form which we shall call the *nature-inscription*, whose popularity seems to have been proportional to that of eighteenth-century gardens. In Shenstone's *ferme ornée*, The Leasowes, one of the famous show gardens of the time, beautiful prospects were discreetly marked for the tourist by benches with inscriptions from Virgil or specially contrived poems.[3] It was this kind of inscription that provided a pattern for Wordsworth's "Lines left upon a Seat"; though pattern is, perhaps, too strong a term. Wordsworth was able to liberate the genre from its dependent status of tourist guide and antiquarian signpost: he made the nature-inscription into a free-standing poem, able to commemorate any feeling for nature or the spot that had aroused this feeling.

A direct glance at the "Lines left upon a seat" yields many of the characteristics both of the inscription in general and of nature-inscriptions in particular. The swollen title, beside telling us where the poem is supposedly found, reflects the link between inscription and epigram. Since the epigram, especially in the later Renaissance, tended to be as brief and pointed as possible, the particular circumstances which had given rise to it were often placed in the title. There are epigrams with titles longer than the epigrams themselves. The relation between title (lemma)[4] and epigram was quite complex and varied, like the cognate relation between motto and picture in the emblem; and I need hardly add that none of this complexity is found in Wordsworth. But his elaborated title does reflect the tradition of the epigram and may even reproduce, typographically, the effect of an inscription.[5] Most of the concrete detail, however, is included in the poem itself, which is far too lengthy to have been inscribed and resembles the Greek rather than Greco-Roman form of the epigram.[6]

The second feature to be noted is still common to both general and special forms of inscription. I can best suggest it by quoting from Lessing's treatise on the epigram—systematic theorizing about genre was his forte, and in England we find little or no sustained consideration of the epigram-inscription as such. Noting that the modern form of the epigram was derived, primitively, from actual inscriptions, Lessing comments: "The true inscription is not to be thought of apart from that whereon it stands, or might stand. Both together make the whole from which arises the impression which, speaking generally, we ascribe to the inscription alone. First, some object of sense which arouses our curiosity; and then the account of this same object, which satisfies that curiosity."[7]

The relevance of this structure to Wordsworth's poem is obvious. By the title—the admonition "Nay, Traveller! rest"—and indeed by the whole opening (to line 12), it presents an object that should arouse curiosity. It then goes on to satisfy that curiosity by its story of the recluse, except that our attention, far from being dissolved, is steadily deepened. The Yew with its ingrown seat is explained, but not explained away. Our eyes are opened to a truth latent in the simplest feature of the landscape. Wordsworth moves psychology closer to archeology by resuscitating the story of the recluse from a trace strongly merged with nature.

The third feature of the inscription, and perhaps the most intriguing, is related to this sense for a life (in nature) so hidden, retired, or anonymous that it is perceived only with difficulty. This sense of hidden life is peculiar to the nature-inscription and betrays itself also in formalistic ways. There is first the context of anonymity which the poem partially dispels. The lines are "left" upon the seat, and they describe a person who has (1) lived unknown, in retirement, and (2) lived an unknown life. He resembles one of the "unhonour'd Dead"whose "artless tale" Gray begins to reveal in his *Elegy*. The anonymity of nature and the anonymity of the common man join to produce an elegiac tenor of feeling.

There is, moreover, a general convergence of elegiac and nature poetry in the eighteenth century. Poems about place (locodescriptive) merge with meditations on death so that landscape becomes dramatic in a quietly startling way. From it there emanate "admonitions and heart-stirring remembrances, like a refreshing breeze that comes without warning, or the taste of waters from an unexpected fountain."[8] Not only is the graveyard a major locus for the expression of nature sentiment, but Nature is herself a larger graveyard inscribed deeply with evidences of past life. This convergence of graveyard and nature, or of epitaph and loco-descriptive poetry, is consecrated by the success of Gray's *Elegy* (1751), in which the division between countryside and cemetery is hardly felt. We move with insid-uously gradual steps from the one to the other, and Gray enters so strongly into the spirit of his poem that he imagines himself as one of the unhonored dead rescued from anonymity only by his epitaph graved under a thorn. His poem ends, therefore, with an archaic image of itself—an actual inscription for which the whole elegy provides the setting, and this is nature in its most regular, ancient, and oblivious form.

Perhaps the clearest sign of the merging of epitaph and nature poetry is the address to the Traveler with which the Yew-tree poems begins. The "Nay, Traveller! rest" is the traditional *Siste Viator* of the epitaph. We are made to hear the admonitory voice of the deceased or of the living who speak for the deceased. Yet Wordsworth commemorates a strange spot in nature rather than a grave, since the seat in the Yew-Tree is not literally a tombstone. It is solely the poet's imagination which sees that pile of stones as a funeral pile.[9] The rudely construc-ted seat was merely the haunt of the recluse, yet because he used it as an escape, burying himself in "visionary views," and not allowing nature to take him out of his gloomy self, Wordsworth rightly treats it as his tomb. The "Lines in a Yew-Tree" exorcize the spot and rededicate the seat to its proper purpose of marking a beautiful view.

The call from a monument in the landscape or from the landscape itself, which deepens the consciousness of the poet and makes him feel he is on significant ground, is also encouraged by a sister-tradition to the epitaph. Most nature-inscriptions are related to the votive or commemorative epigram, which plays an important role in the Greek Anthology and comes into vernacular literature chiefly from that source.[10] The votive epigram took many forms: it was a simple statement identifying the donor, giving a brief yet lucid picture of place and ob-ject dedicated, and saying to whom they are offered; it was, as in inscriptions of this kind which survive from Theocritus, a poem celebrating a votive painting (statue), or rather animating it; and it could be a short prosopopeia, the voice of the god or genius of the place (genius loci) who warns us that we are near sacred ground. The first kind is strangely and uncertainly naive; and only Marvell uses it in an original way in his mower poems, where he sharpens its naiveté deliciously:

> I am the Mower *Damon*, known
> Through all the Meadows I have mown.

It does not play an important role, after Marvell, in the writing of nature poetry.[11]

The second kind does, for it is part of the tradition of iconic verse. Some of the most interesting descriptive poetry of the eighteenth century enters through such iconic and animating gestures as Behold, See, Mark, or through a rather special and limited genre—the Lines on (first) seeing a picture (artifact), which Anna Seward sometimes converts into "Inscription on the back of a Picture."[12] Since the pictures, at least in Anna Seward's case, are landscapes, a good amount of vigorous and picturesque description enters English poetry in this form.

I want to emphasize the third kind of votive epigram, in which the inscription calls to the passer by in the voice of the genius loci or spirit of the place. Like the epitaph it seems to derive from ritual formulae which admonished strangers not to disturb the remains of the dead. In the eighteenth century we find an extraordinary number of inscriptions for Bower, Grotto, Fountain, Seat, or similar Places of Retreat and Refreshment, which both invite and exhort the world-weary traveler. Pope's verses on his grotto at Twickenham are a familiar example. Such verses were directly encouraged by the interest in gardens and participated in the antiquarian fervor of the century. A disgruntled observer, looking in 1819 through Dodsley's collection, complains among other things about its "inscriptions in grottoes, and lines on fans innumerable."[13] But not many years before this complaint (so persistent is the fashion) we find in *Gentleman's Magazine* a competition for the best English rendering of Latin verses supposedly found on a supposed hermitage.[14]

Despite all misuses, the votive inscription is important for nature poetry in that it allows landscape to speak directly, without the intervention of allegorical devices. The voice of nature that calls us does not have to be formalized or pompously accoutered, although sometimes it is. The simplification in the form responds to a rural simplicity of feeling. We begin to hear and see a nature unobstructed by magnifying artifice. A waterfall may purge, momentarily, our selfish cares:

> Come, and where these runnels fall
> Listen to my madrigal!
> Far from all sounds of all the strife,
> That murmur through the walks of life;
>
> From grief, inquietude, and fears,
> From scenes of riot, or of tears;
> From passions, cankering day by day,
> That wear the inmost heart away;
>
> . . . .
> Come, and where these runnels fall,
> Listen to my madrigal![15]

Or the nymph of the grotto, still somewhat portentous, invites us:

> Come, Traveller, this hollow Rock beneath,
> While in the Leaves refreshing Breezes breath;
> Retire, to calm the Rage of burning Thirst,
> In these cool Streams that from the Caverns burst.[16]

Such moments are rarely deepened and even more rarely sustained.[17] Southey's inscriptions, of which eight were published in the first edition of his *Poems* (1797), often assume the bardic and officious voice of the interpreter instead of letting the genius loci speak directly to us. In this respect they do not differ from odic or iconic modes of nature poetry in which the poet addresses the landscape in his own person, asking woods and valleys to mourn or rejoice or show their splendors or perform in one way or another. Yet the Hellenic originals, or intermediate models, chasten Southey's verse into pictures of nature almost completely free of penseroro chimaeras and allegorical personifications:

> Enter this cavern, Stranger! the ascent
> Is long and steep and toilsome, here a while
> Thou may'st repose thee, from the noontide heat
> O'ercanopied by this arch'd rock that strikes
> A grateful coolness: clasping its rough arms
> Round the rude portal, the old ivy hangs
> Its dark green branches down, and the wild Bees
> O'er its grey blossoms murmuring ceaseless, make
> Most pleasant melody. No common spot
> Receives thee, for the Power who prompts the song,
> Loves this secluded haunt. The tide below
> Scarce sends the sound of waters to thine ear;
> And this high-hanging forest to the wind
> Varies its many hues. Gaze, stranger, here!
> And let thy soften'd heart intensely feel
> How good, how lovely, Nature! When from hence
> Departing to the City's crowded streets,
> Thy sickening eye at every step revolts
> From scenes of vice and wretchedness; reflect
> That Man creates the evil he endures.[18]

One more instance of this increased directness is Coleridge's "Inscription for a Fountain on a Heath," first published in 1802 under the title of "Epigram." It is nothing more than a detailed and affectionate picture of a sycamore, musical with bees, to which a small spring adds its own melody. What differentiates his poem from Southey's is that he not only mutes that sententious moralizing, a relic of medieval Christian debates concerning the active and the contemplative life which is quite foreign to most Greek models, but also, though still speaking in his own person, lulls the reader into thinking that the place itself invites him, so calm and murmuring is his voice:

> Here Twilight is and Coolness: here is moss,
> A soft seat, and a deep and ample shade.
> Thou may'st toil far and find no second tree.
> Drink, Pilgrim, here; Here rest! and if thy heart
> Be innocent, here too shalt thou refresh
> Thy spirit, listening to some gentle sound,
> Or passing gale or hum of murmuring bees![19]

We do not know with certainty how many of the poets were directly familiar with the Greek Anthology, or through what intermediaries its spirit came to them. Professor Hutton, who set out to write a history of the Greek Anthology in England, found himself obliged to write it first for Continental literature, since the Anthology came to England via the Continent. But the temptations of the way were so great that he did not end where he began, and we still have no report on England.[20] From my limited perspective, therefore, I can only say two things. The general change from Neoclassical to Romantic style parallels curiously the difference between the brief, witty, pointed epigram of the Latin tradition, influential on the development of the heroic couplet, and the simpler, more descriptive, anecdotal epigram which is a staple of the Greek Anthology.[21] A conscious attempt to recall the virtues of the simpler model is made early by Thomas Warton the Elder, who translates three epigrams from the Greek with the advertisement that they can serve as "a Pattern of the Simplicity so much admir'd in the *Grecian* Writings, so foreign to the present prevailing Taste, to the Love of Modern Witticism, and *Italian* Conceit."[22] His first example is an inscription on a cave (see above, p. 36); his second a votive epigram from Theocritus; and the third, also from Theocritus, a little picture or anecdote. Warton's versions are not particularly felicitous—the Grecian simplicity is exaggerated into a muscular coyness and the couplet form still thrusts that simplicity into a Procrustean bed—but the very attempt is important. It is something of a shock to realize that the Grecian simplicity admired by Warton may have been achieved by Wordsworth in a poem like "Old Man Travelling." This piece could easily be taken as an epigram à la grecque—as an anecdote in plain language and with a muted point. The speech of the Old Man, its strangely quiet character, replaces here the ingenious final turn of the witty epigram.

My second remark concerning the possible influence of the Greek Anthology on nature-inscriptions and the Romantic style is that there seems to have been at least one important intermediary: Mark Akenside. As far as I know Akenside was the first, except for Shenstone, to formally print a group of poems under the collective title "Inscriptions": six poems appear under that heading in Dodsley's

Collection of 1758, and two are added in the 1772 posthumous edition of his poetry.[23] Southey acknowledges that his own earliest inscriptions were inspired by Akenside, and it is also interesting that one of Coleridge's first publications is an "Elegy imitated from one of Akenside's Blank-verse inscriptions."[24]

This title, in fact, gives us one clue to Akenside's importance. His inscriptions created a new short form of poetry for blank verse. Prior to Akenside, blank verse was almost purely a dramatic, epic, or didactic measure;[25] lyric indeed, was invariably in rhymed form, and rime tended to emphasize point. But Akenside, by his inscriptions, suggested the possiblity of a short form free of the obligation of closing the sense with couplet or quatrain, though maintaining epigrammatic firmness by a subtly latinate syntax. The inscriptions previously cited from Wordsworth, Southey, and Coleridge also break the mold of the *Sinngedicht* (as Lessing called it) in which point is all and the sense is closed at short intervals. From a historical perspective, therefore, the lyrical lyric of the Romantics is a liberated epigram; and H.H. Hudson has said astutely that "the moment an epigram becomes very good—if it is not too funny or too obviously ingenious— it is now in danger of being classed as a lyric."[26]

When to this relative freedom from point, we add a freedom from obtrusive personification, the way is cleared for a direct and sustained nature poetry. There are no persons in Akenside's inscriptions except the spirit of the place (or its interpreter) and the offstage traveler. If this traveler, moreover, is significantly identified as the poet himself, a still closer relation is established between nature and the poet. This is what happens in Akenside's first and last inscriptions, which take the genre a good step toward the Romantic blank-verse meditation. Akenside, in the last inscription, also reverses the pattern in which the genius loci calls to the stranger, for now it is he, the poet, who in his lonely anxiety for inspiration invokes the absent Muses of the bards of Greece:

> From what loved haunt
> Shall I expect you? Let me once more feel
> Your influence, O ye kind inspiring powers:
> And I will guard it well; nor shall a thought
> Rise in my mind, nor shall a passion move
> Across my bosom unobserved, unstored
> By faithful memory. And then at some
> More active moment, will I call them forth
> Anew; and join them in majestic forms,
> And give them utterance in harmonious strains;
> That all mankind shall wonder at your sway.

Yet Akenside's sense of alienation is nothing as sharp as that of the Romantics. I suspect, in fact, that his inscriptions exerted a twofold charm: that of mixing naive feelings for nature with melancholy and self-conscious ones, and that of clearly subordinating the latter to the former. We may recall that Wordsworth's Yew-Tree poem (like Coleridge's "Nightingale" which follows it) is intended to combat the melancholy use of nature, and that for Wordsworth this melancholy is symptomatic of a morbidly self-centered mind. Nature should aid us to go out of ourselves, to broaden our feelings by meditation, and to recover original joy. Akenside's inscriptions, like the best Greek epigrams, subdue sentiment—and sentimentality—to votive calmness of mind.

Through a reuniting, therefore, of elegiac and locodescriptive poetry, and through the strengthening influence of the radically Greek element in the Greek Anthology,[27] a new lyrical kind emerges: the nature-inscription. It is nearest in spirit, form, and potential to the Romantic lyric. I would not go so far as to call it the missing link, but it certainly is a vital intermediary between the conventional lyrical forms of the eighteenth century and the Romantic poem. The reason why it is rarely singled out as a distinctive literary kind is that as a special form of the inscription it was naturally classed among inscriptions in general, and inscriptions themselves were not always distinguished from epigrams. Wordsworth, in 1815, lumps together epitaph, inscription, sonnet, the personal verse epistle, and all locodescriptive poetry under the general category of idyllium.[28] This is not sheer muddleheadedness but a practical grouping that reflected the state of poetry in his time. The nature-inscription was an unstable genre, almost a chance product of the multiplication of inscriptions of all kinds in the seventeenth and eighteenth centuries. Anyone who has worked his way through anthologies of that time knows the inordinate variety of mediocre inscriptions they offer in the form of social verse, iconic verse, elegiac and commemorative verse, jeux d'esprits, and emblems. From these, in their combinations, and by a process at least as mysterious as natural selection, the prototype of the Romantic nature poem arose and was partially stabilized by Akenside's inscriptions in blank verse.

II

It was demonstrated some years ago that Wordsworth's *Lyrical Ballads* were not original in subject or sentiment, or even in many elements of form. Robert Mayo's article on their contemporaneity destroyed the clichés of literary historians who had held that this poetry was too bold for its time.[29] But the question of Wordsworth's greatness, or how his poems really differed from their contemporary analogues, was left unanswered. I would now like to address this question by using Wordsworth's relation to inscriptions as the point of departure.

What Wordsworth did is clear: he transformed the inscription into an independent nature poem, and in so doing created a principal form of the Romantic and modern lyric. One step in this transformation has already been described.

When fugitive feelings are taken seriously, when every sight and sound calls to the passing poet—"Nay, Traveller! rest"; "Stay, Passenger, why goest thou by soe fast?"—then the Romantic nature lyric is born.

A second step in the transformation bears directly on the form of the poem. The inscription, before Wordsworth, is strangely void of natural detail though full of nature feeling, for the reason that the genre still depends on the site it supposedly inscribes. Rather than evoking, it points to the landscape. If it has an expressive function vis-à-vis the feeling of the poet, it has a merely indicative function vis-à-vis its setting. To develop as a free-standing form, the nature lyric had to draw the landscape evocatively into the poetry itself. The poetry, as in Shakespeare, becomes fullbodied when it incorporates or even creates the setting.[30]

Yet much depends on the way the setting is incorporated. The criterion of concreteness has only a limited relevance for the nature lyric. There is more descriptive vigor—more observations and pictures from nature—in an ordinary topographical poem like Wordsworth's own *Evening Walk* or *Descriptive Sketches* than in all of *Lyrical Ballads* together. In "Lines left upon a Seat in a Yew-Tree" the natural setting is drawn into the poetry not so much as a thing of beauty that should startle the traveler but because it mingled with a human life and still mingles presently with the poet's imagination. We are made to see the vital, if perverse, relationship of the solitary to his favorite spot, and to hear the poet's *viva voce* meditation on this: he writes the epitaph before our eyes.

What is truly distinctive, therefore, is Wordsworth's enlarged understanding of the setting to be incorporated. This is never landscape alone. He frees the inscription from its dependence, he gives it weight and power of its own, by incorporating in addition to a particular scene the very process of inscribing or interpreting it. The setting is understood to contain the writer in the act of writing: the poet in the grip of what he feels and sees, primitively inspired to carve it in the living rock.[31]

But the very intensity of the desire for perpetuation produces (or reacts to) a kind of death feeling which Shelley described directly. The writer, in composition, is but a fading coal, and his poem dead leaves. A secondary consciousness of death and change associates itself with the very act of writing. Thus, in Wordsworth, the lapidary inscription, though replaced by the meditative mind, returns as part of the landscape being meditated. The poet *reads* landscape as if it were a monument or grave: this position is common to "Lines left upon a Seat in a Yew-Tree"; "The Thorn" 's letter-like distinctness of pond, hill of moss, and stunted tree; "Hart Leap Well" 's three pillars set, like cairn or cromlech, in a desolate place; and "Michael" 's straggling heap of stones.[32]

The setting Wordsworth recovers is therefore of the most elemental kind. Yet he recovers it neither as pseudo-primitive nor as antiquarian but always as a man dealing with what is permanent in man. Inscribing, naming, and writing are types of a commemorative and inherently elegiac act. Despite this, his poems move from past to present, from death to life, from stone to the spontaneity of living speech. The "Lines left upon a Seat" attempt to be an inscription written in the language of nature: a monument that comes to life and makes nature come alive. His verse, says Wordsworth, using one of the oldest *topoi*, is a "speaking monument."[33] This is also true of such greater poems as "Michael" and "Tintern Abbey."

"Michael" bears an obvious structural resemblance to the Yew-Tree poem. Its two basic parts are again a presentation of the curious object and the story or epitomized biography[34] which that object entails. The object, moreover, is a monument almost merged with nature: to interpret the stones of the unfinished sheepfold is to interpret nature itself. We are made to see the naked mind confronting an anonymous landscape yet drawing from it, or interpolating, the humane story of "Michael." The poem begins in an act of the living mind bent over a riddling inscription, perhaps an inscription of death.

But "Michael" also reveals a historical connection between primitive inscriptions and nature poetry. One of the earliest forms of that poetry actually arose as a modification of the epitaph. The opening paragraph of "Michael" which carefully guides the reader to his strange destination, should be compared to Theocritus' love poem in the form of a wayside inscription, and to the wayside inscription in general. This type of epigram, stemming from the practice of wayside interments, was also used to guide the stranger to suitable watering or resting places; it branched finally into an ideal species that allowed elaborate directions in the form of pictures of nature. The Greek Anthology records many examples of the ideal type. I quote one from Leonidas of Tarentum:

> Not here, O thirsty traveller, stoop to drink,
> The Sun has warm'd, and flocks disturb the brink;
> But climb yon upland where the heifers play,
> Where that tall pine excludes the sultry day;
> There will you see a bubbling rill that flows
> Down the smooth rock more cold than Thracian snows.[35]

Wordsworth gives us stones instead of water, but as he tells his story it is clear what refreshment can flow from them. Robert Frost's "Directive" is a latter-day echo of the genre.

"Michael" leads us unexpectedly to a Greek prototype. To recognize this is to become more aware of Wordsworth's greatness in recovering elemental situations. Yet it is no part of that greatness to oblige us to recognize the specific prototype or genre. On the contrary, because Wordsworth recovers the generic factor, we no longer need to recognize the genre which specialized it. Wordsworth's form appears to be self-generated rather than prompted by tradition; and the greater the poem, the clearer this effect.

This is strikingly illustrated by the "Lines written a few miles above Tintern

Abbey, On revisiting the Banks of the Wye during a Tour, July 13, 1798.'' Of the nature-inscription in which they originate, only the subtlest vestiges remain. The prospect with its monument or ruin is still nearby; the long specific title still indicates the epitaphic origin of the mode, as does the elegiac tenor; and the poem still claims to mark the very place in which it was inspired. But there is no actual corpse in the vicinity, and the historical significance of the spot is hardly felt. Wordsworth again restores the universal and deeply ordinary context: the corpse is in the poet himself, his consciousness of inner decay; and the history he meditates is of nature's relation to his mind. We recognize the archaic setting purified of hortative tombstone. The power to make him remember his end or his beginning springs simply and directly from a consciousness involved with nature.

Yet though it is Wordsworth's supreme gift to purge the factitious and restore the elemental situation—in his poetry every convention, figure, or device is either eliminated, simplified, or grounded in humanity—a distinction should be made between two types of the elemental: on the one hand archaic; on the other archetypal or generic. Without this distinction we can still discriminate between Wordsworth's poems and their contemporary analogues, but we cannot properly separate greater and lesser in his own corpus. It is important to recognize that the Yew-Tree poem is more archaic in its use of particular conventions than "Tintern Abbey," even if the Romantics were occasionally forced to return to the archaic in order to reach a truly universal conception.[36]

The proposed distinction can center on Wordsworth's refinement of the belief in spirit of place—the archaic belief recovered by the Yew-Tree poem. The real sin of the recluse is against the genius loci: that beautiful prospect should have renewed his heart and attuned him to find pleasure in nature. But Wordsworth's belief in spirit of place determines more than the poem's doctrine. It determines, in addition, the form of the poem, and perhaps the very possibility of Wordsworth's kind of poetry. Formally, it is the genius loci who exhorts reader or passerby; and the same spirit moves the poet to be its interpreter—which can only happen if, "nurs'd by genius," he respects nature's impulses and gives them voice in a reciprocating and basically poetic act.

Even a song as bare as "Tintern Abbey" is based on the superstition of spirit of place. The poet reads nature or his own feelings as if there were an ominous, admonitory relationship between this spot and himself. At the end of the poem, moreover, when Wordsworth foresees his death and urges Dorothy to perpetuate his trust in nature, he speaks as if he were one of the dead who exhort the living in the guise of the genius loci. But the archaic formulae are now generated from the natural soil of the meditation. We feel that a superstition of the tribe has been genuinely recovered and purified. There is nothing patently archaic or poetically archaizing in Wordsworth's use of a belief which he grounds so deeply in the human passion for continuity, for binding together the wisdom of the dead and the energy of the living.

It is in the Lucy poems that the notion of spirit of place, and particularly English spirit of place, reaches its purest form. (I am not sure that all of the lyrics originated in the same impulse, and the cycle may have a life of its own which took over from Wordsworth's intentions.) Lucy, living, is clearly a guardian spirit, not of one place but of all English places—you might meet her ("a Spirit, yet a Woman too"[37]) by any English fireside or any cherished grove—while Lucy, dead, has all nature for her monument. The series is a deeply humanized version of the death of Pan, a lament on the decay of English nature feeling. Wordsworth fears that the very spirit presiding over his poetry is ephemeral, and I think he refuses to distinguish between its death in him and its historical decline. The Lucy poems, brief elegies[38] that purify both gothic ballad and mannered epigram, consecrate English spirit of place in suitable English. One could apply to Wordsworth a famous comment in praise of Theocritus: His muse is the muse of his native land.

The Matthew poems, which honor a village schoolmaster, can be our last example. Some of them try to restore the literal integrity of nature-inscription and pastoral elegy, but others almost completely abandon the archaizing mode. In the earlier and sometimes unpublished versions, the notion of spirit of place is used in a primitivistic manner: Wordsworth pretends, for example, that he is moved to write his inscriptions in the very places that had known Matthew best and where his spirit presumably lingers. One elegy is therefore "left in the schoolroom"; another is "written on a [commemorative] tablet" in Matthew's school. And in the most pagan and beautiful of the unpublished elegies, Wordsworth deplores that Matthew is not buried near his favorite tree, on which he proceeds to inscribe an epitaph:

> Could I the priest's consent have gained
> Or his who toll'd thy passing bell,
> Then, Matthew, had thy bones remain'd
> Beneath this tree we loved so well.
>
> Yet in our thorn will I suspend
> Thy gift this twisted oaken staff,
> And here where trunk and branches blend
> Will I engrave thy epitaph.[39]

But in "The Two April Mornings" this sense of a continuity between the noble dead and the noble living is conveyed in a natural rather than artificially naïve way, through a description of a picture (a true ex-voto) that rises in the poet's mind after his anecdote about Matthew:

> Matthew is in his grave, yet now,
> Methinks, I see him stand,

> As at that moment, with a bough
> Of wilding in his hand.

The living substance on which the memorial is graved is now the poet's mind itself, which moves, as in *The Prelude*, from past to present under the continuing influence of the past.

III

The modern lyric attempts the impossible: a monument to spontaneity, a poem that coincides with the act and passion of its utterance. It tries to overcome the secondary or elegiac aspect of language by making language coterminous with life. However paradoxical this project may be, it has redeemed the short poem from the bondage of the pointed or witty style. After the Romantics, of course, and partly in reaction to their fluidities, new restraints are imposed to concentrate the lyric's fire and to recover epigrammatic terseness. The neolapidary style of the Parnassians, the mystical essentialism of the *symbolistes*, the Imagists with a doctrine that helped trim Eliot's *The Waste Land* to fragments not unlike epigrams, and the still prevalent emphasis on verbal wit and metaphor—these are restrictive and reactionary rather than liberative and revolutionary measures. The real iconoclasts are found in the period 1750-1830, which saw the diverse and sometimes volcanic change of epigram into free-standing lyric.[40]

The means by which this change was effected differed from country to country, from writer to writer, and often from poem to poem. Blake, for example, could transform epigrams into proverbs in his *Auguries of Innocence*; he could also (going back to native or pseudoepigraphic sources) make primitive inscriptions of his own as in his pictured emblems and children's poetry; he was not above converting to his faith a Wesley-type hymn in "And did those feet in ancient times"; he recovered the mad songs of Shakespeare; he wrote his own Greek-style epitaph in "O Rose, thou art sick"; and, in the blank-verse lyrics of *Poetical Sketches*, he paralleled Akenside's attempt to develop an unrhymed form for lyric poetry. Herder, in Germany, by expanding Bishop Percy's idea and recovering ballads and reliques from all nations (including epigrams from the Greek Anthology), helped to break the tyranny of the Frenchified song, a tyranny that cooperated with the pointed style. But for Herder, Heine's *Buch der Lieder*, which created a new blend of song and witty style, and such collections as *Des Knaben Wunderhorn* would not have been possible. About Hölderlin, Schiller, and Goethe it is hard to speak in a comprehensive and generalizing way; but the spirit of their effort—a radical classicism opposed to that of the French tradition—is indicted by the fact that Coleridge insisted on teaching Wordsworth (when both were in Germany) the prosody of the German classical hexameter and sent him an illustrative sample of verses:

> William, my head and my heart! dear Poet that
>   feelest and thinkest!
> Dorothy, eager of soul, my most affectionate sister!
> Many a mile, O! many a wearisome mile are ye
>   distant,
> Long, long, comfortless roads, with no one eye
>   that doth know us.

Wordsworth, understandably, is not at all moved by their meter, only by their sentiment. He has already found a style: his letter of reply contains two of the Lucy poems as well as blank-verse episodes later incorporated in *The Prelude*.[41]

Though Romantic poetry transcends its formal origin in epigram and inscription and creates the modern lyric, it still falls short of the latter in one respect. The Romantic poets do not purge themselves of a certain moralizing strain. This is especially true, in England, of the first generation of Romantics. The urbane didacticism of the school of Pope is replaced by an oracular didacticism which the inscription, with its palpable design on the passerby, allowed. The overt interpreter is rarely absent from Wordsworth's poems: a purely lyrical or descriptive moment is invariably followed by self-conscious explication. In "The Old Cumberland Beggar," after passages of description subtly colored by his feelings, Wordsworth turns to the statesmen of the world in a sudden moralizing apostrophe longer than these passages. The poem, as a result, falls strangely into two parts, each having its own life: the first part descriptive and quiet, the second oracular.[42]

Byron deplored the Lake poets' lack of urbanity, while Shelley and Keats tried to purify the Wordsworthian mode of didactic intrusions. "A poem should not mean but be" is a modern dictum which reflects the fact that, after Wordsworth, the only obstacle to the autonomous lyric was its self-justifying dependence on preachment. The cold, lapidary finger of the original inscriptions had turned into the oracular apostrophe pointing to humble truth. The attempt to absorb truth into the texture of the lyric has its own history. It tells of poets in search of a modern equivalent to that fusion of reality and idea which haunted artists and theoreticians from Winckelmann on and which seemed to them the very secret of Greek art. It tells of Parnassians and Pre-Raphaelites endowing poetry with something of the mute eloquence or unravishable meaning of the other arts, of Mallarmé wishing to overcome even this dependence and to specialize the qualities distinguishing poetic speech from pictorial and musical, and of Yeats generating his lyrics by means of an invisible didactic framework which is the grinning skeleton behind their casual beauties. A critique of these developments is still needed: I can mention as a symbol of their limited success Keats's one mature inscription, the "Ode on a Grecian Urn," which turns from being to meaning in the final exhortation spoken by the art object itself: "Beauty is Truth, Truth Beauty." This brief oracle has caused an extended debate that ignored until recently[43] a genre essential to the rise of the modern lyric. Keats uses the genre once more to teach what art can teach.

4
False Themes and Gentle Minds

The writers of the Enlightenment want fiction and reason to kiss. They are inexhaustible on the subject. "Buskin'd bards henceforth shall wisely rage," Thomas Tickell announces, foreseeing a new Augustan age.[1] "The radiant era dawns," writes Akenside, when the long separation of imagination and science shall be overcome, and wisdom shall once more "Imbrace the smiling family of arts."[2] The anonymous French author of *Poésies philosophiques* (1758) admonishes the new school of poets to invent "believable marvels": "Sans marcher appuyé du mensonge et des fables / Venez nous étaler des merveilles croiables." Another explains more curiously his desire for chaster fictions. "Women of today," he writes, "are so sated with fine phrases that there is no way of succeeding with them except to appeal to their reason."[3] The enthusiasm for reason—and reasoning—is so great that Crébillon fils, in *Le Sopha* (1740), a degraded and libertine version of the metamorphosis myth, puts his hero-narrator in jeopardy of having his head cut off should he be tempted to *reflect upon* rather than simply *tell* his story. "By my faith," says the Sultan, "I swear I shall kill the next man who dares to reflect in my presence." Even with this threat, the novel ends on a defeated note. How difficult it is to tell a good, rousing story in the Age of Reason. "Ah Grandmother," sighs the Sultan, thinking of Sheherezade, "that's not the way you used to tell stories!"

It does not prove easy to give up the sophisticated superstitions by which literature had always amused, shocked, or instructed. Writers become intensely conscious of the primitive nature of these beliefs but also ingenious in accommodating them to rationality. In William Collins's *Ode on the Popular Superstitions of the Highlands of Scotland*,[4] the problem is honestly and movingly set forth. Collins feels that he must forbear those great local myths which now live only in the far north and which he encourages his friend Home to keep up:

> Nor need'st thou blush, that such false themes engage
> Thy gentle mind, of fairer stores possest;
> For not alone they touch the village breast,
> But fill'd in elder time th'historic page.
> There SHAKESPEARE'S self, with ev'ry garland crown'd,
> In musing hour, his wayward sisters found,
> And with their terrors drest the magic scene.

This dichotomy of "gentle mind" and "false themes" (where "false themes" means the materials of romance, popular or classical in origin) remains the starting point of the great majority of writers between the late Renaissance and Romanticism.

The story I wish to tell is how that dichotomy is faced and perhaps overcome. Many, of course, accepted the alienation of the literary mind from the "exploded beings" (the phrase is Dr. Johnson's) of folklore or mythology. They knew too well that great literature was magic and that reason could only flee from it, as from an enchanter. But others dared to think that literature might become a rational enchantment. They toyed with forbidden fire (with the "Eastern Tale," the Gothic romance, the Sublime Ode) and called up the ghosts they wished to subdue. In this they followed the example of the great poets of the Renaissance, who had at once revived and purified romance tradition. I begin, therefore, with Milton, the last about whom Collins could have said, as of Tasso: his "undoubting mind / Believed the magic wonders which he sung."[5]

Milton is already belated; and it is his problematic rather than naïve relation to Romance which makes him significant. He somehow transcends the very dichotomy of "gentle mind" and "false theme" which appears early in his poetry. Thus he dismisses as a false surmise his vision of nature spirits lamenting for Lycidas without renouncing that machinery of spirits, that multiplication of persons and gods, which is the clearest feature of romantic art—romantic in the largest sense of the word. He accepts a principle of plenitude which belongs to the Romance imagination rather than to an epoch in Lovejoyean history and which sets all action within a conspiracy of spirits. The world is made new or strange by opening into another world: an overhead—or underground—of mediations, of direct, picturable relations between spirit-persons. In such a world the human actor is only one kind of being, and his mind—or whatever else makes him the king-piece—is the target of a host of contrary intelligences.

Keats, thinking about the Enlightenment (the "grand march of intellect"), said that in Milton's day Englishmen were only just emancipated from superstition. It is true: Milton's consciousness is always ambushed by pagan or Christian or poetical myths. He is important for Collins and the Romantics because he shows the enlightened mind still emerging, and even constructing itself, out of its involvement with Romance. He marks the beginning of modern Romanticism, of a romantic struggle with Romance; and it is as a stage in the growth of the English poetic mind that I now want to present his poetry's earliest magic, the *Allegro-Penseroso* sequence.

You know how each poem opens, with a ritual exordium banning the undesired mood. In the first poem melancholy is dismissed; the second poem, like a recantation, hails melancholy and banishes joy. Milton, it has been argued, wished merely to picture the right kind of joy and a purified melancholy. Yet the dramatic aspect of each poem is the stylistic breach as the speaker turns from anathema to invitation. It is like going from an older world creaking with morality plays and heavy emblems to a brave new world in which man is the master of his mood and his spirit machinery correspondingly fluent. The poet seems as interested in purifying an older style as in purging a humor. The poems are Milton's notes toward a gentler fiction.

If mythology old-style showed the mind at the mercy of humors or stars or heavy abstractions, these personifications of easy virtue, which constitute a mythology new-style, reflect a freer attitude of the mind toward the fictions it entertains. The change from

> Hence loathed Melancholy
>> Of *Cerberus*, and blackest midnight born,
> In *Stygian* Cave forlorn
>> 'Mongst horrid shapes, and shrieks, and sights unholy

to

>> Come pensive Nun, devout and pure,
>> Sober, stedfast, and demure

recapitulates the entire Renaissance movement toward a *dolce stil nuovo*. It recalls the great change in attitudes toward the ancient superstitions, which in the century preceding Milton allowed that freer use of Romance associated with (among others) Ariosto and Spenser.

In Milton's double feature it is not the character contrast of the two personae (melancholy and mirth) which is important, but this newer and emancipated kind of myth-making. Milton uses no fewer than three sorts of mythical persons: established divinities (Venus, Mab, Aurora); personified abstractions (Melancholy, Tragedy, Mirth); and spirits of place (the "Mountain Nymph, sweet Liberty"). He does not encourage us to discriminate these kindred spirits; in fact, by mixing them with a fine promiscuity, he produces the sense of a middle region in which everything is numinous or semidivine. This in no respect demythologizes his poetry but suggests that man lives in easy rather than fearful, and daily rather than extraordinary, intercourse with an ambient spiritworld. He walks in a feather-dense atmosphere among "the unseen Genius of the Wood," strange music, "dewey-feathered sleep," and the phantasms of his own imagination. It is an atmosphere that works against sharp moral or ontological distinctions; when the merry man is said to view

> Such sights as youthfull Poets dream
> On Summer eeves by haunted stream

there is delicate ambiguity, because the sights could be public performances ("mask, and antique Pageantry"), dream thoughts, or a real vision. And when Shakespeare is called "fancy's child," the cliché has power, in this context, to suggest once more an intermingling of gods and men—that numinous half-essence which bathes every feature of these landscapes.

What is the reason for this promiscuous and light-hearted divinization? Milton has created a new and sweeter style, but also one that is peculiarly English. Most of his early poetry moves programmatically beyond the erudite pastoralism of the Italians and toward the fresher pastures of an English lyricism. Yet in *L'Allegro* and *Il Penseroso* Milton does more than state his program. He seems to have found the right kind of spirit, or spirits, for English landscape. He has taken the exotic machinery of the classical gods and the ponderous abstractions of moral allegory and treated them all as, basically, local spirits. In Britain they must be temperate like the British, so that extremes of mirth and melancholy, and even of divinity itself, are exorcized. The genius loci suits the religio loci: Milton's romantic machinery is grounded in the reasonableness of a specific national temperament.

That this reasonableness, this pride in a via media, may be a national myth does not concern us: although it will concern Blake, who rejects Milton's compromise and engages in a radical confrontation of the poetic genius with the English genius. Milton himself takes the issue onto a higher level in *Paradise Lost*, where the old and sublimer mode of myth-making is reasserted. From that post-bellum height, *L'Allegro* and *Il Penseroso* appear like exercises in the minor mode of pastoral romance. Even as only that—as an accommodation of Romance to the English mind—they remain a significant attempt to have this kind of fiction survive an increasingly enlightened climate.

That *L'Allegro* and *Il Penseroso* are a special type of romance appears as soon as we go from the nature of the personifications to that of the persona or presiding consciousness. Who is the speaker here if not a magus, dismissing some spirits and invoking others? If we do not have an actual romance, at least we have a romancer: the poems are thoroughly ritualistic, with their exordium, invocation, and ceremonial tone. But the imperatives ("'Tow'red Cities please us then,'" "There let *Hymen* oft appear") are really optatives, while the tone is lightened by Milton's easy, peripatetic rhythm. His style of address intimates a new power of self-determination vis-à-vis the spiritual environment in which we live and move and have our being. Though that environment remains demonic, the magus is clearly in control: the most formal sign of control is, in fact, the conceit governing his invitations, which reverses the oldest religious formula known to us, the *do ut des*—I give, so that you give. In *L'Allegro* and *Il Penseroso* the poet is not petitioning but propositioning his goddess: you give me these pleasures, and I will be yours. He lays down his conditions and enjoys them in advance. It is his pleasure or option to do these things, to be merry or melancholy—a pleasure of the human imagination.

Thus psyche emerges from the spooky larvae of masques and moralities like a free-ranging butterfly. Though still in contact with a world of spirits, it is no longer coerced or compelled. The spiritual drama is, as always in Milton, seduction rather than compulsion. The poet begins to invite his soul and opens the way to an authentic nature poetry. A similar development takes place on the Continent with Théophile de Viau and Saint-Amant, imitators of the lighter Pléiade strain, and who may have influenced Marvell. Their nature poems are little romances, adventures of the liberated and—as the case may be—libertine spirit.

Our mention of psyche may be more than a figure of speech. According to traditional speculation on genius or ingenium, each person was accompanied by two genii, a good and a bad, a protector and a deceiver. These are important figures in many morality plays and still appear in Marlowe's *Faustus*. Could Milton have changed this feature of popular demonology into his humors or states of mind, which are competing spiritual options? If so, he has adjusted an axiom of demonic religion to a more temperate zone and brought us an essential step closer to the modern idea of genius. By tempering the genii's astral nature, he has made them into attendants of the creative mind.[6]

With Milton the spirit of Romance begins to simplify itself. It becomes the creative spirit and frees itself from the great mass of medieval and post-medieval romances in the same way as the Spirit of Protestantism frees itself from the formalism of temples. *L'Allegro* and *Il Penseroso* are not romances but romantic monologues. They show a mind moving from one position to another and projecting an image of freedom against a darker, demonic ground. Poetry, like religion, purifies that ground: it cannot leave it. The newborn allegoric persons retain, therefore, something of the character of demonic agents even while being transformed into pleasures of the imagination. Indeed, the poems' rigidly stylized form reminds us that the imaginative man must join some god's party: the either/or situation remains; he cannot but assume a persona. Personification is still derived from the persona instead of the latter being freely inferred, as it is in modern poetry, from the projection of living thoughts.

If Romance is an eternal rather than archaic portion of the human mind, and poetry its purification, then every poem will be an act of resistance, of negative creation—a flight from one enchantment into another. The farewell to the impure gods becomes part of a nativity ode welcoming the new god. New personifications are born from old in *L'Allegro* and *Il Penseroso*; and *Lycidas* purges the genii loci of Italian pastoral only to hail a new "genius of the shore." This romantic purification of Romance is endless; it is the true and unceasing spiritual combat. At the conclusion of the first book of *Paradise Lost*, Milton transforms the Satanic thousands into fairies of Albion. Their moony music charms the ear of a belated peasant. It is, surely, a similar conversion of the demons which helps to animate the landscapes of *L'Allegro* and *Il Penseroso*. The haunted ground of Romance is aestheticized; the gods become diminutive, picturesque, charming—in a word, neoclassical. But is this change perhaps a Mephistophelian deceit, a modern seduction? The gentle mind thinks it is free of demons, but they sit "far within / And in their own dimensions like themselves" (*Paradise Lost* 1, 792-93).

It is as if Milton had foreseen the triumph and trivialization of the descriptive-allegorical style. *L'Allegro* and *Il Penseroso* become the pattern for eighteenth-century topographical fancies with their personification mania. His nature-spirits are summoned at the will of every would-be magus. Romance loses its shadow, its genuine darkness: nothing remains of the drama of liberation whereby ingenium is born from genius, psyche from persona, and the spirit of poetry from the grave clothes of Romance. By the end of the eighteenth century poets must begin once more where Milton began, though fortified by his example. They must "in the romantic element immerse" and not be deceived by the neoclassical psyche flitting with faded innocence through gaudy landscapes. Keats's imitation of Milton leads from those superficial bowers to the face of Moneta, dark (like Melancholy's) with excessive bright, from pleasures of the imagination to the burdens of a prophetic spirit. This is the path inaugurated by Collins, who uses the formula of *L'Allegro* and *Il Penseroso* to invite a creative Fear—stronger even in Shakespeare than in Milton—back to his breast:

> O Thou whose Spirit most possest
> The sacred Seat of *Shakespear's* Breast!
>
> . . . .
>
> Teach me but once like Him to feel:
> His Cypress Wreath my Meed decree,
> And I, O *Fear*, will dwell with *Thee*!

The theories accompanying the revival of Romance in the second half of the eighteenth century have often been studied. Van Tieghem's chapter on "La

Notion de la vraie poésie" in *Le Préromantisme* contains in suggestive outline what needs to be known. But a fine essay by Emil Staiger on that strange confectioner of supernatural ballads, the German poet Bürger, takes us beyond theory to the inner development of romantic poetry.[7]

Gottfried August Bürger was a witting cause of the ballad revival in Germany and an unwitting influence on Wordsworth and Coleridge. His ballads, first collected in 1778, sent shudders through the sophisticated literary circles of Europe. Their influence reached England in the 1790s: Scott became a ballad writer because of him, and Anna Seward describes how people petitioned her to read them Bürger's most famous work, the *Lenore*: "There was scarce a morning in which a knot of eight or ten did not flock to my apartments, to be poetically frightened: Mr. Erskine, Mr. Wilberforce—everything that was everything, and everything that was nothing, flocked to Leonora.... Its terrible graces grapple minds and tastes of every complexion."[8] Bürger is like the country boy in the fairy tale who finally taught the princess to have goosepimples by putting a frog in her bed. Yet, like most every poet of the period, his first treatment of supernatural themes was jocose. Staiger shows that what began as a literary flirtation led suddenly to genuine "terrific" ballads. The sorcerer's apprentice is overpowered by spirits he had playfully evoked.

What interests us here is Bürger's literary situation and its difference from that of the English poets. Collins and later writers of the Age of Sensibility were also making mouths at the invisible event. When Gray, Percy, Mallet, Mason, Macpherson, and Blake were not redoing old romances,they inflated the neoclassical "godkins and goddesslings" as giant epiphanic forms—pop art addressing a spiritualistic society. They could risk this because they knew the Enlightenment had gone too far for the old superstitions really to come back. Collins's visionary cry

> Ah *Fear*! Ah frantic *Fear*!
> I see, I see Thee near

invokes an emotion which is truly frantic: it wants to get at the poet, who wishes to be got at, but a historical fatality—the gentle mind, polite society—keeps them apart.

Now Bürger's situation is both more hopeful and more difficult. German poetry had had no golden age, no Renaissance. Hence there was no one between the poet and Romance tradition—no one, like Milton, to guide his steps, but also no one to demonstrate the difficulty and belatedness of such an enterprise. Where are *our* Chaucer, Spenser, Shakespeare, and Milton, Herder asks in an essay of 1777, which commends Bürger.[9] English Renaissance poetry, according to Herder, was reared on the old songs and romances which originally belonged just as much to German poetry, because of a common Nordic heritage and because the spirit of Romance is everywhere the same: "In allen Länder Europas hat der Rittergeist nur ein Wörterbuch." But this heritage not having been mediated by poets like Shakespeare and Milton, the modern German writer has no living tradition of older poetry through which he might renew himself and grow as if on the very stem of national life. With us Germans, laments Herder, everything is supposed to grow a priori ("Bei uns wächst alles a priori").

Thus Bürger must somehow raise the Romance tradition by his own arts. What he knows of that tradition is limited: mainly popular songs and superstitions, copied (so he claims) from songs picked up in city or village streets at evening, in the awareness that the poems of Homer, Ariosto, Spenser, and Ossian were also once "ballads, romances, and folksongs."[10] He is like a Faust who does not need the devil because the *Erdgeist* has agreed to be his spirit.

Among the most famous of Bürger's ballads is *The Wild Huntsman (Der Wilde Jäger)*. It depicts the rising blood-lust of a Sunday morning's hunt, and its tempo is wild from the start:

> Der Wild- und Rheingraf stiess ins Horn:
> "Hallo, Hallo, zu Fuss und Ross!"
> Sein Hengst erhob sich wiehernd vorn;
> Laut rasselnd stürzt ihm nach der Tross;
> Laut klifft' und klafft' es, frei vom Koppel,
> Durch Korn und Dorn, durch Heid und Stoppel.

This breakneck pace augments: two horsemen enter to accompany the earl; the right-hand one counsels him to respect the sabbath and turn back, the left-hand one spurs him on. The hunter overrides every objection; the pack rampages on, over a poor farmer's property, over the very bodies of a cowherd and his cattle; finally the earl pursues the beast into a hermit's sanctuary, violating it and blaspheming God. All at once—the transition takes place within one stanza—the clamor of the chase is gone, everything is vanished except the earl, and a deathly silence reigns. He blows his horn, it makes no sound; he halloos, no sound; he cracks his whip, no sound. He spurs his courser: it is rooted in the ground, stock-still. The silence is that of the grave; into it comes, from above, a voice of thunder condemning the hunter to be the prey of an eternal and hellish hunt until the Last Judgment.

The poem is totally steeped in myth and superstition: there is the motif of the blasphemy immediately answered (call the devil, etc.); that of the ride ending in the grave, perhaps indebted to the Nordic myth of Odin, who rides in the sky with his troop of dead souls; and, above all, the theme of the hunter lured by his prey beyond nature into visionary experience.[11] Bürger wants to pack as much Romance as possible into each poem, as if to make up for Germany's lost time. He even classifies the ballad as a lyric kind of epic, not so much to stress that it must tell a story as to emphasize its ambition. The ballad is an epic in brief, a romance in brief. It sums up a life, a destiny, a whole ancient culture.

Yet behind these ballads is a pressure not explained by this ambition, which shows itself in their precipitous, "Würfe und Sprünge," the speed of action ("gesagt, getan"), the heroes' reckless *amor fati*, and everything else that tends to minimize the reflective moment. Here there is no shadow between the conception and the act, or even between life and afterlife. No sooner has the earl blasphemed than he reaps his blasphemy; and Lenore's bitter yet innocent deathwish is rewarded in the same gross way. The mind is not given enough natural time in which to reflect.

Indeed, time in Bürger is intrinsically demonic. Although the supernatural erupts only at the climax of the action, it is there from the outset. One cannot speak of development: the earl is a hunted man from the first lines, a fated part of horse and pack and spurring sound; and the fearful symmetry, whereby hunter and hunted are reversed in the second part, appears like a natural rather than supernatural consequence. The first open hint of the supernatural is, of course, the appearance of the right and left horsemen, whose intrusion is so easy because in a sense they have been there all along. They are clearly the good and evil genii; and we see how externally, even superficially, the theme of reflection is introduced. There is only token retardation: the action consists of incidents arranged in climactic order with time moving irreversibly to the point of retribution. Having reached that point, the nature of time does not change: the hunter has simply run into himself. After a moment of absolute silence, which is like entering the looking glass, the reversed image appears and time continues its avenging course. There is no reflection and no true temporality: only this eschatological self-encounter.

Thus Bürger ballads are ghostly in the deepest sense. But are they romantic? Are they not gothic—or, if you will, gothic romances? They belong to the world of that *Totentanz* explicitly evoked in *Lenore* and not absent from the mad and macabre ride of the earl. Death marries the bride, Death leads the hunt. This is not the world of the romances, not chivalry, and not *Rittergeist*.[12] There is little of genial digressiveness, courtesy, or natural magic. Instead, the classical unities of action, time, and place become the strait and narrow road leading to a single, surreal, pietistic confrontation. The space for reflection is tighter than in Poe's *The Pit and the Pendulum* and more stingily inauthentic than in Kafka. Bürger did create a new visionary form, but at a certain cost. The false theme triumphs at the expense of falsifying the mind, which has become a mere reflector of compulsions and spectator of fatalities.

To turn from *The Wild Huntsman* to Wordsworth's *Hartleap Well* (1800) is to know the rights of the mind—the pleasures and pains of ordinary consciousness—fully restored. No ballad could be more parallel, and more opposed. The first lines strike the keynote of difference:

> The Knight had ridden down from Wensley Moor
> With the slow motion of a summer's cloud. . . .

We begin with the chase almost over; that dramatic accumulation of incident, so essential to Bürger's pace, is at once subordinated to what Wordsworth named "character," but which is more like a consistent weather of the mind.[13] His first image therefore describes a mood as well as a motion and places both into encompassing nature. The stanzas that follow explicitly defuse Bürger's climax by incorporating it in the features of a natural scene:

> But, though Sir Walter like a falcon flies,
> There is a doleful silence in the air
>
> But horse and man are vanished, one and all;
> Such race, I think, was never seen before.
>
> Where is the throng, the tumult of the race?
> The bugles that so joyfully were blown?
> This chase it looks not like an earthly chase:
> Sir Walter and the Hart are left alone.

The silence means only that Sir Walter has outdistanced his helpers; there is nothing supernatural in it. Yet it does lead to an unearthly moment of solitude and reflection. There is something mysterious in the staying power of the stricken animal and in the knight's joy which overflows in a vow to commemorate the hunt. His joy, even so, may be consonant with a chivalric ethos, while the strength of dying creatures is proverbial. A naturalistic perspective is maintained. What hidden significance there may be must await the second part of the ballad, which is purely reflective.

This part introduces no new incidents. The poet, speaking in his own person and not as a naïve bard à la Bürger, reveals that the story just told was learned from a shepherd he met on the way from Hawes to Richmond while pondering in a desolate spot marked by ruins. The natural and the contemplative frame of the story come together as he and the shepherd exchange views in the very spot where Sir Walter was left alone with the Hart. If part one is action, part two is reflection; yet part one was already reflective in mood. Hunter, shepherd, poet: all are contemplatives.

Their contemplations, however, are of a deeply primitive kind. They center on a feeling of epiphany, of revelation associated with a particular place: here a revelation of nature as a sentient and powerful being. Sir Walter erects his pleasure-house on a spot where a natural power verging on the supernatural was manifested. The peasant thinks the spot is cursed because nature sympathized with the agony of the beast. The poet also thinks its death was mourned by "sympathy divein," by "The Being, that is in the clouds and air, / That is in the green leaves among the groves," but he refuses to go beyond what nature itself suggests, beyond the simple, imaginative feeling of desolation. He rejects the idea that there is a blood curse. Thus the poem is really a little progress of the imagination, which leads from one type of animism to another: from the martial type of the knight, to the pastoral type of the shepherd, and finally to that of the poet. And in this progress from primitive to sophisticated kinds of visionariness, poetic reflection is the refining principle: it keeps nature within nature and resists supernatural fancies.

Wordsworth's animism, his consciousness of a consciousness in nature, is the last noble superstition of a demythologized mind. All nature-spirits are dissolved by him except the spirit of Nature. His poetry quietly revives the figure of *Natura plangens*, one of the great visionary personae of both pastoral and cosmological poetry.[14] This link of Wordsworth's Nature to the Goddess Natura makes the formal moral of *Hartleap Well* almost indistinguishable from that of Bürger's poem: the one turns on "the sorrow of the meanest thing that feels"; the other on "Das Ach und Weh der Kreatur."[15] But while Bürger's demoniacal horseman parodies the chivalric spirit (the *Rittergeist*), Wordsworth accepts chivalry as a false yet imaginative and redeemable way of life. In Wordsworth the new and milder morality grows organically from the old: there is no apocalyptic or revolutionary change, just due process of time and nature.

Now this kind of continuity is the very pattern, according to Herder, of the English poetic mind, which builds on popular sources and so revitalizes them. By giving the ballad precedence over his more personal reflections and allowing the characters of knight and shepherd their own being, Wordsworth exemplifies a peculiarly English relation of new to old. The internal structure of his poem reflects a historical principle of canon formation. Even when, as in *The White Doe of Rylstone*, he begins with personal speculation rather than with an impersonally narrated ballad, the essential structure remains that of the reflective encirclement and progressive purification of symbols from Romance.

There are, in the Romantic period, many variations on this structure. The emergence of the gentle out of the haunted mind is not always so gradual and assured. Coleridge's *Ancient Mariner*, a "Dutch attempt at German sublimity" as Southey called it, follows the Bürgerian model. Yet it has, in addition, something of the meander of Romance and of that strange interplay of dream vision and actual vision found in Malory or Spenser. It is clear that Milton is not the only master for the English mind. But he is among those who assured the survival of Romance by the very quality of his resistance to it.

5
Wordsworth and Goethe in Literary History

Whatever the sources of historicism, the Ossianic fragments and similar "Lieder der Wilden" were of decisive importance for the person we consider its principal founder. "I may soon persecute you with a Psychology drawn from the poems of Ossian," Herder warns the reader in his letters on German Art published in 1773.[1] The psychology he refers to is clearly what we now call historicism. "The human race is destined to undergo a procession of scenes, of types of culture and manners: woe to the man who does not like his part in the drama in which he must act out and consummate his life! Woe also to the humane or moral Philosopher for whom the scene he appears on is the only possible one, and who always misunderstands the first scene as the worst! If all participate in the totality of the ongoing drama, then each will evince a new and remarkable aspect of humanity." In explaining why these primitive songs had affected him, Herder adds a second strong metaphor, of shipwreck, or being lost at sea, to that of the theater of history. An amazing confessional passage recaptures in its very swell the sense of danger and disorientation in this cultural traveler, this German Sinbad, when exposed to a northern version of the Arabian Nights:

> To be ejected, all at once, from business activities, from the tumult and mimicry of rank prevailing in the bourgeois world, from the armchair of the scholar and the soft sofa of social life, to have no distractions, libraries, scholarly or unscholarly journals; exposed on the open, infinite sea...in the midst of a totally different theater of events, an alive and active Nature; hanging between sky and deep, encompassed daily by the repetitive, eternal play of the elements, except for glimpsing

intermittently a new and distant shore or cloud or mental horizon—
reading now the songs and deeds of the ancient Scalds, one's soul completely absorbed in them and the places where they were formed—here
the cliffs of Norway . . . over there Iceland . . . passing at a distance the
shores where Fingal wrought and Ossian sang his melancholy
strains . . . then, believe me, Skalds and Bards were experienced differ-
ently than under the auspices of the Professors!

Even at the moment of writing, his calmer mind is colored by that experience.
"Und das Gefühl der Macht ist noch in mir, da ich auf scheiterndem Schiffe, das
kein Sturm und keine Flut mehr bewegte, mit Meer bespühlt und mit Mitternachtwind umschauert, Fingal lass und Morgen hoffte."[2]

Did that morning come? Though the transition was a stormy one in Germany,
it took less than half a century to achieve. Under Herder's influence—reinforced,
of course, by many currents, Klopstock's Nordic phase, the reviving interest in
Gothic architecture—Bürger began to flirt in the 1770s with the demonry of the
ballads; while Goethe, in his programmatic imitation of the older verse forms,
also helped to recover that "Fortgang von Szenen, von Bildung, von Sitten"
which in Herder's vision of things comprised the destiny of mankind. Thirty years
later, Arnim and Brentano dedicate their collection of old German songs, *Des
Knaben Wunderhorn*, to his excellency, Geheimrat von Goethe; and in another
twenty years, his Excellency actually pronounces himself glad that his passion for
the Northern Muse is over. "Das Teufels- und Hexenwesen machte ich nur ein-
mal; ich war froh mein nordisches Erbteil verzehrt zu haben, und wandte mich
zu den Tischen der Griechen."[3]

To some extent, then, it was a false dawn. When the sun rose in Germany, it
was still Homer's sun. "Und die Sonne Homers, siehe! sie lächelt auch uns." Yet
Schiller's verse (the last of *Der Spaziergang*, 1795) may be echoing a book which
had precipitated the interest in Northern Antiquities. "Time produces strange
revolutions," P.H. Mallet (or one of his translators) wrote in the eloquent conclusion to the *History of Denmark and Monuments of the Celts*. "Who knows
whether the Sun will not one day rise in the North?"[4] By the nineteenth century
this Northern sun was shining with more than borrowed light. Wilhelm Grimm's
introduction to *Altdänische Heldenlieder, Balladen und Märchen* (1811) shows
that the Herderian view has triumphed, but in an image far removed from the
stormy pathos of Herder. "Und doch hat die Sonne Homers auch über diese
Eisberge ihren Glanz, und über die bereifte Thäler ihre Edelsteine ausgestreut."
The sun shines on all alike; there is one creative spirit at work everywhere. But
this no longer argues the supremacy of the Classical Muse, or the conformity with
it of true genius. Rather, that each culture has its own classics or genius loci.

I propose to apply the historicist imagination to the age of historicism. In particular, I would like to explore the different impact on a German and an English

ballad poem of the *Northern Enchantment*. It is well known that the idea of a characteristic literature of the North, which Mme de Staëhl championed with late and efficient clarity, helped to break the tyranny of France over Germany, but what role did it play in England? I cannot give for England a sketch of the importance of the Northern Enchantment except to remind you that the success of Macpherson's Erse fragments made Thomas Percy consider publishing in 1761 (the year in which Gray wrote his odes "from the Norse tongue") *Five Pieces of Runic Poetry Translated from the Islandic Language*,[5] and that Percy's translation of Mallet's book under the title *Northern Antiquities* (1770) extended its influence to, among others, Blake.

Wordsworth, Burns, and Scott came from the North Country; and of these Wordsworth made the most determined effort not only to respect the Matter of the North but also to modernize it. Choosing two poems, one by Wordsworth and the other by Goethe, may be too selective a procedure, but it enables me to attempt in a short essay what E. R. Curtius characterized as an essential task of comparative literature: to study the relation between the historical development of a culture and its ideology or self-interpretation. There is a potential "Theory of English Literature" in Wordsworth's poetry as there is a "Theory of German Literature" in that of Goethe.

II

Let me begin, then, with an English poem written in Germany during the very last year of the eighteenth century. It was first called "A Fragment" because the author, immersed in the ballad revival which had moved from England to Germany, thought of it as the "prelude to a ballad-poem." The later title of this lyric also points to the impact of the ballads or of the Northern Enchantment. Wordsworth, for he is the author, eventually named the poem "The Danish Boy"; and it is clear that the shadowy harper he evokes, sitting solitary, and close to the sky, in a spot washed clean of all images except mountain flowers, rills, a tempest-stricken tree, and the cornerstone of a hut, would have sung us a ballad ghostlier, or at least more spiritual, than any found in M.G. Lewis's *Tales of Wonder* (1801)—a collection that contains such "Danish" morsels as "The Water King" and "The Erl-King's Daughter," following on a version of Goethe's "Erl-King."[6] What the Danish Boy in his sacred isolation sang to the flocks and mountain ponies on neighboring hills we shall never know, any more than what songs the sirens warbled to Odysseus; for the actual ballad, to which this portrait is a prelude, was left unwritten. Yet there was a voice out of silence, and the silence knew it, and was pleased (see Appendix 1).

I say this unmystically because elsewhere, too, in epitaph-inscription, prelusive biography, or ballad proper, Wordsworth summons that voice out of the silence of a nature-buried past, out of the rocky, half-animate landscape of a region, which, Northern or English, is a no-man's-land between earth and sky, life and death, memory and oblivion, tautology and muteness. What is that other Boy doing, in a fragment also composed in Germany during this time, when he blows "mimic hootings to the silent owls / That they might answer him"? The Boy of Winander fragment opens with a formula which does not differ from the "There was" or "It was" of the anonymous ballad; and despite nature's generous, wild, even frighteningly deep response to the Boy's call, everything returns to silence. The curious apostrophe which interrupts Wordsworth's opening formula, "ye knew him well, ye Cliffs / And islands of Winander!" suggests not only that the Boy could wake the pastoral echoes but also how enclosed his life was, a mere interruption of nature's silence. Like Lucy he lived unknown, and few (perhaps only that rocky shore) could know when he ceased to be. His brief moment of vocal challenge—it cannot even be termed song—proves to be a deceptive mimicry, ending in muteness. "Oftentimes / A full half-hour together I have stood / Mute—looking at the grave in which he lies."[7] The vale that gave birth to the Boy also buries with him his potential songs; and however different those two Boys or fragments of destiny, both utter a strange or "forgotten" tongue and dwell in a "sacred" spot as close to silence and death as to life:

> The lovely Danish Boy is blest
> And happy in his flowery cove:
> From bloody deeds his thoughts are far;
> And yet he warbles songs of war;
> They seem like songs of love,
> For calm and gentle is his mien;
> Like a dead Boy he is serene.[8]

Wordsworth's poetry has many such figures, neither quite alive nor dead: Lucy and the Leechgatherer date from near this period. Yet in the case of the Danish Boy there is a literal reason for describing him as a visionary "shadow" or "spirit" who both "seems a Form of flesh and blood" and resembles the dead. For, according to a Cumberland superstition, he *is* dead: a ghost or revenant haunting that spot. Wordsworth identifies him in a later note as a "Danish Prince who had fled from Battle, and, for the sake of the valuables about him, was murdered by the Inhabitants of a Cottage in which he had taken refuge. The House fell under a curse, and the Spirit of the Youth. . . haunted the Valley where the crime had been committed."[9] The cornerstone mentioned in the first stanza links up with this story of a cursed place. The poem, therefore, belongs with "The Three Graves," the "Ancient Mariner," "Hartleap Well," and several other ballads in telling of a crime against nature which results in doer or place falling under a curse.

Yet Wordsworth spiritualizes the superstition of curse and revenant: he makes the ghostly harper into the genius of a landscape which is haunted only in the sense that it inspires the poet. The poet's mind is already the "haunt and the main region" of his song. The unwritten ballad might well have been, like "The Thorn," an invention serving to express the mysterious impact on Wordsworth of a spot in nature. That Wordsworth is haunted by the spot argues the truth, though not literally so, of the superstition he preserves. To put it in another way: the superstition allows him to honor what omens and intimations flow from nature.

The strange persistence of the Danish Boy thus resembles the persistence, shadowy and residual, of the spirit of poetry itself. To envision the harper in that place means that he has survived from the time of the Danish invasions. No wonder, then, his flowery cove is also a grave, and that someone so young is already becalmed. He must be as old as the northern ballads which never grow old. The mystery of this Old Boy is resolved more easily than that of Lucy or other border figures.

We are dealing, of course, with the *idea* of the northern ballad, with its "burden" on the consciousness of a poet deeply concerned with the vocation and survival of imaginative power. The question facing Wordsworth is whether this power is dead or obsolete; and if not, how the enlightened mind can accommodate it. The encounter of old and young in his verse expresses this problem of transmission, or, to put it strongly, of succession. The poet creates scenes parallel to that in which Elijah's mantle passes to Elishah. In Wordsworth, of course, there is no open vision but hints of power failure and diminishment. This does not make our analogy of the poetic to the prophetic situation any more disproportionate than it must always be. Part of the problem, in fact, is that the analogy so vividly survives; that the prophetic ideal will not give up; even though Wordsworth meets neither Elijah nor Milton in those border regions but only this marvelous Boy or a poor man hunting leeches or a pedlar nurtured on, and perhaps hawking, the old ballads.

"The Danish Boy" is, actually, the closest Wordsworth comes to a supernatural or explicitly visionary poetry. Yet it seems just one more ballad suggesting the spell or curse which makes a ghost of all of Wordsworth's sufferers—including the narrator himself. Consider that Wordsworth does more than empty the traditional ballad of multiple dramatic *incidents* in favor of an emphasis on *character*: for, without admitting it, he also divests character of its palpability. What "character" can one ascribe to the Danish Boy or Lucy or Matthew or indeed the narrator himself? As elemental as nature-spirits, yet wandering far from their home-element, these ghostly yet human beings are characterized by no qualities other than persistence, imaginative fixation, and the sadness of incompletion. They do not escape a silence from which an anonymous or obsessive voice redeems them. The tone of narration fails to embody the narrator, to characterize him, to present him as authoritative author. It shuttles between overintimacy and detachment, evidential claim and legend, classical and colloquial diction, personal and impersonal modes of rhetoric.[10]

Critics have puzzled over this narrative tone which is neither personal nor yet impersonal—just as the beings described are often neither alive nor dead. The style, clearly, is not, or not yet, the man: it evades impersonating the author. Wordsworth, one must conclude, has not found his own voice or else his character (identity). He can be, of course, natural and direct, when he allows the lyrical ballad to become a dramatic monologue and present a shepherd's or mother's complaint. But in his more peculiar productions, such poems as "Simon Lee," "The Thorn," "The Idiot Boy," and "The Danish Boy," the narrator's presence is both overstated (leading to Keats's charge of "palpable design") and understated—in short, embarrassed. Thus, with plot and character and even narrative voice attenuated, what remains is indeed

> A tale of silent suffering, hardly clothed
> In bodily form, and to the grosser sense
> But ill adapted, scarcely palpable
> To him who does not think. . . .
>
> ("The Ruined Cottage")

III

One wonders what "thinking" meant for Wordsworth. The mind is his haunt, he informs us; and "The Boy of Winander" episode ends with an emblem of reflective man, looking mutely at a life fallen into muteness. If we had "such stores as silent thought can bring," the author of "Simon Lee" admonishes us, then we would find "A tale in everything."

A strange antinomy that, of "silent store" and story ("tale"). It is remarkable how often in Wordsworth this reading of "silent characters" is referred to.[11] Perhaps his mind dislikes a vacuum and strives to convert absence into presence, or silence into restituted speech. Yet the ethos of story-telling is a complex thing: it involves, as "The Ruined Cottage" so finely shows, a respect for the compact silence being disturbed. Fiction treads as gently as on the grave of people whose lives were unconsummated. It should not be a false completion but rather a requiem acknowledging the unsatisfied nature of their lives and the restlessness of their ghost.

Given Wordsworth's scruples about fictionalizing the dead, it is amazing he can write narrative at all, even in the minor form of the ballad. He does it, in effect, by exposing the ghostly interstices of narrative. If stories give events an afterlife, it is because they enable the dead to haunt the living; and if that is so, it is essential to understand the relation of life to afterlife, or of those "silent characters" to the poetic speech they nourish. Indeed, as Wordsworth enters the haunt of his mind, a powerful confusion about what is living and what is dead—what is past and what is present—often takes hold. This confusion usually comes in the form of a disturbing image from legend or personal history, an image which has such usurpatory power that the poet's time-sense is bewildered. He feels "lost," "stopped," "halted," split into separate beings. These heightened moments of self-awareness, mainly from the *Prelude*, are much better known than subtle but equally perplexing "fits" which phantomize his narrative elsewhere and bring it to a halt. After recalling, for example, a pathetic speech of Margaret's, the pedlar says to the listening poet:

> Sir, I feel
> The story linger in my heart. I fear
> 'Tis long and tedious, but my spirit clings
> To that poor woman. So familiarly
> Do I perceive her manner and her look
> And presence, and so deeply do I feel
> Her goodness, that not seldom in my walks
> A momentary trance comes over me,
> And to myself I seem to muse on one
> By sorrow laid asleep or borne away,
> A human being destined to awake
> To human life, or something very near
> To human life, when he shall come again
> For whom she suffered.
>
> ("The Ruined Cottage")

Margaret, in this trance, is seen as a person who will awake from the sleep of death to an afterlife which is not more than human, but merely human. Her humanity was not able to realize itself during her life, so that if the narrator's spirit clings to her, her spirit also clings to him, still hoping for completion. Margaret's fictional presence is simply an extension of the consuming ghostliness of her desire. She dies into the pedlar's mind like Lucy into the poet's. The tale is her haunting.

Poetry thus becomes a commemorative rite, a ceremony to evoke and at the same time appease the perturbed spirit. At the end of the pedlar's tale, the poet is so deeply moved that, he confesses, "with a brother's love / I blessed her [Margaret] in the impotence of grief." A difficult response, for the grief and love elicited are not unlike Margaret's own, which cursed rather than blessed the place in which he stands. Yet blessing and cursing are reactions appropriate to the appearance of spirits: Margaret's story, her passion here revived, is so strong and ambiguously spiritual, it exacts this kind of acknowledgment.

How well Coleridge knew the curse, whose Mariner is never fully released from it! Or Shelley, who prefaced *Alastor* (1815) with lines taken from "The Ruined Cottage" ("Oh Sir! the good die first / And those whose hearts are dry as summer dust / Burn to the socket"), and who relates an even darker version of the loss of Margaret's garden in *The Sensitive Plant*. What of the narrator who spots the Danish Boy near that other ruined cottage? Or the poet who contemplates the Boy of Winander's grave? Are they seeing spirits too? "Vision as thou art," says Wordsworth of the Highland girl, "I bless thee with a human heart." Visionariness and human-heartedness are not easily reconciled. In the curse ballads, as even perhaps in the Lucy poems, the human element ("I had no human fears") is spirited away.

If imaginative power is to survive, this "curse" of the spirit— of the ever-unconsummated spirit—must be acknowledged. It dooms the boy to remain a boy because it is immemorially older than the philosophic mind into which he appears to die. The imagination outlives both boyhood and manhood, as if its imperishable restlessness, which links story to story in a rhapsode's chain, were the one form of immortality granted to human beings. The teller's touch makes all nature kin. It restores the "family," broken by desertion or death, at the level of imaginative sympathy.[12] Though the pitcher breaks, though the container is destroyed by what it contains, from the shards ("the useless fragments of a wooden bowl") a poet somewhere raises Margaret's story.

Wordsworth's new ballad, then, is still a ghost story, like so many traditional ballads or even Coleridge's "Ancient Mariner." The poet is not interested, however, in the supernatural as such. He deals with a contagion of the mind by human materials that exert a supernatural effect. The phantomization which occurs is ultimately that of a person drawn into a deeply imaginative yet antinatural frame of mind. The story, or the ghostly idea it contains, wants to carry the narrator off: it is after his soul, and desires an incarnation as dangerous to him as consorting with nature-spirits.

Wordsworth must hold onto his mind, stand firm in it, gain a foothold on this treacherous realm where ecstasy and bathos alternate. "For I must tread on shadowy ground, must sink / Deep—and, aloft ascending, breathe in worlds / To which the heaven of heavens is but a veil." Even in "Tintern Abbey" that "shadowy ground" is felt. The poet's act of emplacing himself remains uncertain, precarious. His psyche is encircled by the psychic from which it draws its being.

All the more so in "The Danish Boy," where both observer and observed remain shadowy. To what sacred or demonic ground are we being led so insistently? Who is speaking, who is directing us there? The narrator has no real "character": this voice out of silence can only be that of an eccentric guide or of some ghostly being. Follow that voice at your risk. We can think of the story as a local tradition retold, like "The Thorn," by a disordered or infected imagination; but we can also think of it as a visionary seduction, the poet-traveler waylaid by the spirit of the place, or the Mind of Man by an image out of balladry's *anima mundi.*

IV

No one, so far as I know, has set "The Danish Boy" to music. But Goethe's "Erlkönig," first recited during a *Singspiel* at Weimar in 1782, has haunted the musical as well as literary interpreter. It, rather than Wordsworth's poem, should be called a *lyrical* ballad. The poem is in several distinct voices, which alternate, rise to a climax, and cease.[13] To characterize those voices is relatively simple because of the lyric's dramatic structure: one voice is anonymous, that of the ballad narrator; the others are the personal voices of father, son, and Erl-King. If the poem evokes, like Wordsworth's ballad, the presence of the demonic, or of a mind prey to the demonic, this does not embarrass the narrative or lead us to puzzle about the "character" (psychology) of the narrator. However eerie a silence from which these voices arise, they are so clearly typed, so bonded to role, that when Goethe's spectacle of sound is over they seem to have fulfilled a destined play; and the ending, though it involves a child's death, satisfies curiously our imagination (see Appendix 2).

It might have been a more disquieting ballad. Its atmosphere, certainly, is visionary enough. We are reminded of Herder's "Gefühl der Nacht," his reading Fingal and hoping for sunrise "mit Mitternachtwind umschauert." It is as if some passage-trial were taking place: the rider must run, with the boy in his arms, a gauntlet of ghostly trees. No doubt Gundolf exaggerates when he talks of "Locken, Raunen, Dämmern, und Weben des Wassers und der Luft, zu Elementargeistern verdichtend, aus dem Grauen heraus ballend."[14] Yet the boy's death is difficult to explain except as a victory of the *Elementargeister*: have they not succeeded in stealing him away, in kidnapping his imagination? As in "Der Fischer," the victim lives between two realms, nature and supernatural, reasonableness and ecstasy; and he fails to maintain his separateness. Two fathers struggle for Goethe's Danish Boy; and however we interpret the outcome—whether we accept the supernatural intimation or rationalize it as the product of a fearful or feverish mind—the natural father here is not powerful enough to save his child.

Both poems, then, Goethe's and Wordsworth's, evoke a border-region or no-man's-land between natural and demonic; both are mysterious rather than mystical. Let me emphasize this similarity a moment. It is clear that, unlike Bürger, neither poet yields up his naturalism to the ghostly ballad. So Wordsworth's comment on "The Thorn" and Goethe's on "Der Fischer" can be harmonized. The origin of the English poem was a natural impression heightened by atmospheric circumstances. "Cannot I by some invention . . . make this Thorn permanently an impressive object as the storm has made it to my eyes this moment?"[15] Goethe, for his part, wished to express through his poem "das Gefühl des Wassers...das Anmutige, was uns im Sommer lockt, uns zu baden." Does not the "Erl-King" also depict "das Anmutige," or an ominous variation of it: the ghostly solicitation of trees on a windy night?[16]

Yet it is not really wind and trees which emanate the dangerous charm. It is Voice. In Wordsworth, voice is ghostly because it is a wandering sound in search of character or completion. We are compelled to ask: what does voice want? What is the point or hidden intent of the supposed narrative? Why does it haunt this place? But in Goethe's ballad, voice is ghostly because overdefined—so essentialized, so voice-like, it does not require localization. We are as close to *seeing* voices as is possible. More is involved, however, than Goethe's plastic power, a classicist will-to-form that seeks to dominate even a romantic-ghostly situation. The impression conveyed by the minimal art of this great artist is of voices overheard in the dark, therefore at once clear and obscure, piano and forte, individuated yet merging back into night, nature, and wind. They create as they speak the world of which they speak, as if it were through voice we reached the concept of being. The two fathers become simply two voices in the ear of child and reader. There is nothing else but this ghostly *Nachtmusik* in which difference of being is reduced to difference of voice.

Goethe's poem, thus, eliminates narrative by absorbing it into voice. The disappearance—classical, musical, dramatic—of the narrator into his voices evades the very issue haunting Wordsworth, that of the complicity of art and artist, or of the psychology of narration. Only at the end is Goethe forced to revert to narrative and so to raise the question as to which "voice" has mediated the other voices. The author's disappearance is modified by a "remainder" of which we are not aware till that last stanza; and even there it is so carefully managed that it betrays less the invisible author than a directorial skill of near-magical proportions.

On analysis, Goethe's first stanza is already a play of voices, though we do not know precisely who asks or who replies, or whether it is one voice or two. The emphasis is clearly shifted by his prelude from narrative to voice; and within this from the expressive pathos of each voice to a question-and-answer, or cry-and-reply, structure. The division of voices, in short, is as impersonal or modal as that between tenor and bass or parts assigned different instruments. Only in the second stanza do we feel this musical partition becoming a real division; and even here an ideal symmetry or balance of tones modifies the impression of *Zwiespalt*. There is, momentarily, a sense of containment: the father's words, which begin and end the verse, hold the boy as firmly as do his arms.

But the next lines complicate the cry-and-reply pattern. The Erl-King's voice takes over a whole stanza: it is put in its own, uninterrupted vocal space, apart from that of father and child, ominously complete. The middle of the poem (stanzas 4-5) repeats this pattern of a divided stanza followed by a whole; the movement seems to begin again with stanza six, but in the climax of the seventh the Erl-King's threat is followed at once by the boy's cry, which is followed, instead of by the father's words, by no reply at all. It is the narrator who takes over in a final stanza, which is the only strictly narrative portion of the ballad.

How do we interpret this narrative "remainder"? It heightens the impersonal mood and seems to confirm the poem as a masterful development of the impersonal ballad. But we can insist, at the same time, on the movement from voice to voice, and ask what kind of voice might have followed the climax of the seventh stanza. Narrativity then appears as a voice-substitute: a speaking silence which takes over when a voice fails or a new voice is wanting. The author shows his hand but not his voice.

What makes one shudder like the father ("Dem Vater grausets") is the role of the author rather than the situation itself. The author seems to be in control to the very end, to the last syllables of the poem, in suggesting that the child might come through, "In seinen Armen das Kind," still raises a glimmer of hope, "war tot," extinguishes it. The shudder comes when we realize that we know from the start a sacrifice would be required: that the boy must die, and voice fail. Something in the form itself compels this awareness. "Wer reitet so spät durch Nacht und Wind?" is, in retrospect, more than a functional device allowing the narrative to unfold. It is as much a challenge as a question, a *qui vive* indicating a satisfaction to be exacted, if only in the form of an appropriate answer. And the answer we then hear is indeed strangely impersonal, cold, ritualistic. Does it imply a judgement that father and son are trespassing on ghostly ground? Or is it, potentially, an intercession: doom-words which might still turn into pass-words?

All we hear is voices, as if the action were to be played out on that level—yet if that is so, the expectation of a transcendent voice, redeeming or resolving, is raised without being fulfilled. The middle of the poem does waver subtly between personal and impersonal constructions, but the concluding stanza returns to impersonality. The *er*, dominant in the first stanza, then receding uninflected into Vat*er*, or hiding in *Er*lkönig, is sharply obtruded once more: "*er* reitet . . . *Er* hält . . . *Er*reicht." No password or saving voice has appeared. The "remainder" is like the corpse brought home.

The withholding of personal voice is, therefore, a formal triumph or else the price Goethe pays to wrest this genre from the past. Perhaps both are one; perhaps what Henry James called "the coercive charm of form" has here become an *amor fati* related to Goethe's sense of artistic and historical vocation. Let us recall the context. Goethe is directing a "Wald- und Wasserdrama," and he opens it with the "Erlkönig." The form he revives is a *Singspiel* in small, performed at Weimar, where less than ten years before Wieland staged an *Alceste* inspired by Gluck. Is not Goethe enacting something Orphic himself in leading this form, these voices, out of the silence of the past? If so, his orphism belongs to art alone: the artist is the only magus; the show begins and ends according to his will. "May I be bold to think these spirits?" Ferdinand asks Prospero in *The Tempest*, when shown another kind of "harmonious" vision. And Prospero replies: "Spirits, which by mine art / I have from their confines call'd to enact / My present fancies." Goethe's art is equal to the spirits he conceives. The literary form itself is the magic formula.[17]

Let us reflect further on Goethe's orphism. By 1780 his program for the renewal of letters in Germany had outgrown its nationalistic or Nordic phase. He engages in a ransacking of North, South, East, and West which will culminate in the great Helena episode of *Faust*. "Bildung" is all; history itself is but a "Bildungsroman"; William must become "Master." Yet in 1827, the year in which he sends the *Helena* to press, Goethe still complains: "Wir Deutschen sind von gestern." How can someone born yesterday be reborn through art, and become, like the French or English, "ein Stück Geschichte"?[18]

Hence there is something magical in Goethe's genius, in his orphic katabasis, even if he stresses, like Hegel, *Werden, Bildung, Meisterschaft*. Instant history is impossible; culture does not come out of the mouth of a gun;[19] yet the very need of it goads him like Faust into magic reanimations. What are ghosts but reanimated ideas, abstractions with a face, a void full of voices?

The difference, in this respect, between Goethe and Wordsworth is telling. Wordsworth did not have to call up ballads from the vasty deep: despite a hiatus usually blamed on the school of Waller or of Pope, the ballad was not only around him in popular and debased form but its spirit had been taken up into literature by Shakespeare. Many of the Renaissance poets, in fact, provided a pattern (as Herder remarked) for the symbiosis of popular and sophisticated fiction, a symbiosis which enabled Friederich Schlegel's famous definition of Romantic poetry as "progressively universal," and which was also one of the sources of Goethe's concept of *Bildung*.

Wordsworth feared above all the demonism of an imagination that might leave us naked of nature or culture; but for Goethe whatever heritage might have existed is so alienated, so far in the dark backward and abysm of time, that scholarly effort and revivalist affirmation are insufficient to bring it to life.[20] Goethe must produce a culture twice-born from the start, for the historicist or antiquarian impulse can only evoke animated abstractions which he discounts under the name of *allegory*. What he dignifies by the antonym *symbol* is based not so much on history as on natural history, and suggests a productive or generative principle by which dead matter is made organic once more. This *natural magic* merges with the "mystery" of a craft called art which at once organizes and organicizes a past so discontinuous with the present, that, but for it, only volcanic (storm-and-stress) historicism or a new religious incarnation could re-present it.

Two conclusions from this. We see, first, why Goethe's ballad is not primarily an accommodated northern form. It cannot be assigned to one era, to Nordic rather than romance stirrings, to German rather than French culture, or even to an inspired, superconscious syncretism. It arises out of all this historical experience, all this "enormous labour of the world-spirit," as Hegel called it, and yet out of nothing—out of nothing more, that is, than misty trees on a windy night.

We also understand why Goethe's attitude toward the demonic is so much freer than Wordsworth's. The rebuilding of culture in Germany is a Magian enterprise. Yet Goethe defines the demonic as a magic inherent in nature. The demonic is not ultimately distinguishable from the productive power of nature, and is called the demonic simply because adversity and death may accompany its energetic drive. So Goethe's admiration for Napoleon and Byron includes their ruin as well as their achievements. The demonic enlarges character as fate: it is genius in its human form.

Compare the tradition that goes from Wordsworth to Keats. It is deeply uncertain of the "character" or "identity" of the poet. What kind of labor is imaginative labor? The charge that poetry is an ignoble or idle dreaming—"Thou art a dreaming thing; / A fever of thyself"[21]—is never far from the English consciousness. But Goethe's labor is cut out for him. Could anyone be more productive than this demiurge who works at catching culture up; who builds *Bildung* with devilish energy of purpose? What a supremely confident maker!

We must not simplify, however: in one respect he, too, is wary of all this dream-work. He knows that many persons of demonic character are not interested in culture as such but exclusively in rejuvenation, or what we today would call youth-culture; and his own ideal is almost the opposite of that. He wants young persons to be so in touch with the cultural heritage that they and it would be mutually renewed. A purely demonic ideal, in contrast, tends to become eudaemonic: eternal youth is sought for its own sake, not for the sake of a productive life. What the Erl-King promises the child is not unlike what Faust bitterly requests of that demon-king, Mephistopheles. The phantom seems to say to the boy, "Verweile doch, du bist so schön." He is luring him into eudaemonia, or arrested youth.

If for Wordsworth voice is demonic, for Goethe it is eudaemonic. Wordsworth's "still sad music of humanity" wants to chastize voice, to ground its ghostliness, to endow it with the reality of character. But Goethe wants to make voice more genuinely demonic, orphic, productive. The Word must become Act. The demonic in man must triumph over the eudaemonic. Musicality must become characteristic and voice release itself from the Italian charm.[22]

It has become customary to use *voice* as a metonymy for *character*, but this may conceal more than it reveals. I have tried to uncover an opposition which goes deeper than that between lyric and narrative, though related to it. The demonic or eudaemonic charm of voice should be linked, I believe, to the study of character formation as we pass, to use psychoanalytic terms, from the preoedipal to the oedipal phase.[23] The notion of character, in its link to the question of mimesis, then to the problem of the character or identity of the poet, may be the largest subject of a historical poetics.

To connect the psychology of art and the history of art in any methodical way is beset by the temptation of psychohistory. But just as we have used poetry to analyze the notions of "voice" and "character," so we could use it to analyze the notion of "psyche." A psychoanalysis should emerge from this more adequate to art than any so far devised; and these concepts of voice, character, and psyche may then allow us to explore the history of the poets: the relation between the works of an artist and the role he plays or desires to play in literary history.

In this light a final remark on Goethe's poem. Its source was Herder's version of a Danish ballad, "The Erl-King's (Elfking's) Daughter"; and in this ballad Sir Oluf, on the evening before his wedding, happens on the Erl-King's daughter dancing in a fairy circle—a meeting which costs him his life. Although there is a touch of motiveless malignancy in Sir Oluf's fate, we know why he has to die; just as we know why Goethe's Fisherman is fished by his lorelay. The fairies are frigid: they envy human passionateness and destroy what they envy unless permitted to incorporate with it. In short, they cannot be redeemed except by securing that *soul* or *psyche* which they lack. Thus the Erl-King's daughter, like the mermaid in "Der Fischer," commits a *crime passionelle* precisely because she is passion-less; and the vampire maiden, as in Goethe's "Bride of Corinth," is but a variant of this ghostly figure who seeks and cannot receive full earthly pleasure.[24]

But how do we understand, from within this logic of myth, the Erl-King's rape of the child? It strikes one as more brutal, more instinctive even, than those other fatal acts, which contain a clear hint of sexual jealousy. Whatever erotic motive exists is surely secondary to the demon's sheer envy of the "human form divine." It is as if this demon, all ego and no psyche, wanted to seize the psyche itself, to possess it in its purest, most pristine state. Thus by extending the myth Goethe may also have clarified it. My remark, of course, is not intended to link poetry to a pathology of incorporation, although the imaginative gift is obviously a troubled or triumphant form of empathy.

It is, in any case, Herder rather than Goethe who suffers from the ambitious need to really know the soul of every age. Recall how he threatened to persecute us with a "psychology" drawn from Ossian. The frenzy of historicist redemption which possesses him, and which remains, despite all those hyperbolic books, curiously abstract, is reduced by Goethe to humane proportions, that of actual poems. Goethe also wishes to catch up with the past; but he recognizes the quasi-erotic or demonic nature of this quest. His art can be seen as a critique of historicism which at once honors and limits it. He knows the myth of Orpheus

is shadowed by failure, as the parallel myth of Alcestis by human sacrifice; and
this knowledge, this shadow, never leaves the author of *Faust*, who seeks, like
his hero, an eternally youthful psyche which draws him ever on.

APPENDIX 1

The Danish Boy

A Fragment

Between two sister moorland rills
There is a spot that seems to lie
Sacred to flowerets of the hills,
And sacred to the sky.
And in this smooth and open dell
There is a tempest-stricken tree;
A corner-stone by lightning cut,
The last stone of a cottage hut;
And in this dell you see
A thing no storm can e'er destroy,
The shadow of a Danish Boy.

In clouds above, the Lark is heard,
He sings his blithest and his best;
But in this lonesome nook the Bird
Did never build his nest.
No Beast, no Bird hath here his home;
The Bees borne on the breezy air
Pass high above those fragrant bells
To other flowers, to other dells,
Nor ever linger there.
The Danish Boy walks here alone:
The lovely dell is all his own.

A spirit of noon day is he,
He seems a Form of flesh and blood;
Nor piping Shepherd shall he be,
Nor herd-boy of the wood.
A regal vest of fur he wears,
In colour like a raven's wing;
It fears not rain, nor wind, nor dew;
But in the storm 'tis fresh and blue
As budding pines in Spring;

His helmet has a vernal grace,
Fresh as the bloom upon his face.

A harp is from his shoulder slung:
He rests his harp upon his knee;
And there in a forgotten tongue
He warbles melody.
Of flocks upon the neighboring hills
He is the darling and the joy;
And often, when no cause appears,
The mountain ponies prick their ears,
They hear the Danish Boy,
While in the dell he sits alone
Beside the tree and corner-stone.*

There sits he: in his face you spy
No trace of a ferocious air,
Nor ever was a cloudless sky
So steady or so fair.
The lovely Danish Boy is blest
And happy in his flowery cove:
From bloody deeds his thoughts are far;
And yet he warbles songs of war;
They seem like songs of love
For calm and gentle is his mien:
Like a dead Boy he is serene.

   *   *   *

*In the 1800 *Lyrical Ballads*, an additional stanza follows:

When near this blasted tree you pass,
Two sods are plainly to be seen
Close at its root, and each with grass
Is cover'd fresh and green.
Like turf upon a new-made grave
These two green sods together lie,
Nor heat, nor cold, nor rain, nor wind
Can these two sods together bind,
Nor sun, nor earth, nor sky,
But side by side the two are laid,
As if just sever'd by the spade.

APPENDIX 2

Der Erlkönig

Wer reitet so spät durch Nacht und Wind?
Es ist der Vater mit seinem Kind;
Er hat den Knaben wohl in dem Arm,
Er fasst ihn sicher, er hält ihn warm.—

Mein Sohn, was birgst do so bang dein Gesicht?—
Siehst, Vater, du den Erlkönig nicht?
Den Erlenkönig mit Kron' und Schweif?—
Mein Sohn, es ist ein Nebelstreif.—

"Du liebes Kind, komm, geh mit mir!
Gar schöne Spiele spiel' ich mit dir;
Manch' bunte Blumen sind an dem Strand;
Meine Mutter hat manch' gülden Gewand."

Mein Vater, mein Vater, und hörest du nicht,
Was Erlenkönig mir leise verspricht?—
Sei ruhig, bleibe ruhig, mein Kind!
In dürren Blättern säuselt der Wind.—

"Willst, feiner Knabe, du mit mir gehn?
Meine Töchter sollen dich warten schön;
Meine Töchter führen den nächtlichen Reihn
Und wiegen und tanzen und singen dich ein."

Mein Vater, mein Vater, und siehst du nicht dort
Erlkönigs Töchter am düstern Ort?—
Mein Sohn, mein Sohn, ich seh' es genau;
Es scheinen die alten Weiden so grau.—

"Ich liebe dich, mich reizt deine schöne Gestalt;
Und bist du nicht willig, so brauch' ich Gewalt."—
Mein Vater, mein Vater, jetzt fasst er mich an!
Erlkönig hat mir ein Leids getan!—

Dem Vater grausets, er reitet geschwind,
Er hält in Armen das ächzende Kind,
Erreicht den Hof mit Mühe und Not;
In seinen Armen das Kind war tot.

6

Blessing the Torrent

Ein Räthsel ist Reinentsprungenes

Hölderlin

The river is fateful,
Like the last one. But there is no ferryman.
He could not bend against its propelling force.

Wallace Stevens

riverrun, past Eve and Adam's

James Joyce

I

How art thou named? In search of what strange land,
From what huge height, descending? Can such force
Of waters issue from a British source,
Or hath not Pindus fed thee, where the band
Of Patriots scoop their freedom out, with hand
Desperate as thine? Or come the incessant shocks
From that young Stream, that smites the throbbing rocks,
Of Viamala? There I seem to stand,
As in life's morn; permitted to behold,
From the dread chasm, woods climbing above woods,
In pomp that fades not; everlasting snows;
And skies that ne'er relinquish their repose;
Such power possess the family of floods
Over the minds of Poets, young or old!

If the two opening lines of this sonnet had been an untitled fragment, their refer-
ent would be uncertain. Whom is the poet talking to, what "thou" is addressed?
Is the force natural or divine? And why should the act of naming be important?
   But the lines are part of a sonnet titled specifically "To the Torrent at the

75

Devil's Bridge, North Wales, 1824."[1] Moreover, as line 2 runs into line 3, the "force" is identified as a "force of waters," that is, a river or, more precisely, a waterfall. ("Force" was dialect in the North of England for "waterfall.") Describing the impact of a different sight, though it also involved naming or labeling, Wordsworth writes: "My mind turned round / As with the might of waters."[2] In the present poem the verse line itself turns round and naturalizes the poet's wonderment. Uncertainty of reference gives way to a well-defined personal situation that is easily described, though less easily understood.

II

In September 1824 Wordsworth traveled through North Wales on one of the many sentimental journeys he was fond of taking. They were sentimental in the sense of covering old ground in order to reflect on the changes time had wrought in him or the scene; and "Tintern Abbey" was the earliest and most remarkable issue of such memorial visits. On this particular trip Wordsworth saw a friend of his youth, Robert Jones, who had shared with him two determining moments in his life: the ascent of Snowdon in 1791 and the tour of 1790 through revolutionary France and the Alps, with its complex seeding in his mind of experiences in the Simplon / Viamala region. Both journeys were now over thirty years old, and had already been described; the Snowdon climb in Book XIII of the unpublished *Prelude*, and the Continental tour in Book VI, as well as in *Descriptive Sketches* (1793). In 1820, moreover, Wordsworth retraced his journey through the Alps with his sister, Dorothy, and his wife, Mary, both of whom kept journals of this visit.

On a portion of this new trip to Wales the poet was accompanied by Robert Jones; and it was with him (as well as with Mary and Dora Wordsworth) that he viewed the waterfall described in the sonnet. No wonder, then, that as he stands at the torrent's edge, he feels he is back "in life's morn," and what he sees with the eyes of an aging man (he is fifty-four years old) is not a local river but "that young stream, that smites the throbbing rocks, / Of Viamala," which had giddied him when his own mind was young and in turmoil.

We can normalize this sonnet then; and the fact that it is a sonnet, one of so many written during the poet's later career, tempts us to give it a nod of esteem and pass on. There is little on first reading to hold the attention. Formal features of a conventional sort abound: opening and closing apostrophes; a first half comprising a cascade of questions that receive their resolution or coda in the second half, which is introduced by an efficient turn in the eighth line; enjambments that reflect the passion or perplexity of the utterance; and the abbreviated effect of sublimity created by a broken series of descriptive phrases characterizing his memory of the Viamala region (10-12).

In line with this we can also normalize the initial "How art thou named?" as

Devil's Bridge, Wales. John Sell Cotman, from *the Liber Studiorum.*

a rhetorical or animating movement that is a residue of the sublime style and so risks bathos. The poet must have known the name; he is obtruding the question to express a momentary ecstasy or disorientation. Still, this trace of sublime diction makes us uneasy; and the discomfort spreads if we read the letter Wordsworth wrote to his noble painter friend, Sir George Beaumont. We learn that "It rained heavily in the night, and we saw the waterfalls in perfection. While Dora was attempting to make a sketch from the chasm in the rain, I composed by her side the following address to the torrent."[3] There is a calming or distancing effect in the phrase "waterfalls in perfection" that reminds us of Wordsworth's own earlier critique of the picturesque artist's superficial mastery of landscape; there is also the subdued paradox of making "a sketch from the chasm" and "composing" an "address to the torrent."

Devil's Bridge, Wales. From *A Tour Through the South of England, Wales, and Part of Ireland Made During the Summer of 1791 by [Edward Daniel Clarke],* London, 1793.

Teufelsbrücke (Canton Uri). Early nineteenth-century engraving.

Le Pont du Diable. Eighteenth-century French engraving.

Via Mala (Graubünden). Early nineteenth-century engraving.

Little Devil's Bridge over the Reuss above Altdorf. J.M.W. and Charles Turner (after J.M.W. Turner), from *The Liber Studiorum,* 1809. Courtesy the Yale Center for British Art, Paul Mellon Collection.

Even if "compose" is used here without the overtone of "repose," two further sonnets written during the visit to Wales stress that "expression of repose" with which nature or time endows wild places.[4] And there is, I would suggest, something faintly absurd about an "address to the torrent." How does one address a *torrent*? To do so, one hears Alice or some Wonderland Creature saying—to do so one must have its name and know where it lives. And, indeed, Wordsworth is not asking for an actual name. His opening question is in search of something existential rather than informational. If Lucy lives among untrodden ways near the Spring of Dove, where do I live? Where now, in 1824? Near what springs or feeding-sources? Like the torrent itself, he seems uncertain of origin or direction, and the questioning mood of the next lines confirms that.

Yet his opening cry is not "What art thou?" nor as in a moving poem of Hölderlin's "Where art thou?" ("Wo bist Du? Trunken dämmert die Seele mir . . ."). It is "How art thou named?" What force, then, lies in the naming of a force? One of the other sonnets written in Wales describes a stream that mingles with the Dee and flows along the "Vale of Meditation," or "glyn Myrvr"—a "sanctifying name," comments Wordsworth. As in his early "Poems on the Naming of Places" (1800), he then invents a name in Welsh for the place he wishes to single out. Yet the sonnet before us bestows no name, even though "Devil's Bridge" and "Viamala" might have encouraged a man called Wordsworth.

To "address the torrent" means, clearly enough, to domesticate the sublime:

to contain it in the form of picturesque sketch or reflective sonnet; and the opening exclamation, at once perplexed and marveling, is expressive of Wordsworth's problem. The sublime, moreover, is not a quality of place alone but also of time: a bewildering memory seems to decompose the name of the torrent or any that might be given. Though the sonnet as a form is a domesticating device and though Wordsworth emulates Milton's "soul-animating strains" when he first chooses the sonnet as a verse instrument, his diction falters or condenses under the strain. But the significance of this cannot be discussed without attending carefully to the strangeness of Wordsworth's later verse, indeed to the verbal style of the sonnet in its entirety, from title to final exclamation. The title already suggests the problems of (1) naming and (2) localization. It anticipates the question of how a "force" can be localized in place, time, or language.

III

It is when we realize what naming implies that this poem betrays its significant failure, its capable negativity: it cannot name the stream. Acts of naming and, by extension, of address localize a subject (votary, speaker, writer) and a subject matter (river, river-god, thoughts). In the present case such localization is thwarted by a streamy "force." The poet is carried away from British soil to a point far off in space and time. Though not a drunken boat, he has lost his anchor. The river itself seems to transport him. When he finds stability again, after several surmises, he is in the Alps and in "life's morn"—reliving, that is, an experience lodged thirty-four years in the past. "There I seem to stand"; but even this anchoring phrase, this "Stand" as the Sublime Ode might have termed it, together with the "*As* in life's morn," is carefully infirm. We ask ourselves: Where is "There"?

The perplexity remains, of course, formal. We have said that the poem breaks almost at midpoint; the turn occurs in the overflow segment of line 8, when the speaker's surmise reaches the word "Viamala." Formally, then, "There I seem to stand" refers to the halted surmise of the mental traveler. Surmise is replaced by a pointed and inward *nunc stans*. The word "Viamala" has punctuated a pathfinding movement of thought and suggests a final station or resting point as it turns the sonnet toward the description of a single scene—though a scene that turns out to be a prospect rather than a terminus, with features that reach beyond time.

"Viamala," then, the strong name, stands metonymically for the entire experience that has flowed into the present and confused the poet's consciousness so that he cries "How art thou named?" Yet, is "Viamala" the sought-for-name; is it not rather a surrogate of some supercharged vocable, not utterable or available? "Viamala" leads through itself to an infinitizing perspective if we perceive this double metonymy. It localizes the experience, but only like the sonnet of which it is the pivot: a sonnet whose "narrow room" strangely resembles the "narrow chasm" through which the travelers of 1790 passed.[5]

IV

If "Viamala" does not answer "How art thou named?" what does? The sonnet's second half yields a kind of response. Not that Wordsworth finds or bestows a name. Instead he explains the question itself, the emotional reason for the quasi-sublime apostrophe. He grounds his apostrophe to the Unnameable in the emotional fact that an involuntary memory has phantomized the torrent or made it appear to be in a different place. This other place then recalls by its very features the "Characters of the great apocalypse" (1805 *Prelude* VI, 570) or the radical homelessness of imagination.

Thus the sublime opening, once opened, is not closed by the sonnet's "narrow room." Wordsworth's apostrophe, residue of a poetic diction he had in earlier days wished to purge, reveals its truth by refusing any ground except the "language of the heart." The sublime formula is grounded only in the sense that as a heartfelt cliché it allows the poet's dislocation to found, as well as founder in, the sonnet's precarious continuum.

I conclude that what is exemplified here is the topos of the sublime as such, of the *atopic*. Though the river has a name, and the title specifies that Wordsworth knows where he stands, something—call it "Imagination," as in the Simplon / Viamala episode, where the topic of naming is broached ("Imagination! here the Power so called / Through sad incompetence of human speech")—rises in the traveler's path, takes the name away, or produces a powerful conflation of Viamala (the "Bad Way") and Devil's Bridge. As if it were the poet's fate to be subject to such "shocks" (6), this doubling of name and place, buffered by intervening allusions that provide a false east for the disoriented mind,[6] uncovers a *traumatological* structure. River, road, and narrative path always lead, in Wordsworth, to an abruptness of this kind—to a chasm that is like a chiasmus in the way it both narrows and opens up. "How art thou named?" is abrupt enough, and by suggesting a sublime aphasia, it almost closes the poem; yet its rhetorical force carries the sonnet toward the more literal "chasm" experience of line 10, which then opens onto an "everlasting" scene. So Wordsworth saves, even as he confesses, the "incompetence of human speech."

V

Though the rhetorical question with which the poem begins is a sublime cliché,[7] its very character of diction or cliché is deceptive. The reader discovers in the formulaic phrase an unapparent meaning. This other meaning is not secondary or subordinated, nor yet in brilliant tension with what comes first. No vivid or subtle effect of irony, ambiguity, or paradox is produced. There is simply the sublime diction—"solar junk" as Wallace Stevens once called it—in an incongruously domesticated form, as if Wordsworth were writing a sonnet rather than a sublime ode, which is what he is doing.

Let us continue this line of inquiry. Nothing could be more of a cliché than "in life's morn"; and the Reverend W. L. Bowles employs it in "To the River Itchin," one of his *Sonnets Written Chiefly on Picturesque Spots, during a Tour*.[8] It is not even sublime diction, although "life" and "morn" yoked together are disparate measures of time and may have given someone somewhere a rise. What is peculiar about the phrase is that it refers to both (1) 1790, the dawn of Wordsworth's mature life or poetic career ("Bliss was it in that dawn to be alive"), and (2) the dawn of human life itself, since this pomp of snows, floods, mountains, and woods is everlasting. The cliché takes us in the manner of the entire sonnet on a temporal fugue from a specified moment at Devil's Bridge, North Wales, 1824, to Viamala in 1790 and thence into the "Dark backward and abysm of time" as well as into "the forward chaos of futurity." This fugue characterizes many poems of Wordsworth: "Tintern Abbey," for example, also a poem of revisitation beginning with the flow of time and the sound of a stream; or 1805 *Prelude* II, 213ff., which keeps reaching backward from the thought,

> Who that shall point as with a wand and say,
> "This portion of the river of my mind
> Came from yon fountain?"...

to "How shall I trace the history, where seek / The origin..." (365-66).

"How art thou named?" is also, implicitly, a question about origins, and it leads to a "dread chasm" (10) not easy to locate as a specific point on the map. We have seen that "in life's morn" looks toward the dawn of life itself; if so, the "dread chasm" from which the poet is "permitted to behold" this "everlasting" landscape suggests a birth channel. Less, perhaps, the "narrow chasm" of the womb (or the alliance of some memory trace of that first labor with the sense of being in a defile) than the "gloomy strait" through which we pass into an ultimate "repose."[9] Dread chasm, dead chasm: we know from many other instances that Wordsworth's imagination flows toward a funerary and ghostly place of this kind. "Origin and tendency," Wordsworth writes in a passage we shall soon quote more fully, "are notions inseparably co-relative." The grave questions that begin the sonnet ask something for which the answer could never be simply names on a map. They are eternally childlike, sublime, spiritual:

> Never did a child stand by the side of a running stream, pondering
> within himself what power was the feeder of the perpetual current,
> from what never-wearied sources the body of water was supplied, but
> he must have been inevitably propelled to follow this question by
> another: "Toward what abyss is it in progress? what receptacle can
> contain the mighty influx?" And the spirit of the answer must have
> been, though the word might be sea or ocean accompanied perhaps

with an image gathered from a map, or from the real object in nature—these might have been the *letter*, but the *spirit* of the answer must have been *as* inevitably,—a receptacle without bounds or dimensions;—nothing less than infinity.[10]

Another cliché that evokes, not surprisingly, a similar fugue or vanishing point is "the family of floods" (13). We recognize it as a metaphor extending or intensifying the "family of rivers" topos. Yet the change from rivers to floods, however slight, suggests an incongruity strengthened by the alliteration: how can floods be a family? Wordsworth's figure redomesticates an element that has just shown its "force" or "power." The word "family," moreover, is still evocative of time, of duration through lineage; though we hardly feel this aspect of the metaphor. Only when apposing to it the opening address of another sonnet, written in this period, do we sense fully the depth of the modified cliché.

The sonnet begins "Rotha, my Spiritual Child!"; and for a moment we are confused, thinking Wordsworth has become truly daring and reversed a venerable poetic topos that depicts genius as an offspring of native place or stream (so Shakespeare is the "Swan of Avon," and Wordsworth himself suggests that Derwent, "the fairest of all rivers," is a nurse or foster mother with its "ceaseless music that composed my thoughts / To more than infant softness"). The river Rothay that feeds into Windermere from Grasmere and Rydal becomes the poet's child by a figure that bespeaks the responsive generosity of the aging bard: he renews the image of nature, of this stream, to our mind; he keeps alive the music that, in infant days, composed his thoughts. He fosters nature even as nature has fostered him. In reality, the sonnet is addressed to Rotha Quillinan, his godchild, daughter of the man his own daughter was to marry some twenty years later.

TO ROTHA Q—

Rotha, my Spiritual Child! this head was grey
When at the sacred font for thee I stood;
Pledged till thou reach the verge of womanhood,
And shalt become thy own sufficient stay:
Too late, I feel, sweet Orphan! was the day
For stedfast hope the contract to fulfil;
Yet shall my blessing hover o'er thee still,
Embodied in the music of this Lay,
Breathed forth beside the peaceful mountain Stream
Whose murmur soothed thy languid Mother's ear
After her throes, this Stream of name more dear
Since thou dost bear it,—a memorial theme
For others; for thy future self, a spell
To summon fancies out of Time's dark cell.[11]

How complex these kinship terms become! Can they ever be fully sounded? Family romance merges with "localized romance"; and the act of naming, in the Rotha sonnet's context of baptism or second birth, evokes an animism more elemental than is afforded by either natural or supernatural religion.

VI

Naming is a family matter; it brings nature into the family of man or acknowledges that nature's life and human life are bound together. I have written elsewhere about Wordsworth's fear that nature might die to the human mind. In another famous address to a river, the "After–Thought" of the River Duddon series, he uses so intimate a language that he could be talking to Dorothy or Coleridge:

> I thought of Thee, my partner and my guide,
> As being passed away.[12]

The ominous thought is soon set aside; the sympathies that produced it are labeled "vain"; and the poet affirms, with a half-subdued pun, "Still glides the Stream, and shall for ever glide." In the Devil's Bridge sonnet, similarly, the concluding lines are upbeat indeed in their finality. They assert the deathless power of nature over the mind of poets.

Once again, however, an unapparent meaning modifies the final ring of these verses, and the sonnet remains open despite its assertive close. For we cannot be sure that "possess" is in the indicative. It might be read as an optative or wishful imperative: May the family of floods possess such power, etc. The ending would then suggest a sort of blessing—a counternaming to the name "Devil's Bridge." The magical hint in this is intensified if we understand "possess" as a transitive verb whose subject is "power": May such power possess (like a divine spirit) the family of floods.... Though this further reading does not harmonize grammatically with the line that follows, it may hover over it as an inward possibility.[13]

It is uncanny that a poem so commonplace in diction and sentiment can yield so deep a wishfulness and evoke the issue of naming in its psychic, magic, and religious context. "How art thou named?" may involve, ultimately, all the namings of language. Is language a blessing or a curse; can it still be used—given Wordsworth's darkening sense of his era as well as of his mortal being—as a blessing? "With a brother's love," the young poet of 1798 writes of Margaret, whose story has just been told, "I blessed her in the impotence of grief."[14] In 1824 he blesses the torrent, with a brother's love, and not without impotence.

VII

In Wordsworth's style, early or late, the fallen sublimity of classicizing or poetic diction blends with the naturalism of elemental speech-acts of wishing, blessing, naming. Faded figures, and archaic or trivialized fragments of high style, are naturalized in a way that remains undramatic, and even, at times, awkward. If there is sublimity here, it is of the kind that students of Longinus saw in the Bible, in such supremely simple utterances as "'Let there be light.' And there was light." It is a sublimity without glitter but also without false naïveté. It deals with natural light or "the speaking face of earth and heaven" or "the fellowship of silent light / With speaking darkness."[15]

To some extent, as I have argued, what we experience is the "Schicksalslied" of language itself, as it turns on and around the consciousness of change or instability."[16] But to the younger Wordsworth this signaled itself as a diminution in his powers of feeling, as a perplexing loss of nature's light, glory, aura. He undertook to reverse the divine command, so that it would read: "And there was light. Let there be light (again)." His foreboding bodied forth such blessings as "let the moon / Shine on thee in thy solitary walk; / And let the misty mountain winds be free / To blow against thee" ("Tintern Abbey"), in which we hardly feel the biblical sublime as it blends with a neoclassical formula that represents natural events as having to be permitted.

Yet my point is not the survival or later resurgence of classical diction in Wordsworth, as he reaches for a natural mode of sublimity. It is, rather, to show how the poet aspires to identify naming and blessing, to be a light bringer despite an opposite, or *luciferic*, moment in which a man feels he is changed, or even a changeling.

He often stands, then, on some "Devil's Bridge." The first time is in the Viamala episode of *Descriptive Sketches*. Retracing the Alpine journey Wordsworth asks whether "led where Viamala's chasms confine / Th' indignant waters of the infant Rhine" (184-85) he should "Bend o'er th' abyss?" He pictures a Grison gypsy wandering solitary in a landscape filled with surreal yet natural phenomena, and especially a torrent:

> The torrent, travers'd by the lustre broad,
> Starts like a horse beside the flashing road;
> In the roof'd bridge, at that despairing hour,
> She seeks a shelter from the battering show'r.
> —Fierce comes the river down; the crashing wood
> Gives way, and half it's pines torment the flood;
> Fearful, beneath, the Water-spirits call,
> And the bridge vibrates, tottering to its fall.

> (207-14)

So both names, "Devil's Bridge" and "Viamala" (the Bad Road), are literalized. And the light here—"fiery clouds" (206), "lustre broad," "flashing road"— though real enough, is equally the component of a superstitious or luciferic imagination. It is a "fearful light" emitted also, as previous verses show, by the indignant river: "The else impervious gloom / His burning eyes with fearful light illume" (186-87). "Impervious" has "via" (road) in it: the "unpassable" gloom refers to the darkness of the chasm or *Verlorene Loch*: the "lost hole" through which the river falls at this "via mala" point.[17] The very image of progress—river, path, bridge—is obscured.

The "Shall we . . . bend o'er th' abyss," which imbues Wordsworth's sketch with a note of picturesque progress and falsely elegant surmise—positing the tourist's freedom to taste nature's scenery at will—is totally transformed in *Prelude* VI, where Imagination rises from the mind's abyss in a moment of involuntary divination. Also in the perplexity of "How art thou named?" forced from a poet who is swept away by imagination, and who barely keeps a hold on reality via this beachhead or bridge. If there is an answer to "How art thou named?" it might be, once more, "Imagination!"

The luciferic moment is obviously a "vocable thing" and cannot be separated from the apostrophic sublime, or divinatory gests of speech. In language "darkness makes abode, and all the host / Of shadowy things work endless changes" (1850 *Prelude* V, 598-99). So Lucifer, fallen angel or star, the one who is changed yet will not admit the change and who curses the light (*Paradise Lost* IV, 35ff.) that reminds him his own light has passed away, is above all the image of a voice. "How art thou named?" may echo not only the "quantum mutatus" ("O How fallen! how changed," *Paradise Lost* I, 84) but also "How art thou fallen from heaven, O Lucifer, son of the morning" (Isaiah XIV, 12). The river near "Devil's Bridge" seems to fall from the sky, "From what huge height, descending?" (cf. 1805 *Prelude* VI, 561), and the poet, no longer a son of the morning, stands once more "As in life's morn."

Let the interpreter take some responsibility. Let him venture the thought that "How art thou named?" is addressed to the power of imagination, or the place (home) it seeks. How can imagination, its source, destiny, or Progress, be named by me, fallen or changed as I am? is what Wordsworth seems to be saying. But if the subject addressed is imagination, the predicate is an involved series of quotations. Their "homeless sound" is what ultimately affects us like the "homeless voice of waters" or a "homeless sound of joy."[18] The poet's imagination, divining its "force" and thronging with sublime echoes, must decide to bless or curse itself in this place of involuntary insight.

The interpreter may feel that the mode of being of Wordsworth's poem is inward, so enclosed in a circle of prior texts and experiences, that it is scarcely recognizable as a "creation." Moreover, what tumult there is gives way to a proleptic or unprogressive calm, as if the poet's homing and sabbath instincts coincided. The later poems often require from us something close to a suppression of the image of creativity as "burning bright" or full of glitter and communicated strife. Wordsworth's lucy-feric style, in its discretion and reserve, appears to be the opposite of luciferic. Can we say there is blessing in its gentle breeze?

7
Words, Wish, Worth

Thinking of walking with Dora in the English countryside, Wordsworth is way-laid by a Miltonic image from *Samson Agonistes* that makes his twelve-year-old daughter an Antigone leading the blind Oedipus:

> *A LITTLE onward lend thy guiding hand*
> *To these dark steps, a little further on!*[1]

Wordsworth suffered from severe eye-strain and feared to go blind. The fact is alluded to when he calls himself "not unmenaced" (9), but this merely qualifies a surprise he insists on: the usurpation of that text on his voice, and the antici-patory, proleptic nature of the thought. He records an involuntary thought having to do with privation, and which implies a halted traveler. He looks for-ward to the pleasure of walking with Dora, and instead of an easy progression from thought to fulfillment, from innocent wish to imaginative elaboration, something interposes darkly and complicates the sequence. The movement of fantasy is momentarily blocked; it no longer rises as easily and naturally as dawn but must precipitate itself as a Morning Voluntary: "From thy orisons / Come forth; and while the morning air is yet / Transparent as the soul of innocent youth, / Let me, thy happy guide, now point the way" (20-23).

Yet this active gesture or call—a kind of antistrophe to the opening invoca-tion which had blocked him, for it restores an image of the poet as "natural leader"—this excursive voice is soon halted once more by images which revive, thematically now, and from within the wishful narrative, the anticipatory, even vertiginous power of imagination:

> Let me, thy happy guide, now point thy way,
> And now precede thee, winding to and fro,
> Till we by perserverance gain the top
> Of some smooth ridge, whose brink precipitous
> Kindles intense desire for powers withheld
> From this corporeal frame; whereon who stands
> Is seized with strong incitement to push forth
> His arms, as swimmers use, and plunge—dread thought,
> For pastime plunge—into the "abrupt abyss,"
> Where ravens spread their plumy vans, at ease!
>
> (23-32)

What happens here seems ordinary enough because it does not inspire an ecstatic utterance. There is no address to Imagination, as in *Prelude* VI: "Imagination—here that Power. . . That awful Power rose from the mind's abyss. . ." But imagination, of course, has already risen from the "abrupt abyss" in the form of a voice, the quotation from *Samson Agonistes*—echoing back to *Oedipus at Colonus*—which opens the poem. It disturbs the course of time and nature, not only by foreshadowing a Wordsworth who is old and blind but also by reversing the roles of child and father. Though Wordsworth tries to normalize this sense of reversal (4-10), the disturbance lingers on, and his mood soon rises again to a prophetic pitch ("Should that day come"). At that point the halted voice turns deliberately outward and imports sounds from nature in order to restore its faith in natural continuity:

> Should that day come—but hark! the birds salute
> The cheerful dawn, brightening for me the east;
> For me, thy natural leader. . .
>
> (12-14)

The sun always rises, eventually, for Wordsworth. But the phantoms of imagination—glimpses of glory or privation, ancestral voices, blind thoughts—continue to cast over the cheerful scene a mingled light. Wordsworth's steps remain devious and halting, "dark steps," uncertain of a progress he affirms. Nature proves to be a temple (35ff.) or school of awe, and the poet is drawn as if compulsively toward some "abrupt abyss," or "center whence those sighs creep forth / To awe the lightness of humanity" (*Ode to Lycoris*).

It is a sighing yet awe-inspiring voice which opens this poem. If Wordsworth's poetic thought has a beginning, it is in such a voice, or the visionary stir produced by it. We can give the voice a context, of course, yet we cannot humanize it completely. As its "invisible source" "deepens upon fancy" (*Ode to Lycoris*), the poet may associate it with oracular cave or Egerian grot or other sacred place or omphalos. What is "a little further on" if not a *templum*: a destined, clearly demarcated spot, the locus of a death, and perhaps an exaltation? The opening quotation, like the poem as a whole, borders on that space: we hear a voice that is scarcely human speaking in words that are all too human. An afflicted man, part beggar, part prophet, looks from the extreme edge of his mortal being toward justification.

These liminal words, then, are close to being final words. They overshadow the poem and compel Wordsworth to an interpretive or reflective, rather than freely fictive, response. There cannot be many poems that begin with a quotation and develop against or in the shadow of it. Perhaps every poem does so, in the sense that the effaced or absorbed memory of other great poems motivates its own career. The status of poetry becomes uncertain here, since poetry seems to be neither oracular-visionary speech nor a purely reflective, mediated kind of language. It is both, undecidably: the poet being Major Man, free of guidance, and the source rather than the dupe of oracles, but also one who continues to live in this problematic area of divine intimations.

There is indeed something oracular (inaugural may be the proper word) about the beginning of the poem. It is as if Wordsworth's spirit had been unconsciously playing at Sybilline leaves with Milton or the Classics. It is not the first time, of course, that the poet's voice is usurped by a visionary reflex or "trick of memory." Yet here the quasi-oracular source proves to be, via Milton, from the Classics, and is not only a passage but also a passage-way he must negotiate: the words perplex the poet like a dark omen whose psychic antecedent remain as obscure as the cry recorded in "Strange fits of passion."

Through the "dark passage," then, of a text surfacing in his mind, Wordsworth struggles to find a "passage clear" (52) that would lead him and Dora to a sublimer scene. That scene may possibly be the Alps (34-39) which he will visit on an anniversary trip in 1820, and toward which his thought turns after the war with France. But a repetition of the wish to guide Dora evokes at the end "heights more glorious still" and "shades more awful" (53ff.) that seem to lie beyond nature. If Wordsworth is repeating his Alpine journey of 1790 in the spirit, he foresees a still further journey, until the image of blindness, so charged yet absurd at the beginning, reveals its truth at the close. For each new journey could increase his sense of loss. *Tintern Abbey* already suggests that loss and the need for borrowed sight: "and in thy voice I catch / The language of my former heart, and read / My former pleasures in the shooting lights / Of thy wild eyes." In the present poem we are "a little further on." There is no repetition in a finer tone but rather a "mournful iteration"—a phrase even more telling if it contains a pun on *iter*, the Latin words for journey.

II

...the childhood shows the man

As morning shows the day
Milton, *Paradise Regained*

Interpreters have commented adequately on the poet's return to Nature or memories of childhood and somewhat on his return to the writers of Reformation
England. Equally remarkable is his regression, after 1801, to the Classics. It
begins with a renewed interest in the poets of the Reformation, who were also
poets of the Renaissance—who managed, that is, to revive the Classics as well
as Scripture.

The Classical sources, though, are almost as dangerous as Imagination itself.
Do not brood "o'er Fable's dark abyss," Wordsworth solemnly cautions us in
1820. It may be like the abyss from which imagination springs in *Prelude* VI, or
the "abrupt abyss" that kindles "intense desire for powers withheld" (27). The
voice of Samson-Oedipus, rising so forcefully from the mind's abyss, could
represent the felt though repressed power of pre-Christian literature: a power
which, like Imagination, points to the possibility of unmediated vision. Samson-
Oedipus himself, at this juncture in the drama, approaches divine status.

"A little onward" starts with a private psychic event, a well-known text flashing on the poet's mind, yet ends with a peroration that shows unmistakably how
intensely Wordsworth felt about both Classical wisdom and Scripture. The peroration combines two inherited notions: that of the Book of Nature which lies
open to all eyes, and that of the Reformers "opening" the Book of God for all
to read:

> Now also shall the page of classic lore,
> To these glad eyes from bondage freed, again
> Lie open; and the book of Holy writ,
> Again unfolded, passage clear shall yield...
>
> (49-52)

Wordsworth stops short of suggesting that the Classics are a kind of scripture,
but he extends a principle shared by Milton, the Reformers, and the great scholars
of the Renaissance, that we must go directly to the sources. Only then does reading lead to inspiration. When freed like Holy Writ from false mediation, classic
lore may open itself to the private conscience as forcefully as at the beginning of
this poem.

Wordsworth's movement toward the Classics is virtually as daring as his
movement toward childhood. To reintegrate the Classics is not unlike reinte-
grating a childhood conceived as the heroic age of the psyche. But the association
between childhood and early literature is not the usual primitivistic one. That
would be impossible with the Classics which are called such because they appear
to us incredibly mature. The reason for linking the Classics with youth or
childhood is that pagan fable, rhetoric and history, were the literary staple of the

young poet. Though trivialized by school routine and eighteenth-century usage, Wordsworth's republican sympathies and Milton's example kept them alive. And when childhood comes back, they come back. Commenting in the 1830s on the *Ode to Lycoris*, composed within a year or so of "A little onward," Wordsworth remarks: "Surely one who has written so much in verse as I have done may be allowed to retrace his steps in the regions of fancy which delighted him in his boyhood, when he first became acquainted with the Greek and Roman poets... Classical literature affected me by its own beauty. But the truths of scripture having been entrusted to the dead languages, and these fountains having been recently laid open at the Reformation, an importance and a sanctity were at that period attached to classical literature that extended, as is obvious in Milton's *Lycidas*, for example, both to its spirit and form in a degree that can never be revived."

Yet the insistence of the Classics is not explained so easily, even if the poet himself could fall back on associationist psychology. There is very little urbane classicism in Wordsworth; and nothing, or almost nothing, of hellenistic "beauty" as Winckelmann conceived of it, and which affected so many European and English writers. I would guess that Keats and Shelley were less radical in their understanding of the Classics than Wordsworth, though they were also less defensive. In Wordsworth's recollection of Classical texts there is often something involuntary, a sympathy not agreed to, or painfully hedged about. His difficult reserve has a pathos of its own that seems to go beyond the ordinary type of Christian scruple. Milton's use of the Classics recall to him a more absolute beginning: a point of origin essentially unmediated, beyond the memory of experience or the certainty of temporal location. A "heavenly" origin, perhaps, in the sense of the myth (already a mediating device) that the *Intimations Ode* presents, and which makes a heuristic use of Plato's notion of preexistence. This recession of experience to a boundary where memory fades into myth, or touches the hypostasis of a supernatural origin—as well as complete respect for that boundary—is what preoccupies the psyche of the poet. Only that boundary, uncertain as it is, separates in his mind childhood, the Classics, and divinization. The Classics, then, reach beyond religious or temporal mediation toward a dubious and dangerous point where "all stand single" (1850 *Prelude* III, 189).

The scene from Sophocles has, of course, a near-Christian pathos: humiliation precedes exaltation. Yet in terms of the poem, the reversed roles of daughter and father are what is most affecting, and carry us back to a famous text from Wordsworth's own poetry. Did he not write at the very onset of his reviving passion for the Classics, "The Child is Father of the Man?" And does this not disorder our temporal and genealogical perspective? If the thought becomes an axiom for modern developmental psychology, and for the poet himself the stone that marks a boundary he will not cross, it remains as scandalous a paradox as ever founded a poetry of experience.

The riddling image is part of an "extempore" lyric of 1802, "My heart leaps up when I behold / A rainbow in the sky." It affirms what Wordsworth calls "natural piety." Piety comes from a sphere of virtues associated with Classicism, and "natural piety" suggests something inborn, a gift of nature which should protect nature. In 1816 "natural piety" is still there, in the image of Antigone as a "living staff" helping her father; and though the poet's heart sinks rather than leaps up when the image of the blind Oedipus comes into his mind, at least there is a strong "extempore" response: a negative leaping rather than none. That leap could well go "beyond" or "outside" (ex) time: it points to a more absolute power to begin, or to posit a beginning—as in the poem of 1816. What seems to have changed, or intensified into a haunting symbol, is the poet's fear that the time may come when, blind or not, he will be spiritually blind to nature, autonomous even beyond his desire.

This fear is no late birth, however: it can be found in Wordsworth's earliest poetry, pervades *Tintern Abbey* and the blind beggar episode of *Prelude* VII, and is inevitably mingled with thoughts of Milton, or what would happen to his own "genial spirits" were they to "find no dawn" (cf. *Paradise Lost* III, 24). Until nature blanks out under the influence of imagination, or of "The prophetic spirit...Dreaming on things to come," Wordsworth invokes no mediation except nature. And even when obliged to recognize the future necessity of a wisdom that is "blind" in the sense of being purely an inner light, he still portrays it as dependent on nature as Oedipus is on Antigone.

"The Child is Father of the Man"—Antigone leading her father, or childhood nature returning upon the poet to guide him, are different emblems of one truth. Childhood, or its continuous role in the growth of the mind, is the truth Wordsworth discovers, and in the light of which he rejects all heroic and classicizing themes; but what is rejected returns and discovers itself as a yet deeper childhood, capable of reaching through time and renewing itself in the poetic spirit. If that is not the Wordsworthian Enlightenment, it must be the Wordsworthian Renaissance.

III

Wordsworth's poetry often describes a flashing on the inward eye. An after-image or memory surprises the mental traveler. A wish that has formed, sometimes unconsciously, or at least so naturally that no thought is taken of it, is suddenly made conscious by being defeated, crossed, or fulfilled in an unexpected way. The emphasis is on the strange fulfillment rather than on defeat; but precisely because of that, every anticipatory movement of the mind is attended by "anxiety of hope" (1805 *Prelude* XI, 372). The wish, whether active fantasy or vague daydream, tends toward fulfillment. Wordsworth screens, therefore, even the most innocent "leaping up" of eye and heart. Many of his poems, in fact, are simply reflections on "wayward" motions of the mind. The result is a consciously minor poetry, depressed yet psychically fascinating, which enacts that very distrust of *enthusiasm* limiting the greater part of eighteenth-century verse.

That the flash should take the form of a quotation clarifies further Wordsworth's relation to eighteenth-century verse: that is, to post-Miltonic or post-visionary writing. How much of it tends toward the condition of quotation, attenuated allusion and paraphrase! It has been argued that the sonnet by Gray severely criticized in the Preface to *Lyrical Ballads* should be read with quotation marks around its phraseology. Gray, it is suggested, knew the inadequacy of those words in the face of death. But what of the "sad incompetence of human speech" (1850 *Prelude* VI, 593) in the face of imagination? The visitings of imaginative power in Wordsworth put quotation marks even around nature. Thus the lines from *Samson Agonistes* that usurp the beginning of Wordsworth's poem are a fulfillment of literary velleities: they exalt the "borrowed voice" of eighteenth-century poetry. They give the glory to Milton, and to an imagination as privative as it is prophetic.

To represent Wordsworth as a Jonah evading the divine Word, or a privative imagination, may seem melodramatic. There is here no city, no Nineveh to prophesy against. But there is Wordsworth's knowledge that the imagination may not be on the side of nature. The voluntary or involuntary utterances that rise in him are not allowed to gain even an artificial ascendancy. He both acknowledges and refuses their vehicular, visionary power. Quotation or exclamation marks keep them in quarantine: no easy, integrating path leads from the absolute or abrupt image to the meditation that preserves it. Wordsworth does not solicit metaphors for poetry.

"A little onward" remains a *conspicuously* secondary response. The gambit offered by imagination is declined, and so, ultimately, is the opening toward a radical Classicism. Though the poem implies the wish, "Where Imagination was the Classics shall be," Milton and Scripture and perhaps the strength of the Classics themselves interfere, and the wish becomes, "Where Imagination was, quotation shall be." An unmediated psychic event turns out to be a mediated text: words made of stronger words, of the Classics and the Bible, and suggesting even by their content the need for mediation. Wordsworth records scrupulously an inward action: *the incumbent mystery of text—as well as sense—and soul.*

IV

The relation of "text" and "soul" is the province of a theory of reading. Although there have been many attempts (from I.A. Richards through Norman Holland, Stanley Fish, and Wolfgang Iser) to understand the reading experience, and to draw a theory from actual or reported acts of reading, the matter is usually studied in divorce from the history of interpretation. Even when history enters, it does so as the social record of *Rezeptionsgeschichte* or as the structural record of the particular work's "indeterminacy," and not in connection with great movements in theology or political philosophy.

However, we must be able to talk of the reader both intrinsically, or as he is in himself, and historically, as someone set concretely in a changeable field of influence. Many contemporary thinkers are therefore not satisfied with viewing reading as a "practical" matter to be corrected or improved by some sort of training. They see it rather as a vital "praxis" imbued with theory, or ideological values. The rise of Protestantism, for example, is not irrelevant to the reading experience, in Wordsworth's time or now. The claim that Scripture contemplated by faithful minds would prove inspiring—that a priestly or institutionally sanctioned hermeneutic was not a necessary mediation—is at least analogous to our modern prejudice in favor of "critical" reading and against methodological machinery. There has been, of course, a recent revival of methodology, owing to the parascientific disciplines of structuralism and semiotics, on the one hand, and increasing interest in medieval (Christian or Jewish) allegorical exegesis, on the other. But this has merely sharpened the conflict between two types of reading: the direct or "inner light" approach, inherently critical when applied to secular works, because it pits the wit ("ingenium," "natural light," "good sense") of the reader against a text considered as potentially crucial or influential; and the learned, scientific, or philosophical approach, which sees all works, secular or sacred, as deeply mediated constructs, not available to understanding except through a study of history or of the intertextual character of all writing.

Wordsworth's poem suggests that we must read the writer as a reader. The writer is a reader not only in the sense that he must have read to write, and so is "mediated," however original his work. He is a reader because of his radically responsive position vis-à-vis (1) texts, and (2) an inner light—or inner darkness— that enables his counter-word, the very act of interpretation itself. Reading is a form of life whether or not correlative, as in Wordsworth, to a specific theology. But if we take Wordsworth's poem of 1816 as paradigmatic, it suggests that when a theology exists, even should that theology affirm direct inspection and the efficacy of a principle of inner light, it requires historical study to be appreciated. So that the conflict between direct and mediated types of reading continues to operate.

The complexities do not end here. For there is, of course, a metaphor in the concept of "inner light." Though it plays an important role from Augustine through Descartes, assumes a salient position in the Reformation, and is continued in such derived formulations as Heidegger's "*Lichtung*," one wonders why the correlative metaphor of "inner voice" was not found to be as appropriate.[2]

The emphasis on "light" rather than "voice" may be an unconscious and simple falsification. But it may also point to the repression of the oracular or enthusiast element in the reader. That is certainly the case in England where a conservative or Catholic protestantism is especially sensitive to the un-English nature of any ideology of inner voice. T.S. Eliot, whose poetry pastures on voices of all sorts—aurality being an essential aspect of its aura—still tries to disqualify, and savagely, the concept of inner voice as politically and religiously subversive. He attacks Middleton Murray who had claimed that "The English writer, the English divine, the English statesman, inherit no rules from their forebears; they inherit only this: a sense that in the last resort they must depend on the inner voice." Eliot smells a Romantic, populist and even daemonic heresy in this. "My belief is that those who possess this inner voice. . . will hear no other. The inner voice, in fact, sounds remarkably like an old principle which has been formulated by an elder critic in the now familiar phrase of 'doing as one likes.' The professors of the inner voice ride ten in a compartment to a football match at Swansea, listening to the inner voice, which breathes the eternal message of vanity, fear, and lust."

I have quoted this skirmish to show how easily this idea of inner light when reconnected with that of inner voice becomes ideologically sensitive again. The metaphor is an explosive one. Yet we must honor the fact that Wordsworth's poem of 1816 begins with an "inner voice" usurping his voice. That inner voice also proves to be a text. It is the textual voice of Milton evoking the agony of Samson for whom the sun is dark, and "silent as the moon." It seems like a giant and awkward step to go from this to the Snowdon episode at the end of *The Prelude*, where the "voice of waters" roars up to the "silent light" of the moon. The circumstances on Snowdon are, Wordsworth explicitly states, unusually awful and sublime (1805 *Prelude* XIII, 76); perhaps, then, the inner rising of Milton's voice, as in the poem of 1816, was more usual.

In any case, this silencing of light—the removing, by a kind of negative metaphor, of sound from light, or the addition to light of a now separated sound—is more than a figurative depiction of blindness. It occurs (very subtly circumstanced) in the opening stanzas (1, 2) of the *Intimations Ode*—and there too sound returns. Though no overt reversal (as on Snowdon) is found in the *Ode's* third stanza, there is a feeling of discovery and relief. An inner source opens: it is as if Wordsworth, in the absence of "a sound–like power in light" (Coleridge), had uttered internally the wish "Let there be light," or more precisely, "Let there be sound, and light from sound." Not so much *son et lumière*, but the illumination that sound is. The reader's fiat, "Let the sources be opened," and the poet's "Now also shall the page. . . Lie open," begin to coincide when we shift to the "oracular cave" of the ear: "Strict passage, through which sighs are brought, / And whispers for the heart, their slave" (*On the Power of Sound*, 6-8).

V

These lines, however, when followed by "And shrieks, that revel in abuse / Of shivering flesh" etc., suggest something quite specific, which explains why the ear's "oracular cave" is "dread...to enter" (ll. 5-6). Wordsworth evokes sounds of lust or passion ("How oft along thy mazes, / Regent of sound, have dangerous Passions trod." ll. 81-82), with a reserve that intensifies rather than veils the affect. One cannot separate in his description love-ecstasy from religious ecstasy or martial frenzy. We are in the realm of the passions, perhaps of their tenuous sublimation; and it is the stricken ear rather than stricken eye that leads us there, via resonances of other great Music Odes of the eighteenth century, including Collin's *The Passions, an Ode for Music*.

The "dread" is more than an abstract anxiety, then: the "strict" of "strict passage" points at once to the ineluctable modality of hearing, its "constricted" nature which overdetermines sounds that all pass through the same narrow channel, and to the burden on heart and conscience, on moral response, which is imposed. The "incumbent mystery of sense and soul" includes the charged relation of "passion" to voice and hearing. "Strange fits of passion have I known: / And I will dare to tell, / But in the lover's ear alone, / What once to me befell."

"The sounding cataract haunted me like a passion," also foregrounds the word. These uses share an ambiguity: "passion" seems to mean a passionate utterance, as when someone is said to "fall into a passion." The word joins emotion and motion of voice. The "power in sound" takes a form that is vocal as well as verbal, like song—except there is no song, only a movement of voice heard internally, or in revery, or one that "[vexes] its own creation" (1805 *Prelude* I, 47). Perhaps the term "lyrical ballad" indicates this excess of voice-feeling over the articulate word. The "power in sound" is the severe music of the signifier or of an inward echoing that is both intensely human and ghostly.

"Passion," in any case, is generally used in this meaningful way. Wordsworth begins *The Prelude* with an extempore effusion whose special character he then points out. He calls it, in fact, a "passion" (1805 *Prelude* I, 69) and even within the extempore passage the word is not unambiguous ("Pure passions, virtue, knowledge, and delight, / The holy life of music and of verse" [1805 I, 53-54]). Wordsworth's narrative can almost be said to begin with "an Ode, in passion utter'd" (1805 V, 97), which the poet holds to our ear.

This intricate press of meanings in "passion" emerges explicitly later in *The Prelude*:

> whatsoe'er of Terror or of Love
> Or Beauty, Nature's daily face put on
> From transitory passion, unto this

> I was as wakeful, even, as waters are
> To the sky's motion; in a kindred sense
> Of passion was obedient as a lute
> That waits upon the touches of the wind.
>
> (1805 III, 132-38)

Here the word is first used in its conventional sense of an elevated if volatile mood, then "in a kindred sense" of a passively evoked spontaneous utterance, analogous to that of the wind harp. The latter "passion" had inaugurated *The Prelude*. "O there is blessing in this gentle breeze" shows the poet responsive to "the touches of the wind." He expresses an aeolian mystery to which we now turn, that purifies the ear by its gentle touch, and removes us from heavy to lighter breathing.

<h2 style="text-align:center">VI</h2>

> . . . my ear was touched
> With dreams and visionary impulses.
>
> Wordsworth, *To Joanna*

To what extent is poetry the working through of voices, residues as explicit and identifiable as the usurping passage from Milton, or as cryptically mnemonic as rhythm and dream phrase? Freud insists that direct speech, when it occurs in dreams, is something previously heard, however radically the dream-work may change its context. Ideas of the inspired poet or the dictating muse also point to this realm where words are as ineluctable as images: we cannot choose but hear.

The poet, a famous definition holds, dreams with his eyes open, yet this latent pressure of voices or texts suggests he dreams with open ears. "The winds come to me from the fields of sleep" (Wordworth, *Intimations Ode*). The winds must carry intimations, but do they come from fields in the poet's dream, fields that are asleep because their virtue lies unregarded, wintry fields now moving towards new life, or fields elysian? What aeolian mystery is here? The context of the line in Wordsworth's *Ode* yields nothing but the surround of sound: trumpeting cataracts, mountain echoes, the shouts of a shepherd boy. These sounds open his ears, as if a luster that had faded from the eye could be restored through aural intimations: winds, words, echoes. The ear, naturally dark, searches a darkness that has befallen sight. "To the open fields I told / A prophecy" (1805 *Prelude* I, 59-60) reverses gratefully, or gives back amply, what has been received: the breeze, the winds, their words, now come from within the poet himself.

> Visionary Power
> Attends upon the motions of the winds
> Embodied in the mystery of words.

> There darkness makes abode, and all the host
> Of shadowy things do work their changes there.
> (1805 *Prelude* V, 619-23)

Between the visionary power ascribed to words and the working dark of aural experience there must be a relation. Very often ears become eery in Wordsworth. "With what strange utterance did the loud dry wind / Blow through my ears!" (1805 *Prelude* I, 347-38). "At that time," Wordsworth adds, "I hung alone," just like an aeolian or abandoned harp, the poet's ears being the wind instrument. The actual context is his hunting for ravens' eggs, when he finds himself on a "perilous ridge" between earth and sky, "ill sustain'd" and "almost suspended by the blast." Sense itself, the direct referential meaning, is "almost suspended" by a curious verse-music that then leads into the simile: "The mind of Man is fram'd even like the break / And harmony of music" (1805 *Prelude* I, 351-52). We hear, as well as see, the "motion mov'd" and the "loud" in "clouds." We wonder if ears and eyes have not opened beyond the "open fields."

Yet Wordsworth's prophecy to the fields is never formalized as a visionary distortion of words and world. The words remain familiar, and what their motion opens up is still fields and clouds. That there is referentiality, that we find some stability in this world, is the end that is praised. The means are troubling, however, that move the poet toward this happy end. "Ah me!" he sighs, enumerating the "discordant elements" that have interfused in his mind. Nature's means are visitations both gentle and severe, but even the gentle ones are described in terms that contain power. From earliest infancy Nature "doth open up the clouds, / *As at the touch of lightning*" (1805 *Prelude* I, 363ff., my italics). That phrase approaches paradox, like "blast of harmony" (1805 *Prelude* V, 96.)

Is there an equivalent in sound to this "touch of lightning"? A flash of sound, or thunder touch? I think this is what the poem of 1816 shows when it begins with the voice of Milton's Samson. Here too referentiality is maintained, in the sense that the usurping voice is referred to a specific text. It is not a floating, ghostly intrusion: a hollow voice from some mysterious spot in the landscape of the mind. The intertextual referent delimits the ghostliness as we see *through* the text. Milton's voice opens up an ear in Wordsworth not blinded (darkened beyond memory) by that revelation.

We are close now to understanding Wordsworth's style: more precisely, the relation between textuality and referentiality. The poet's words are always antiphonal to the phoné of a prior experience. Or, the prior experience is the phoné.

> [I] Have felt what'er there is of power in sound
> To breathe an elevated mood, by form
> Or image unprofaned; and I would stand

Beneath some rock, listening to sounds that are
The ghostly language of the ancient earth,
Or make their dim abode in distant winds.
Thence did I drink the visionary power.

(1805 *Prelude* II, 324-30)

By phoné I mean voice or sound before a local shape or human source can be ascribed. Wordsworth's antiphonal style—his version of "ecchoing song"—limits by quotation or self-institutionalizing commentary a potentially endless descent into the phantom ear of memory. We almost forget that, in the poem of 1816, something has reached through historical and personal time to claim a second embodiment. The moment is comparable in its very difference to when Milton falls into Blake's left tarsus and inspires a Christian pseudopod that marches on (*Milton*, Plate 15). The Miltonic voice becomes Blake's phantom limb. Yet Wordsworth's footing is radically different from Blake's: it has nothing of the confidence of "And did those feet in ancient times / Walk upon England's pleasant green." Wordsworth's voice has lost, or is always losing, its lyric momentum; formally it is hesitant, disjunctive, "dark steps" over places in nature or scripture aware of the "abrupt abyss" that may, again, open up.

It is Wordsworth's own writ, his own poem, that should be disclosed, yet by a fate for which the word Oedipal is appropriate, an oracular "Discourse of the Other" interposes, one that involves the relation of child and parent, or younger poet and elder. Reacting to these inner "passions" Wordsworth projects nature as something that speaks "rememberable things," as something that textualizes phantom voice: perhaps "the ghostly language of the ancient earth," perhaps the language of dream image and phrase. The result is lyric poetry precariously extended, even *The Prelude's* stumblingly progressive form: a lengthened night music, the residue of a long day's night.

VII

O first-created beam, and thou great Word,
Let there be light

Milton, *Samson Agonistes*

In Wordsworth trembling ears and enlightened ears go together. The path toward enlightenment leads through dark passages filled with strange sounds. To characterize what is heard as a "ghostly language" is already to humanize it by a metaphorical act that engages the drift of the entire *Prelude*. "My own voice cheered me," the poet says candidly at the outset, because it is a voice rather than the mutterings, sobbings, yellings, and ghostly blowing echoes that are his ear-experience. When he adds, "and, far more, the mind's / Internal echo of the imperfect sound" (1850 *Prelude* I, 55-56) he suggests not only his hope for a perfected voice, his "cheerful confidence" that he will advance beyond the prelusive strains of this perambulatory pastoral (*paulo majora canamus*), but also his hope that he will master the echo-sphere—darkly numinous after-effects evoking the "dim abode" of a visionary geography which "unknown modes of being," "mighty Forms that do not live / Like living men" (1805 *Prelude* I, 425ff.) inhabit. Poetry is echo humanized, a responsive movement represented here in schematic form.

This progress toward a language which is human and timely, a word that dwells with and between men, remains uncertainly fulfilled. For the "power in sound" cannot be humanized by a sheer act of will or the arbitrariness of metaphorical speech. And the doctrine of the Logos ("In the beginning was the Word"), which evokes a parallel enlightenment ("A Voice to Light gave Being" is Wordsworth's allusion to it in *On the Power of Sound*), remains caught up in mystery. The Logos dwells with God and when it comes to men is not understood. The Light to which it gives Being lights a darkness that is uncomprehending. In the vision on Snowdon, however, which is the finale to *The Prelude*, Wordsworth recovers the "fellowship of silent light / With speaking darkness." The poet ascends the mountain and brings back the word. Yet even here sound does not come first but in the form of an antiphonal response from the abyss. What Wordsworth brings back, then, is a second that becomes a first: an antiphony that reverses the priority of "silent light" and shows itself to be coeval, even ante-phonal. The poet brings the speaking darkness to light; he transforms the power in sound into enlightened sound.

Thus Snowdon is a vision of mastery, though a peculiar one. The power in sound and the power in light, or ear and eye, or nature and mind, are asymmetrical elements that struggle toward what Wordsworth calls "interchangeable supremacy," "mutual domination." There is no single locus of majesty or mastery: it is doubled and troubled by shifts in the poet's interpretation of what he experienced. Though light begins by usurping the landscape (both internal and external), sound roars up in reclamation; and no cosmological or ontological position is reached that would resolve the conflict. Wordsworth's manuscript revisions also suggest radical metaphoricity rather than mastery: power is not unified or localized as the property of one place, organ, or element; it is as "homeless" as the "voice of waters" itself. He may insist in the commentary (1850 *Prelude* XIV, 63ff.) that what he saw was the "type" of a "majestic intellect," yet the most striking feature or "soul" (1805 *Prelude* XIII, 65) of the vision is an instance of *timely utterance* (*Intimations Ode*, I, 23).

I borrow this phrase to characterize the voice of waters roaring to the sky and into the poet's moonstruck mind. The force of their utterance replaces timelessness with timeliness. And what we hear, as these not-so-still and not-so-small voices break in, proves timely in three ways: they release the poet from a fixation, they make him stand in time once more, and their delayed response (their seeming untimeliness) is what endows them with timely, that is, antiphonal effect. They seem to make literal the logos-power as Wordsworth conceives it: "A Voice to light gave Being; / To Time. . . ."

VIII

On Snowdon hearing replaces a state of non-hearing as a "voice" is disclosed. To say the voice is intelligible or that what is heard is readable would move beyond Wordsworthian premises, even if we accept the conjunction of ideas of time and voice in "timely utterance." For this phrase tells us nothing specific about what was uttered or whether what was uttered had an intelligible, that is, human language content.

I want to insist, however, that the reversal of "powers" on Snowdon includes the poet as reader of a prior and sacred text. There is a "first" text to which his stands as a "second," but this relation is reversible and the later utterance achieves its own firstness. What Wordsworth has done is to raise the antiphonal cues in his precursor text(s) to a new, a "second" power. He has created his own text by a verbal geometry that extends the lines of force in a prior scripture. The scripture in this case is Scripture.

For the "timely utterance" of the voice(s) heard on Snowdon parallels principally the *Let there be light* of Genesis, the first divine utterance that emerges from the brooding over chaos, and creates at once language and light. Light is uttered, and with light, time (the division of day and night), and with light and time the Word that the Gospel of Saint John rightly extracts from that fiat as having been "with" God. But in Wordsworth, and it constitutes a reversal, the breaking through of speaking darkness to silent light presupposes a separate fiat that had been overlooked and which rises up to claim equality or primordiality. It is as if the instancy of light—"For instantly a light upon the turf / Fell like a flash" (1850 *Prelude* XIV, 38-39)—had satisfied one wish in the psyche, but had roused another, which then suggests an infinite repetition (*Prelude* XIV, 71). *Let there be light* is the first wish, not consciously voiced by Wordsworth, but recalled into existence by the effect, *And there was light*.

Perhaps the very fact that light was given without a conscious or wishful motion of the voice raised in the poet the question of the status of voice. Prevenient light elides or usurps the consciousness of voice; the flash is there, magically, before one is aware of having wished or asked for it. There is likewise no explicit reflection that precedes the poet's consciousness of the voice of waters. Instead of *Let there be voice*, which must have been doubly intense if unuttered in Wordsworth, because the voice of that wish was elided both by the prevenience of light and the silent sky, we find that *And there was light* is followed as suddenly by *And there was voice.*

Thus two things are silenced in the episode: voice (temporarily) and the wish or fiat-form itself. Another way of putting it is to say that "Let there be" as a primordial wish and "Let there be" as a primordial speech act (*voicing* desire) converge in the vision; that this convergence is felt to be dangerous; and that an unauthorized or ur-fiat is repressed. Instead of the voice of Wordsworth's wish only the responsive or antiphonal word is given, and not so much as a word but as the image of a voice; and this pattern is continued in Wordsworth's commentary on the vision, which again prevents the coming to conscious voice of a primordial and wishful calling. Though this calling is suggested (1850 *Prelude* XIV, 93-99) and even viewed as the basis of poetic power, it appears in the main angelic and soothing, as if it took away rather than imposed the consciousness of human autonomy, creative or willful. The 1805 *Prelude* talks of "peace at will" (XIII, 114), an ambiguous formulation that while it stresses a "sovereignty within," calming the will at will, also suggests an ultimate renunication of sovereignty ("Let Thy will be done"). The 1850 version clarifies that pacific urge:

> Hence, amid ills that vex and wrongs that crush
> Our hearts—if here the words of Holy Writ
> May with fit reverence be applied—that peace
> Which passeth understanding, that repose
> In moral judgements....
>
> (XIV, 124-28)

Yet Nature, however strong its presence, does not extinguish the creative principle in the poet. The after-thought, by interpreting the spectacle on Snowdon as a grand emblem of responsive verse—as a magnified Davidic psalm, caught at the source, at psychogenesis—allows Wordsworth to authorize himself in a movement analogous to the responsive *And God saw. . . that it was good.* In his commentary Wordsworth blesses his own vision.

IX

There darkness makes abode
Wordsworth, *Prelude* V

Is there in Wordsworth a silenced ur-fiat? Considered in itself "Let there be" mingles desire and speech in a way that defeats ontological or even grammatical specification. "Let there be". . . what? Can an *object* be supplied that really completes the fiat: that makes it a sentence? "Let there be" is so basic a "passion" that to add the word "voice" as its object sentences it to redundance, while all other objects delimit it. One feels that not an object of desire is called for but "something evermore about to be" (1850 *Prelude* VI, 608); and that the mood of the phrase at once goads and restrains the reality-hunger of an infinite will desiring omnipotent and manifest fulfillments. Yet fulfillment cannot be separated from responsiveness if "Let there be" asks for a response which is the object still to be created. Creation and response merge, even as imagination (infinitely wishful brooding) and intellectual love (socializing and excursive thought) cannot stand "dividually."

To separate out the verbal form of "Let there be" has its own precariousness: it is a peculiar form and if sounded reflexively could lead to self-cancelling equivocations. Perhaps it is enough to suggest that Wordsworth was haunted by the fiat as such, and sought to convert a divine or willful imperative into a responsive or timely utterance—picking up toward this cues from sacred texts: from Genesis, Psalms, and *Paradise Lost* as a creation epic.

I leave moot the questions of whether there is a semiotic way of describing the demand-and-response structure of this word (the fiat) that is also a wish. What we do know is that as a word-wish it is always queered on its way to an utterance that might bring fulfillment. Utterance itself, that is, blocks or delays the wish or alters it. At once fiat and fit (read: "Strange fiats of passion have I known"), the status of the word-wish remains unresolved.

Every "passion" of words, then, is under the shadow of being a "strange fit"—or not fit at all, because the correspondence (the expected harmony) between word and wish has been disturbed. The blocking of the wish in utterance is also explicit at the beginning of "A little onward." The most intriguing episode of this kind, however, happens to be associated with Snowdon by contiguity and theme: it occurs during the poet's experience of creative power on Salisbury Plain and is recorded in the penultimate book of *The Prelude* (1850 XIII, 318-35). Wordsworth describes himself falling into a revery or trance about the British past while traveling solitary over the desert-like plain:

> Time with his retinue of ages fled
> Backwards, nor checked his flight until I saw
> Our dim ancestral Past in vision clear;
> Saw multitudes of men, and here and there,
> A single Briton clothed in wolf-skin vest,
> With shield and stone-axe, stride across the wold;
> The voice of spears was heard, the rattling spear
> Shaken by arms of mighty bone, in strength,
> Long mouldered, of barbaric majesty.
> I called on Darkness—but before the word
> Was uttered, midnight darkness seemed to take
> All objects from my sight; and lo! again

> The Desert visible by dismal flames;
> It is the sacrificial altar, fed
> With living men—how deep the groans! the voice
> Of those that crowd the giant wicker thrills
> The monumental hillocks, and the pomp
> Is for both worlds, the living and the dead.

"I called on Darkness" is a fiat-style wish followed by immediate fulfillment. And it is as dramatic an episode of omnipotence of voice as Wordsworth's poetry affords. As a "fit," moreover, it is strange enough. Fulfillment comes in a peculiar and perhaps unexpected manner, "before the word / Was uttered." This may indicate nothing more than instantaneity. The 1805 version omits the phrase. But it may also indicate that, had it been uttered, the wish might have been blocked or tangled up in sublime feelings—as when an unconscious wish, hinging on the idea of Crossing the Alps, becomes conscious during the composition of the Simplon Pass episode in *Prelude* VI.

Or Wordsworth's utterance was not in time, and the darkness that came was not the darkness called. Unless he yielded to the horror encroaching on him during his trance, unless he became its accomplice (which is a possible interpretation), one could have expected him to wish for blankness, that is, a blanketing sort of darkness. But if his call was not uttered in time the darkness which came may have been the one that was to be averted, and he found himself in the grip of a vision of human sacrifice. (One darkness forestalls another, as one type of light another for the travelers who set out to see the sun rise from Snowdon.)

Equally remarkable is (1) that the episode shows a decreating rather than creating word, and (2) that whereas on Snowdon a timely utterance revealed "speaking darkness," here the poet speaks the darkness. Instead of uttering the primal fiat which conflates light and the word, Wordsworth may have approached an "unutterable" fiat conflating darkness and the word. This would explain the blocking or eliding of wish or fantasy (any "Let there be") in Wordsworth. The fiat is waylaid on its way to utterance because the poet is anxious lest he speak the opposite of a creating word—an untimely or "apocalyptic" word. He fears that "Let there be voice" will conflate with "Let there be darkness" to produce a "speaking darkness" and a flight of time (1850 *Prelude* XIII, 318-20) that may continue unchecked.

As Wordsworth, then, approaches the Apocalyptic there is his concern that "the furnace shall come up at last" (Christopher Smart). And that is what happens on Salisbury Plain almost as literal vision:

> and lo! again
> The Desert visible by dismal flames;
> It is the sacrificial altar, fed

> With living men—how deep the groans!...
>> (1850 *Prelude* XIII, 329-32)

"The Desert visible..." is a version of Milton's hell, "No light / But rather darkness visible." The "dismal flames," moreover, lead us back to the theme of voice, its mystery and efficacy. Druidic sacrifice is portrayed as the efficacious sacrifice of human voices:

> ....how deep the groans! the voice
> Of those that crowd the giant wicker thrills
> The monumental hillocks, the pomp
> Is for both worlds, the living and the dead.
>> (1850 *Prelude* XIII, 332-35)

It is as if the assumption of visionary status by the poet (see 1850, XIII, 300ff.) must revive voices like these, ancestral, fearful, unenlightened. The tale punishes the teller: it is the price he pays for aspiring to potency of voice. That groaning or speaking darkness seems but an extension of his own voice which also spoke darkness.

Snowdon at once deepens and modifies dread of voice. It suggests that the *shift* from speech-act to spoken, from visionary voice to visionary text, is part of a vast metaphoric activity identifiable with creative power itself. To become "A power like one of Nature's" (1850 *Prelude* XIII, 312) is to produce such "mutations" or "transformations": "to one life impart / The functions of another, shift, create...." Creativity appears as metaphoricity, and lodges in such shifts from voice to image and vice-versa.

The blocked or elided fiat in Wordsworth may therefore be described as a "mutation" that is muted. The fiat, whether considered as a primal text or as a primordial speech-act, expresses metaphoricity by lodging it in the formulaic and performative utterance of a sacred voice. Yet on Salisbury Plain, Snowdon, and in the poem that provided our starting point, the fiat is merely a "dark passage." Metaphoricity cannot terminate in the "dark deep thoroughfare" (1805 *Prelude* XIII, 64) of such texts, each of which discloses a radical shift that recovers from the primal fiat the image of a voice that called on darkness: whether to delimit it, or to honor its prior claim.

X

> ...divine respondence meet
> Spenser, *The Fairie Queene*

The phrase "timely utterance" can be applied both to the fiat ("Let there be...") and to such ordinary wishes as "Let me, thy happy guide, now...." Whatever the difference in imaginative intensity between extraordinary and ordinary wishes, there is a common link which extends also to the simplest form that wishing takes: "Good morning," or "This morning gives us promise of a glorious day." Greetings and blessings of this kind maintain their connection with the highest, most elaborate verbal forms: for example, with Milton's *On the Morning of Christ's Nativity*, which is but another "Good Morning" or "timely utterance." The poet, in the prologue to the hymn, puts the question to himself whether his voice can join the angel quire and honor the greatness of the event. "This is the month, and this the happy morn." He should, he must respond; and in Wordsworth, where ritual occasions are not so manifest, where a "living calendar" replaces that of fixed feasts, the burden of responsiveness is more continual, indefinite, self-imposed.

But if the poet is always under this obligation of "timely utterance," if "Let there be verse" is always incumbent, then the power of imagination cannot be only a blessing. It may come to vex its own creation (1805 *Prelude* I, 47). The creative will, or the wish to respond with timely utterance, and even to renew time by means of it, may become willful and turn against what it wishes to bless; and "thereof come[s] in the end despondency and madness" (*Resolution and Independence*). The imagination may feel like Hamlet: "The time is out of joint. O cursed spite / That ever I was born to set it right."

The problem of response, in the case of Wordsworth, is not made easier by his understanding of the "power in sound." Ultimately or primordially this is the fiat power. It is not, then, only a matter of response but also of demand and potency. The fiat as a wish does not take the form of a blessing except retrospectively: it is a compelling call, a force exerted to make something, even time itself, conform. "There was a time, when. . . ." Then let that time come again.

It may be an innocent wish when Wordsworth looks forward to walking with his daughter in the English countryside. But his looking forward is also a looking back at scenes involved with memories and associations: he attempts to recapture the time that was, to read in Dora's eyes as in Dorothy's (*Tintern Abbey*, 117ff.). The utterance that darkens his wish, the usurping memory of Milton's text, is an obscure judgment on him which he answers in verses more reflective than imperious, verses that merely gain time by a characteristic *whiling*. His poem to Dora becomes a lingering, wayward iteration, a thrice-wishful journeying to transform a failed "Good Morning" into a blessing of what caused it to fail: that disconcerting and usurping Miltonic quotation. For the close of the poem joins not only Dora's and William's hands but also Classical and Scriptural sources of inspiration. Text calls unto text, and Milton's assumption of the Classical tradition is involved. The bar, at least the literary bar, between Classical and Christian has been removed.

But what of the bar between father and daughter? Dora has entered her twelfth year, she is on the threshold of puberty. The Oedipal situation is there, whether or not it prompts those opening words from the literary unconscious. The displacements are complex yet it would not be difficult to understand them as an elaborate disguise of the incest wish. Dora emerging into womanhood may be assuming in the poet's mind a supportive role not unlike Dorothy's. The "guiding hand," by a crude if powerful reduction, would then point to a wished-for touch; the "intense desire for powers withheld" to what is repressed or prohibited; the final "hand in hand" to a union that looks beyond earthly and kinship bars (lines 43-48 would imply that the father prefers his daughter to with-draw as a nun rather than emerge from her orisons / horizons, cf. *Hamlet*, act 3, sc. 1). Through this Oedipal reading the timely utterance points to a transcen-dence or transgression of time, even as we recover the life-situation it responds to. The wish reveals a double structure of sublimative and regressive motivation; and the poet's voice darkens understandably as it verges on the unutterable bless-ing that consecrates union with Dora.

XI

Why then I'le fit you

Hieronymo, in Kyd's *The Spanish Tragedy*

It would be hard to distinguish, therefore, the wish for a "Now" from the wish for a "Thou" in the "timely utterance" of poetry. We have been concerned to reveal the structure, or phenomenology, of the word-wish in the form of the fiat, and also in the form of blessing (or curse). But "Now" and "Thou," those mutually echoing words, also play their part. I have elsewhere described their contribution to a "western," or residually epiphanic, style; and a full account would have to include their transmission through the predication language of both Classical and Christian hymnology.

Some theology is indispensable here. So Jacques Lacan, for instance, has tried to understand the "imperative Word" as it founds or maintains us in time. His theory of symbolic mediation, based at once on Freud and semiotics, views sym-bols as enveloping "the life of man in a network so total that they join together, before he comes into the world, those who are going to engender him 'by flesh and blood'; so total that they bring to his birth, along with the gifts of the stars, if not with the gifts of the fairies, the shape of his destiny; so total that they give the words that will make him faithful or renegade, the laws of the acts that will follow him right to the very place where he *is* not yet and even beyond his death; and so total that through them his end finds its meaning in the last judgment, where the Word absolves his being or condemns it—unless he attain the subjec-tive bringing to realization of being-for-death." Through such a theory we touch again the lost imagination of theology, or what used to go under the name of a "theology of the poets." Carlyle does not do better in *Sartor Resartus*.

To many contemporary thinkers theology remains a junkyard of dark sublimities. Littered with obsolete and crazy, or once powerful now superstitious ideas, it emits at best no light but rather darkness visible. The contemporary mind prefers a semiotic theory of symbolic mediation, however complicated by Freudian insights. Yet there has been a discernible movement of recovery, to which, in addition to Lacan, such different rabbis as Gershom Scholem, Owen Barfield, Walter Benjamin, Erich Auerbach (on "figura"), and Kenneth Burke (on Augustinian "logology") have contributed.

The most effective *countertheological* movement at present is Jacques Derrida's post-Heideggerian analysis of voice, or "timely utterance." It focuses on the deceptive relation between speech acts and being-in-time. Utterance discloses the relation of human wishes to existence yet also complicates rather than resolves wishing, for the latter does not disappear into time. It reveals, through such phenomena as texts, an "untimely," that is, residual and deferred element. The eclipse of voice by text is valorized, in the wake of Heidegger's analysis of temporality and of the "call" (*Ruf*) or "voice" (*Stimme*) of conscience. Heidegger describes conscience as a mode of discourse not dependent on vocal utterance, but which "in calling gives us to understand" (*Being and Time*, paragraphs 55ff.). This silent discourse (Derrida will see it as characteristic of textuality) reveals that the "voice" of conscience, or the guilt and care inherent in human nature, are not echoes of prior events, that is, prehistorical or pretemporal constitutions. They are characteristics of *Dasein*, human existence in time, and are inauthentically interpreted by theological, historical and psychologistic positivisms.

Though Heidegger, then, cannot avoid the metaphor of "voice," he effectively cancels its divine or psychogenetic status. His analysis of the discourse of conscience is of something that "speaks silence," that mutes the directly communicative, affective or performative, word. According to Heidegger even inner speech, or the dialogue of self with self, may be an evasion of human responsibility. (We can think of the clammy intimacy of certain novels or interior monologues, which evade guilt by means of their contagious, all-embracing confession.) Structures of congruence or correspondence, which substitute harmony for hierarchy—demand satisfied, expectation fulfilled, or the desired convergence of voice and act in utterance—reveal not truth but rather untruth: the failure to "overhear" oneself, or an erroneous "mishearing" (mistaking of the self, *Sichverhören*) which shows we cannot seize ourselves in time. We have no authentic way of passing judgment on ourselves. We must continue to live, *unpurged by voice, ours or another's*, in guilt or debt or responsibility. We live with these death-feelings, then, toward a death that resolves them.

The prematurity of voice—its pathos of presence, its peculiar, proleptic ecstasy, its capable self-exculpation—is exposed also by Derrida's technique of "deconstruction." Yet the greatest deceit voice has practiced is to represent itself as repressed by the written word. Derrida argues that it is writing that really suffered the repression, by being considered a mere reduction or redaction of the spoken word. So the interpreter zealously redeems the buried voice of the text instead of understanding how texts eclipse voice and speak silence. There is no authentically temporal discourse, no timely utterance, except by resolute acts of writing. It is in writing that the "subjective" attains, to quote Lacan's paraphrase of Heidegger, a "bringing to realization of being-for-death." Writing, as an individual or collective process, defers utterance of the definitive *parole* or password—from generation to generation.

Against Husserl, Heidegger, and a certain kind of philosophical technique, I hope to have shown that it is not necessary to bracket "natural experience," psychology, or ordinary language, in order to disclose the structure of "timely utterance." (Derrida's bracketing, his parenthesis style, is both more sly and obvious: every referent or "thing" is deferred, and this movement of *différance*, identified with writing, discloses no "thing.") By starting with a simple if miscarried wish, a given of human nature as universal as can be found, it was possible to trace the complex interactions of poetry with that wish. I had no recourse to a special interpretive system like psychoanalysis, although taking a wish as my starting point, and recognizing its devious connections to voice and time, were prompted by that movement. Yet I did not try and reduce the wish to something prior or deeper; and I made no decision, in particular, on the priority of wish to word. The notion of word-wish, and of its prototype in the fiat, may be useful for a future reflection on the relation of wish, speech act and text, especially when the text is poetic or visionary. But again, while appreciating the area of concern focused on in speech act theories, I have not depended on them.

Wordsworth wrote in his famous "spousal verse" published as a Prospectus to the uncompleted *Recluse*:

> . . .my voice proclaims
> How exquisitely the individual Mind
> (And the progressive powers perhaps no less
> Of the whole species) to the external World
> Is fitted:—and how exquisitely, too—
> Theme this but little heard of among men—
> The external World is fitted to the Mind. . . .

Annotating this Blake commented: "You shall not bring me down to believe such fitting & fitted I know better & Please your Lordship." Blake is not wrong. He sensed the debt this passage owed to the theological and rhetorical principle of accommodation. God's truth, any great truth, must be accommodated—fitted—to human understanding. Like Heidegger, Blake rejected this principle (or idiom) which claimed to redeem what the former calls "natural experience" and the latter "natural man." But their rejection is itself strongly redemptive: it rids us also of a condescending view of human power ("bring me down," "Please your Lordship") implied by the need to accommodate truth to human perception. We might put it this way: fitting has to do with tailoring, not with creating.

Yet the content of the passage in Wordsworth is creation: "the creation (by no lower name / Can it be called) which they [the Mind and the external World] with blended might / Accomplish." Wordsworth's "fitting and fitted" tries to respect the "blended might," that is, the "interchangeable supremacy" or "mutual domination"—the mobile, responsive, reciprocal factor—in the fiat; and he goes so far as to say, in verses introducing the visionary experience on Salisbury Plain (but more apt for what follows on Snowdon), that there is a creative passion in both nature and the mind:

> I felt that the array
> Of act and circumstance, and visible form,
> Is mainly to the pleasure of the mind
> What passion makes them; that meanwhile the forms
> Of Nature have a passion in themselves,
> That intermingles with those works of man
> To which she summons him. . . .
>
> (1850 *Prelude* XIII, 287-93)

Strange fit of passions, indeed! The poet like the prophet, he continues, has a peculiar faculty, "a sense that fits him to perceive / Objects unseen before" (1850 XIII, 304-5). Though the meaning of "fits" is plainly enough "accommodates," can we avoid hearing "that causes fits to fall on him, like on prophets of old, visions that make him perceive. . . ?" That the word "fit" should become so divided against itself, capable of expressing both responsive adaptation and imaginative frenzy, points to the problem of all poetry with a creative or visionary claim. The fiat, its pressure on vision and utterance, can become a fit that nothing on earth could modify. Against that possibility Wordsworth writes, wishfully perhaps, yet consuming only the voice of his wish.

XII

I end by returning to a beginning: that of *The Prelude*. This poem opens like "A little onward" with a quotation. But the poet quotes himself, not Milton; and the "passion" expressed is that of poetry as it seeks to be an extemporaneous response to "present joy." The Wordsworthian text inspires itself before our ears: made of nothing more than a breeze, a feeling, a minimalist impulse ("saved from vacancy"), it is shadowy and insubstantial without being overtly visionary. The fifty-odd verses of this prelude to *The Prelude* are but a recovered or extended breathing ("I breathe again!" 1805 I, 19), and can be compressed into a sentence made of their first and last lines:

> 1   O there is blessing in this gentle breeze
> 54   The holy life of music and of verse.

What does it amount to? The breathing apostrophic O, the facticity of "There is" (cf. *"Es gibt,"* or the balladic "There is," "It is"), the sense, in this present, of not being able to distinguish between the pure movement of a voice that blesses and the prompting impulse, so that voice and blessing, voice and wish, become as one, the wish being for voice elaborating the wish—it adds up to nothing progressive, to nothing but a new, confident, even self-originating textuality. The text is built almost *ex nihilo*, yet exposes in its course (it finds, as it goes on, feeding-sources in the Classics, Scripture, and Milton) the problematic of giving and receiving, of nourishing and being nourished, of self-tasking and being tasked, which is the dilemma of emergent maturity (the growth of the poet's mind) as well as a point at issue between Coleridge (the friend addressed) and Wordsworth.

If, in the event, Wordsworth fails to make a "present joy" the "matter" of his song, it is because a "present," in the sense also of "gift" (cf. the virtual pun in Milton's "Say heavenly Muse, shall not thy sacred vein / Afford a present to the infant God?"), proves to be an effect of grace and not of work, of divine rather than human and self-inaugurated power. The question is again that of achieving a "timely utterance" rather than an involuntary or self-provoked one. Is there a present (time) that is a present (gift) without detracting from the mind's reciprocal, reciprocating power?

Poetry, in Wordsworth, names that ideal moment of "blended might" or "interchangeable supremacy." Yet despite "Eolian visitations" (1805 *Prelude* I, 104), the poet's time may not have come. In Milton's *Nativity Ode*, the time is given ("This is the month, and this the happy Morn") and justifies the poet who joins his voice to the sacred quire. In *Lycidas*, however, the occasion though solemn is less compelling: there is doubt expressed in "forced fingers rude" and "season due": perhaps *Lycidas* is a pretext for a questionable trial of strength (cf. 1850 *Prelude* I, 94ff. "my soul / Once more made trial of her strength. . . . "). It is not a "timely-happy" moment and Milton calls for "lucky words."

Compared to *The Prelude*, "A little onward" begins with an *untimely* utterance. Though the latter is still in the form of a quotation that represents a direct movement of speech, the words seem to have come, extempore, to the wrong voice and confuse the speaker's relation to time. Elsewhere too Wordsworth records utterances which make it hard for him to read the time. "The clock / That told, with unintelligble voice, / The widely parted hours," as he watches (outside Gravedona) the "dull red image of the moon" from "hour to hour... as if the night / Had been ensnared by witchcraft" (1850 *Prelude* VI, 700-22), almost literalizes that kind of experience. Has he called on darkness without knowing it? He seems to have become, like Hamlet, "cursed" in a time out of joint.

Indeed, there are Shakespearian as well as Miltonic echoes evoked by this sense of the untimely event. A famous "spot of time" (1805 *Prelude* XI, 345-89) recounts how the young Wordsworth climbed a crag overlooking the meeting-point of two highways to watch for the horses that would take him home for the Christmas vacation. There he waits "in anxiety of hope," a single sheep on his right hand and a whistling (1850: blasted) hawthorn on his left. He is, as it were, at the crossroads of a stark clock. He strains his eyes, watching the mist advancing on the line of each of those two roads in "indisputable shapes"—an episode followed shortly by his father's untimely death. "You come most carefully upon your hour," one guard says to the other near the beginning of *Hamlet* as they wait for the "questionable shape" of Hamlet's father's ghost. The boy's wish, innocent enough, that the time pass quickly, that he see what is to come, darkens retrospectively into a sense of his transgressive relation to time, associated with Shakespearean complexities. One event follows another too fast, like the marriage the funeral in *Hamlet*. The boy's father dies; and the boy feels obscurely that he called on darkness without knowing it, that he cursed the time which now curses him. It is "desire," i.e. the omnipotence of thoughts or imagination, that is corrected. "How awful is the might of souls / And what they do within themselves" (1850 *Prelude* III, 180ff.). Such childhood experiences provide a basis for the poet's sublimely absurd invocation of the Child as "Mighty Seer" in the Great Ode.

Perhaps the strangest of these episodes is a poem composed "almost extempore" in the groves of Alfoxden and included in *Lyrical Ballads* of 1798. This poem, *The Idiot Boy*, finds its climax in an "answer" to a "question" which the mother puts to Johnny after his abortive night ride. "'Tell us Johnny, do, / Where all this long night you have been, / What you have heard, what you have seen.'" But the poet himself had already given up this wish for a story. "O reader! now that I might tell / What Johnny and his horse are doing! / What they've been doing all this time..." He cannot tell; he feels unable to pursue a "delightful tale" (despite some speculation on his part), because what may have happened is inward to the idiot boy. We, the reader, learn nothing of all that adventure except the women's anxiety as Johnny fails to return—an anxiety linked to the clock ("The clock is on the stroke of twelve, / And Johnny is not yet in sight")— and the few words Johnny utters:

'The Cocks did crow to-who, to-who
And the sun did shine so cold.'

Is this not the very type of an "untimely utterance," this quotation which is "all his travel's story," and which hovers undecidably between mournful and gleeful iteration?

In a peculiar and moving comment on idiots, Wordsworth remarked that their life was with God. We are bound to ask, after our lengthy analysis of "A little onward," where the life of such a poem is. For it is both a minor *poem* and a considerable *text*. In this case, the order of poetry and the order of texts seems to diverge. It is just possible, of course, that the distinction will prove false. We may have to conclude either that such poems are weak, and redeemed only by the responsive interpreter, or that they have the sort of strength we are not yet fit to perceive: that our present image of great poetry stands in the way of their peculiar textual quality. Eventually there might be a new convergence, and certain of Wordsworth's minor poems might be seen for what they are, and accorded the esteem that accrues, say, to Milton's minor pieces.

Time will tell. Yet time, precisely, is at issue. The life of Wordsworth's lines is often uneasy and as if somewhere else: still to be manifested by the action of time or the utterance of future readers. One could apply to Wordsworth what he says of the idiot boy: "You hardly can perceive his joy." We should not forget that Wordsworth's greatest poem remained hidden, and that its power and authority (in the light of which we *now* read everything else) was but alluded to in the rest of his oeuvre. At its curious worst this allusive manner can produce the stylization we find in ll. 34-39 of "A little onward" (referring to the Alps); but there is also a general effect of indirect or inner reference. Keeping *The Prelude* in reserve, almost like God his own Son, Wordsworth reposed on a text-experience whose life remained with God. He delayed becoming the author of a poem so original that it could not be accommodated to known forms of Christianity. In what he does publish, then, the relation of author to poem is often the strangest mixture of knowingness and childlikeness—it is, in short, a divine idiocy. The intertextual glitter of Milton, his blended might of Scripture and Classical lore, is but an undersong to Wordsworth's intratextual strain that repeats something already begotten in himself.

TEXT OF POEM
AND BIBLIOGRAPHICAL NOTE

For the text given below, see E. de Selincourt, *The Poetical Works of William Wordsworth*, vol. 4 (Oxford: Clarendon Press, 1947), pp. 92-94 (by permission of Oxford University Press). In his Notes to the same volume de Selincourt lists other echoes of Milton (p. 422). There are also curiously inwrought allusions to scenes involving the blinded Gloucester in Shakespeare's *King Lear*. I discuss these in "Diction and Defense" (see Chapter 8 of this book). Coleridge's fragmentary *The Wanderings of Cain* (composed in 1798, during the ferment leading to *Lyrical Ballads*) had already imitated that pathetic "A LITTLE further...." The allusion to Antigone is reinforced by the original version of line 11, which reads in all editions up to 1850, "O my Antigone, beloved child!" rather than "—O my own Dora, my beloved child!" The only extended discussion of the poem so far is by Leslie Brisman in *Milton's Poetry of Choice and Its Romantic Heirs* (Ithaca, 1973), chapter 5. Brisman emphasizes not only the debt to Milton but also how "Wordsworth achieves some of his finest moments by turning to Milton" and "takes the Miltonic sublime 'a little onward.'" He seeks to modify Harold Bloom's insistence on the sublime but restrictive shadow Milton throws on later poetry. On Wordsworth and voice, the most detailed studies have been by John Hollander: "Wordsworth and the Music of Sound," in *New Perspectives on Coleridge and Wordsworth*, ed. G.H. Hartman (New York, 1972) and his Churchill College Lecture, *Images of Voice* (Cambridge, England, 1970). Cf. also my *The Fate of Reading*, pp. 195ff. and 288-92. Derrida's response to Heidegger on the issue of voiceless voice, conscience and writing is most succinctly set forth in *De la grammatologie* (Paris, 1967), pp. 31ff. For the quotations from Eliot in section IV, see his "The Function of Criticism" (1922), and for the quotation from Lacan in section XI, see his "Discours de Rome" (1953), "The function and field of speech and language in psychoanalysis," *Ecrits: A Selection* (New York, 1977), p. 68. With regard to the Oedipal interpretation of the poem ventured in section X, cf. my "The Voice of the Shuttle," in *Beyond Formalism* (New Haven, 1970), which tries to link a theory of life to a theory of literary condensation. The forbidden convergence of life-lines through the incest wish (more properly phrased, through a desire for union despite kinship bars) elides temporal and historical structures; and poetry's "timely utterance" allows time for that wish to be gratified in the very lineaments of delay.

> "*A LITTLE onward lend thy guiding hand*
> *To these dark steps, a little further on!*"
> —What trick of memory to *my* voice hath brought
> This mournful iteration? For though Time,
> The Conqueror, crowns the Conquered, on his brow
> Planting his favourite silver diadem,
> Nor he, nor minister of his—intent
> To run before him, hath enrolled me yet,
> Though not unmenaced, among those who lean
> 10   Upon a living staff, with borrowed sight.
> —O my own Dora, my belovéd child!

Should that day come—but hark! the birds salute
The cheerful dawn, brightening for me the east;
For me, thy natural leader, once again
Impatient to conduct thee, not as erst
A tottering infant, with compliant stoop
From flower to flower supported; but to curb
Thy nymph-like step swift-bounding o'er the lawn,
Along the loose rocks, or the slippery verge
20   Of foaming torrents.—From thy orisons
Come forth; and while the morning air is yet
Transparent as the soul of innocent youth,
Let me, thy happy guide, now point thy way,
And now precede thee, winding to and fro,
Till we by perseverance gain the top
Of some smooth ridge, whose brink precipitous
Kindles intense desire for powers withheld
From this corporeal frame; whereon who stands
Is seized with strong incitement to push forth
30   His arms, as swimmers use, and plunge—dread thought,
For pastime plunge—into the "abrupt abyss,"
Where ravens spread their plumy vans, at ease!

    And yet more gladly thee would I conduct
Through woods and spacious forests,—to behold
There, how the Original of human art,
Heaven-prompted Nature, measures and erects
Her temples, fearless for the stately work,
Though waves, to every breeze, its high-arched roof,
And storms the pillars rock. But we such schools
40   Of reverential awe will chiefly seek
In the still summer noon, while beams of light,
Reposing here, and in the aisles beyond
Traceably gliding through the dusk, recall
To mind the living presences of nuns;
A gentle, pensive, white-robed sisterhood,
Whose saintly radiance mitigates the gloom
Of those terrestrial fabrics, where they serve,
To Christ, the Sun of righteousness, espoused.

    Now also shall the page of classic lore,
50   To these glad eyes from bondage freed, again
Lie open; and the book of Holy writ,

Again unfolded, passage clear shall yield
To heights more glorious still, and into shades
More awful, where, advancing hand in hand,
We may be taught, O Darling of my care!
To calm the affections, elevate the soul,
And consecrate our lives to truth and love.

8
Diction and Defense

Hamlet. Let her not walk i' the Sun; conception is a blessing, but not as your daughter may conceive.

I wish to discuss a poem Wordsworth wrote in 1816, when he was forty-six and his daughter Dora, twelve. We perceive only dimly the personal circumstances: the Continent had opened up again to English travelers after Napoleon's fall; Wordsworth was thinking of going back for the first time since the Peace of Amiens of 1803, when he had visited his illegitimate daughter Caroline (from a liaison with Annette Valon contracted during his 1792 stay in revolutionary France); Dora is approaching puberty; and his eyesight is troubling him. As he is enjoying the idea of walking with Dora in the English countryside one sunny morning, his mind is usurped by a voice: more precisely by the opening lines of Milton's *Samson Agonistes*. They depict Samson at Gaza, blind, humiliated, and having to be led; and the quotation (words within words) echoes the opening of Sophocles' *Oedipus at Colonus*, where the blind Oedipus is guided by Antigone. Wordsworth cannot understand the intrusion of this voice, for what it describes is a situation exactly the reverse of his: instead of a father leading his child into the sunny Lake District, and perhaps into the Alps, the quotation depicts a blind man led by his daughter, a man who is guilt-ridden and burdened by his role in divine history. I quote the first thirty-two (out of fifty-seven) lines of the poem:

> "*A LITTLE onward lend thy guiding hand*
> *To these dark steps, a little further on!*"
> —What trick of memory to *my* voice hath brought

This mournful iteration? For though Time,
5   The Conqueror, crowns the Conquered, on his brow
Planting his favourite silver diadem,
Nor he, nor minister of his—intent
To run before him, hath enrolled me yet,
Though not unmenaced, among those who lean
10   Upon a living staff, with borrowed sight.
—O my own Dora, my beloved child!
Should that day come—but hark! the birds salute
The cheerful dawn, brightening for me the east;
For me thy natural leader, once again
15   Impatient to conduct thee, not as erst
A tottering infant, with compliant stoop
From flower to flower supported; but to curb
Thy nymph-like step swift-bounding o'er the lawn,
Along the loose rocks, or the slippery verge
20   Of foaming torrents.—From thy orisons
Come forth: and, while the morning air is yet
Transparent as the soul of innocent youth,
Let me, thy happy guide, now point thy way,
And now precede thee, winding to and fro,
25   Till we by perseverance gain the top
Of some smooth ridge, whose brink precipitous
Kindles intense desire for powers withheld
From this corporeal frame; whereon who stands
Is seized with strong incitement to push forth
30   His arms, as swimmers use, and plunge—dread thought,
For pastime plunge—into the "abrupt abyss,"
Where ravens spread their plumy vans, at ease![1]

It is hard to know what is most peculiar here. First, why the image of the blind man? Then, is there an emphasis on the very idea of beginning, of taking that step, since it is unusual to have a poem open with a quotation, and even more so to have the reaction to that quotation be part of the subject? Finally, should we explore the similarity of the quotation to an inner voice?

I will offer some thoughts about all these matters, starting with the last. The question of "inner voices" is a large one, and well known to psychoanalytic literature. Poetry, I will surmise, is the working-through of such "voices," which are often projected as coming from the outside, or attributed to supernatural agency. They summon or entice the hearer, they urge him to some fatal step. They come from the "abrupt abyss" (31) or bring him close to it. So in the case of the strange and glorious death of Oedipus at Colonus:

> Suddenly a voice
> Call'd him aloud: awestruck we stood aghast:
> Again, and oft it call'd him, "Oedipus,
> Why Oedipus, delay we to depart?
> Thine this delay. . . ."
>   . . . we backwards turn'd
> Our eyes; the man was no where to be found;
> He was not; but we saw the king [Theseus] alone;
> He stood, and o'er his face his hands he spread
> Shading his eyes, as if with terror struck
> At something horrible to human sight.[2]

The entire speech (by one of the citizens of Colonus) is suggestive, for it shows Oedipus becoming a guide once more, leading his daughters to "the rent rock's craggy verge" and taking his station near "the gulf's yawning mouth" (cf 26ff.). What happens next remains mysterious, but the voice must have done its work, for Oedipus disappears, divine victim or suicide, "haply by the gods / Borne thence, or sinking through the friendly earth, / Which in her deeply-rifted bosom oped / A painless passage to the realms below."

That "passage," in Wordsworth, often leads from eye to ear. Voice, by a strange law of exchange, seems to imply a darkened eye. Sometimes merely an "eye made quiet" (*Tintern Abbey*); at other times, as in a visionary episode of *The Prelude*, nature exhibits the emblem of a mind "that broods / Over the dark abyss, intent to hear / its voices. . . ." It is as if the eye entered the ear to recover a lost conjunction, or to shelter in its darker recess. "Why was the sight," Samson laments in Milton's poem, which provided Wordsworth's opening verses, "To such a tender ball as the eye confined?" The sense of vulnerability, psychic as well as physical, is extreme. Voice exposes that vulnerability yet also evokes a deeper faculty, which is, as it were, an eye without the eyes. Wordsworth's ode *On the Power of Sound* describes it as "The cell of Hearing dark and blind, / . . . more dread for thought / To enter than oracular cave."

"More dread for thought to enter"? Compare "and plunge—dread thought, / For pastime plunge—into the 'abrupt abyss'" (30-31). A katabasis with traumatic implications is suggested. The inner or "abrupt" voice points at one and the same time to an ideal blindness (voice beyond sight), and a terrible blinding (voice purchased by the loss of sight). The dependence on voice has always been symptomatic of an intimate relationship to inspiration or divine guidance (the oracular cave). That presumption is also the danger, call it enthusiasm or ecstasy, delusion of grandeur or omnipotence fantasy, bardic or visionary power. "Visionary power," Wordsworth writes in the fifth book of *The Prelude*, "attends the motion of the viewless winds / Embodied in the mystery of words." The contrast of "visionary" and "viewless" also moves us beyond sight. No wonder Wordsworth is "blinded" by the passage from *Samson Agonistes*.

Not till the very end does the poet foresee a "passage clear" (52); for even after he finds his way again (23ff.) he comes to a "brink precipitous" that halts him once more, like the opening verses. At this point allusions to Milton return: "abrupt abyss" is a conflation of *Paradise Lost* II, 405 and 409; more significantly, the sequence from "whereon who stands" to "plumy vans" recalls *Paradise Regained* IV, 541-83, in which Christ resists the Tempter's voice. Satan asks Christ to show his godhead by casting himself from a pinnacle, and Christ resists that presumption of divinity. It is as if Wordsworth quoted Milton to resist in himself a similar presumption.

Usurpation by a voice, then, is itself a mixed traumatic event. It is both defensive and inspirational. It at once blocks and originates the poem. It breaks into thought in a way that breaks thought, yet it has something of the divinity of oracle or fiat. On the one hand, the carefree wish (restated in l. 20 as "From thy orisons / Come forth...") becomes a burden through the intervention of an ominous quotation. Time is apocalyptically speeded up, the roles of father and daughter reversed, and Wordsworth approaches the position of Samson and Oedipus just before their exalted deaths. On the other hand, the poem is launched, and works against that perspective, and establishes a development of sorts. The poet becomes active from passive and voices the voice he hears.[3]

Though we cannot locate the trauma with precision, because diction and interdiction, or the ideal and terrible in this "dictation," blend so intricately, the traumatic effect can be described further. What is wounded here? The answer must be *human time* itself, or *growth* considered from a psychic and developmental perspective. Wordsworth finds himself in the situation of a man who, because of the shock he has suffered, moves as if the ground before him were not reliable. He takes "dark steps," and so does his language, which seeks to recover its previous state related to the innocence of wishing and walking. Yet it remains "diction" rather than "language." Now this is still very abstract, but it becomes telling when we recall that Wordsworth had been thinking about his daughter and that the blocking quotation links his thoughts involuntarily to the story of Oedipus as well as Samson.

In both these stories there is guilt, and a guilt partly linked to sexual transgression. In the case of Oedipus there is unconscious incest. Incest is itself a collapse of human and developmental time: it merges lifelines that should be kept separate. Wordsworth was, in fact, too separated from one child, Caroline; he has also passed through an extraordinary union, through what can only be called a symbiotic relation, with his sister Dorothy ("She gave me ears, she gave me eyes"). Is he uncertain and anxious about his future relations with Dora? The proleptic image of blindness that comes to him in the form of Milton's voice (the blind Milton, whose daughters became his amanuenses) may indicate a guilt of the eyes, a fear for their punishment or "castration," or the wish to avoid such a trial by an imaginary exclusion of the guilty organ, by its ideal "sheltering" or "immunization." The fear may not be directly connected with sexual thoughts; rather with the wish to be so closely in touch (the poet guiding the thoughts or hands of Dora) that the eyes are actually wished away.

In this overdetermined situation there can be no single resolving hypothesis. The situation is further entangled by the fact that Wordsworth had real eye trouble, whether or not it was psychogenic; and that the association of blindness and prophetic power was a literary commonplace. Are we confined, then, to impotent speculation?

I think not. The maze has to be respected; yet the very act of limning it, of making it visible, leads out as well as in. We have not yet taken up the peculiar emphasis on beginnings in this poem; the Miltonic verses are so strong that all the rest appear to be commentary, or revision. Whatever the private psychic reason for the usurping lines, they make Milton's beginning Wordsworth's beginning. What is the connection between this emphasis on beginnings, the theme of blindness, and the father-daughter relation?

It is important to observe that though "In the beginning was the Word" is true of this poem, an absolute beginning in terms of literary sources is hard to locate. Milton's lines reiterate those of Sophocles; and this leading back is not the end of the matter. For the words of Oedipus or Samson form a highly allusive quotation which evokes something just beyond: a dangerous and sacred space, a fatal threshold or *templum* of some kind. ("A little onward" is an ambiguous phrase, moreover, when referred back to *Oedipus at Colonus*, for there a similar plea occurs twice, when Oedipus asks Antigone to lead him *into* the sacred grove at Colonus, and then when he is led, at the insistence of the Colonians, *out of* that sacred plot.) In short, there is so remarkable an abbreviation or condensation of several contexts that no one literary source can be cited as the original, even though all the contexts together drive us back (like the Oedipus myth itself) to beginnings, and project the image of a potent place where something "original"—theophanic—is to happen.

This structure, however paradoxical, establishes words—or their potential of condensed, literary expression—as a boundary beyond which the empirical search for origins—as when psychoanalysis locates the cause of a trauma— becomes mythicizing in its drift. "Each most obvious and particular thought," Wordsworth writes in *The Prelude*, "...hath no beginning." The quotation that begins the poem of 1816 acts as a boundary that limits and even admonishes our desire for self-inauguration: for being present in or at the origin. The intertextual condensation, moreover, displayed by literature, is an opacity akin to blindness. It reinforces the ceremonious "diction" by means of which liminal anxieties are raised and the threshold becomes a dwelling place. We cannot step beyond it into unmediated vision.

In the Romantic period, and still today, the faculty that moves us toward original or unmediated vision—vision more intimate and direct than even the eyes afford—is given the name of *imagination*. Wordsworth once called it an "unfathered vapor." It tends to block as well as facilitate; to take away fatherhood (authority) as well as be a fathering power. To think of it in these terms, in metaphors derived from the family nexus, is bound to produce a contradiction, because imagination, like Freud's Eros, drives beyond the natural family and toward more ultimate or exalted form of union.

The first step in "A little onward" goes backward, toward beginnings. It is a quotation, an unfathered (psychically abrupt) yet unoriginal fragment, that reveals a verbal abyss (words within words). The poem's second step is equally dark and backward. Wordsworth's querulous reflection,

> What trick of memory to *my* voice hath brought
> This mournful iteration?

embodies a further quotation, more covert than the first, yet raising with equal force the issue of beginnings.

These lines contain not only a significant pun but also a far-reaching echo of Shakespeare's *King Lear*.[4] They dislocate the words of another blinded man, Gloucester, when he meets a Lear now driven mad by the cruelty of his elder daughters as well as by the memory of his own cruelty to his youngest daughter. Gloucester says:

> The trick of that voice I do well remember.
> (IV, vi, 105)

In the context of the outrageous wordplay that characterizes this scene and focuses through the puns on what eyes see or cannot see—

> *Edgar.* O thou side-piercing sight!
> *Lear.* Read.
>
> . . . .
> *Gloucester.* What, with the case of eyes?
> *Lear.* Oh ho, are you there with me? No eyes in your head,
>   no money in your purse? Your eyes are in a heavy case,
>   your purse in a light; yet you see how this world goes.
> *Gloucester.* I see it feelingly.
> (IV, vi, 85, 141-47)

—in this context, "trick" meaning habit or characteristic trait, moves toward "trick" meaning trickiness or deceiving quality. "Give the word" says Lear (IV, vi, 92),[5] recalling the play's first scene, in which everything had been made to depend by him on a *trick of speech*.

That first scene opposed Cordelia's "Nothing" to Lear's "Speak." Lear's command is a kind of fiat; and from this beginning everything devolves, as from the "dark and vicious place" where Gloucester begot Edmund. Sexual force is, in fact, more potent than the fiat in human relations. Lear cannot force Cordelia.[6] Lear wants love and speech, Eros and Logos, to coincide; but there can be no fiat in the sphere of the emotions. The defeat of the "omnific word" (Milton's phrase for the fiat), especially in the bosom of the family, means that Logos has brought death, not love. Cordelia fails to be the daughter of Lear's word.

With this defeat of the fiat the problematic of self-inauguration comes into view again and explains Wordsworth's borrowing of Milton's and Shakespeare's hand. Both allusions, one too explicit, one too implicit, not only reinforce the theme of blindness but associate it with the pressure of imagination: its drive toward originality or self-inauguration. The repressed and repressive fiat shows *its* hand as a "trick of memory," allied to what today is called unconscious process. The fiat is, of course, a word in the beginning, one that creates what it inaugurates; and its conflation with the theme of blindness expresses the poet's anxiety about the "awful power" of imagination. The father's wish to guide his daughter—no more dangerous, surely, than Lear asking for words of love— betrays a fantasy about the fathering power of words. Even, perhaps, an omnipotence fantasy, a desire for "powers withheld / From this corporeal frame" (27-28), which would allow the poet to transcend natural limits or social taboos. The end of the poem (52ff.) seems to consecrate the union of daughter and father, as they advance "hand in hand" into a beyond.

It is well known that Wordsworth, who rebelled in the name of Nature against the artificiality of eighteenth-century "poetic diction," returned to a comparable style in such poems as "A little onward." My analysis suggests that his language here is indeed a diction, yet not a relapse into conventionality. The new diction, in its allusive and condensed character, creates time for the poet: it slows down something precipitous, it allows him a response. In the poem of 1816 the compelling element is a voice or a blind thought; it may also be, as in other poems, a "glimpse of glory" that comes unbidden, or a "spirit" that leaps out from the past, recalling and even radically modifying his memory of an event.

Also modified is his understanding of the poetic diction previously rejected: the attenuated and conspicuously secondary style imitating the great poets of the English Renaissance. Wordsworth revalues the relation of diction and defense. Poetic diction, as it develops after Spenser, Shakespeare, and Milton, is a compromise with them, which incorporates in an urbane and distanced, rather than open and creative way, many of their "tricks." Originally creative, the fiat can also be a decreating word—as in *Lear*, and perhaps in the pressure of poet on poet. Harold Bloom insists that what is defended against is always the overwhelming solicitation of a precursor poet: the voice of Milton, for instance, which initiates this very poem.

Yet in this area more care is needed. The inner voice has a traumatic resonance that evokes the exchange of eyes for ears, as if a blinding of that kind could restore Voice to its most powerful mode, that of Logos or fiat. Hearing voices implies a backward journeying, through mourning or mania (the "plunge" of II, 30-31, where "pastime" is also "past time"). For what comes back with those voices is the dream of divinity, of our unmediated or self-inaugurated power. "By our own spirits are we deified," Wordsworth writes in *Resolution and Independence*, a poem about the fate of poets.

It is, however, the defeat or impotence of the fiatlike voice—its deadly rather than loving effect in the context of family life—which causes grief and puts the vocation of the poet in doubt. In his earlier and more famous poetry, Wordsworth is very subtle in terms of passives and actives, and seems to escape from fiat into an atmosphere where everything is reciprocal, at once given and received, or half-perceived and half-created. Surely the Wordsworth who renews poetic diction is on the defensive once more: cornered by the repressed strength of the fiat in him, arrested by an image of Voice he cannot evade. Yet it remains a strong defense, as they say in chess, because his diction is also genuinely neoclassic, not only defensive but mediational. Through Sophocles and others he absorbs a sense of nature like his own, of the earth as having, or having had, a "lustre too intense / To be sustained" so that "Mortals bowed / The front in self-defence" (*Ode to Lycoris*, 1817). As he walks through the Lake District, his steps may suddenly become dark in that knowledge, and the mild English countryside may disclose an oracular cave:

> Long as the heat shall rage, let that dim cave
> Protect us, there decyphering as we may
> Diluvian records; or the sighs of Earth
> Interpreting; or counting for old Time
> His minutes, by reiterated drops,
> Audible tears, from some invisible source
> That deepens upon fancy....
>
> (*Further Ode to Lycoris*, 1817)

A final remark on the "defensive" character of Wordsworth's allusions to Shakespeare and Milton: the allusions to Milton are interesting yet patent. Why, then, a "viewless," or devious and inwrought, diction when it comes to *Lear*? It seems to me that Wordsworth approaches Shakespeare *through* Milton. The overt presence, Milton's, may be the less dangerous one: it is possible that the real block, or the poet defended against because of the power of his word, or the way he represents its wounding effect—wounded eyes and ears pictured by means of brazen pun and stage spectacle—is Shakespeare. In the poem of 1816, at least, Milton is a screen, or part of the "outwork" (Freud's metaphor) erected by

Wordsworth's imagination to keep it from a starker scene. The poet's tribute to the "mystery of words" in the fifth book of *The Prelude*,

> There darkness makes abode, and all the host
> Of shadowy things do work their changes there,

has a Shakespearean rather than a Miltonic ring.

9

The Use and Abuse of Structural Analysis

There is a Yew-tree, pride of Lorton Vale,
Which to this day stands single, in the midst
Of its own darkness, as it stood of yore:
Not loth to furnish weapons for the bands
5   Of Umfraville or Percy ere they marched
To Scotland's heaths; or those that crossed the sea
And drew their sounding bows at Azincour,
Perhaps at earlier Crecy, or Poictiers.
Of vast circumference and gloom profound
10   This solitary Tree! a living thing
Produced too slowly ever to decay;
Of form and aspect too magnificent
To be destroyed. But worthier still of note
Are those fraternal Four of Borrowdale,
15   Joined in one solemn and capacious grove;
Huge trunks! and each particular trunk a growth
Of intertwisted fibres serpentine
Up-coiling, and inveterately convolved;
Nor uninformed with Phantasy, and looks
20   That threaten the profane; a pillared shade,
Upon whose grassless floor of red-brown hue,
By sheddings from the pining umbrage tinged
Perennially—beneath whose sable roof

Of boughs, as if for festal purpose decked
25   With unrejoicing berries—ghostly Shapes
May meet at noontide; Fear and trembling Hope,
Silence and Foresight; Death the Skeleton
And Time the Shadow;—there to celebrate,
As in a natural temple scattered o'er
30   With altars undisturbed of mossy stone,
United worship; or in mute repose
To lie, and listen to the mountain flood
Murmuring from Glaramara's inmost caves.

I

Michael Riffaterre's essay on Wordsworth's "Yew-Trees" is, in substance, the best commentary on that poem yet written and ranks with the best commentaries on any Wordsworth poem.[1] Moreover, in the exposition of a method of analysis, it is an equally impressive act, whose significance for the study of poetry—not only descriptive poetry of Wordsworth's kind—is considerable. My own comment here can only be supplementary to Riffaterre's, but it will try to locate certain limits of the structural-semantic method he employs. I am also interested in the role played by history—or assumptions about it—in this kind of analysis.[2]

It is a truism, of course, that no method can guarantee an interpretation. At most it can assure an open, articulate, and transferable kind of analytic procedure. But two specific remarks can be made of all methods or techniques of analysis, including Riffaterre's: (1) They are unable to determine, qua method, what finding is to be emphasized. (2) Methods are backed up by methodizers: there is a person in the machine. Consequently, even where the method successfully disciplines the personal factor, the latter can still make its appearance, as in the choice of the object of analysis: this poem rather than that. Without claiming that Riffaterre's analysis could not yield significant results when applied to other Wordsworth poems, one suspects that "Yew-Trees" cooperates with the method because there is a harmony between the curious impersonality of this "descriptive" or "nature" poem and the desired impersonality of structural-semantic analysis. Yet precisely here, on this matter of what happens to "person" or "subject" in the method or in the poem, Riffaterre's analysis proves vulnerable, though far from wrong. Let me begin, however, with a synopsis of his findings.

Riffaterre states that (1) even in "descriptive" verse the words are not there only to describe real trees and other objects, but are also part of a "system" with its own grammatical-semantic correlation. He names the belief in the direct signifying function or real reference of words the "referential fallacy." (2) This deflection from referentiality is enabled by the fact that the word system can extend beyond the boundary of the sentence to encompass the totality of the poem. Riffaterre elaborates clearly the advantages of this verbo-poetic logic which he defines as "an ideal model for various chains of . . . associations," "an imaginary space in which . . . components are distributed so as to define their reciprocal functions," "strings of semantic equivalences." (3) Because of this reciprocity or equivalence an overdetermination occurs which both founds meanings and eventually deprives the reader of his interpretive freedom. All functions "converge and concur irresistibly toward the one single significance. . . ." (4) In this particular poem, the structure of significance starts from a chain in which the *tree* cluster of associations issues in the *ghost* variant, at which point (25) meaning is no longer conveyed by richly redundant variations on certain commonplaces. The personifications of lines 25ff. literalize meaning without giving us a symbolic key to it. What is being worshiped by these ghosts? There is something like a riddle here, "circuitous . . . pointers surrounding a semantic hole"; this indeterminacy culminates in a near-onomatopoeic "soundscape" which reinforces the theme of mere-listening-to-sound (the second "action" ascribed to the ghosts [31-33]), and again resists symbolic meaning. "Far from being a letdown after the symbolic meanings of the first part, the strict literalness of the end is a climax. Its significance lies in the meaninglessness of the sound. Sensation is all—which is exactly what descriptive poetry is about."

My excerpting of a long and skillful paper cannot do it justice. There is no doubt that Riffaterre achieves one of the highest aims of commentary: local illumination of the words of a text together with the foregrounding of a structure that provides a skeleton key for other poems and situates the object of analysis in generic terms ("descriptive poetry"). The analysis is at once minute in its attention to particulars and theoretically ambitious.

II. "The Yew-tree had its ghost": *The Prelude*

A more intuitive approach, guided by the genius of Wordsworth's language, could endorse almost all these findings. Riffaterre's key insight—the imbalance between "mere sound" and "the infinity of thought," or the opposition *water murmuring / dulls the pangs of mortality*—is, as he suggests, central to Wordsworth's aesthetics; and even the relatively unsystematic analysis found at the end of my Wordsworth chapter in *The Unmediated Vision* reaches a similar conclusion.[3] It is equally clear, however, that an essential feature of "Yew-Trees" has been slighted. I allude to the poem's elision of the human intermediary or observer:[4] *elision* being a better word than *absence* because the perceptions obviously issue from a speaking source that is human, though not explicitly localized as such.

The elision begins with the opening phrase, "There is," an impersonal notation when compared to, say, "I know of" or "I am told of." The impersonal constructions continue and on occasion strongly animate what is inanimate. It is suggested, for example, that the tree has a kind of will (it is "Not loth to furnish weapons...''); while Wordsworth's image of "sounding bows" is like an ablauted variant of "sounding boughs" and creates an echo-metaphor intimating a magical or superstitious persistence of the yew's life—as if the wood retained its original characteristics even in this changed form.

Only at lines 25ff., when the ghost personifications appear, does Riffaterre note the elision: "The listening subject is normally actualized in the person of the narrator. The difference in 'Yew-Trees' is of course that the narrator's thoughts, the ghosts, take his place as listener." But what is true of the *listening subject* has been true of the *speaking subject* all along. The speaking subject never appears on the scene: of him too we could say that "the narrator's thoughts, the ghosts, take his place." The strong device of personification reveals a more inobvious and deeply sustaining figure. From the very beginning we must accept the voice that speaks as, somehow, akin to the Yew-tree itself in ghostly extension or longevity.

Why has no one raised the question of who is speaking here or whose voice it is? At one point Riffaterre says casually: "The descriptive poem, like most of Wordsworth's texts of this kind, is also a narrative in the first person (implicit here)." This shows the danger of such hypostatized genres as "descriptive poetry." It also supports our contention that no method can determine what findings are to be emphasized. Riffaterre chooses not to develop, on the other hand, such a strong figurative device as the personifications—though here too he fails to remark how unusual personification is in Wordsworth,[5] how Wordsworth's literary polemic is against it, and how this very poem evades explicit personification until the strong lines at the end breach the poet's reserve.

That there is a disturbance centering on the concept of personification is not irrelevant to the question of who is speaking, or why no one has raised that question. Speech is assumed to be human, and where it is not so we expect the poet to indicate explicitly that he is personifying, or using a mythological idea. No one has raised the question because of the convention that what is normal does not have to be made obvious. Wordsworth, or someone like him, must be the speaker: if the title does not specify *quercus loquitur*, we assume *poeta loquitur*. Surely it is no tree spirit or personified guardian whose voice is represented here?

Yet the shadow of an indeterminacy remains, and for equally conventional reasons. There is a poetic tradition in which a tree or long-lived though mute object is made to speak: perhaps an oracular oak, perhaps a ruined castle, perhaps a genius loci.[6] (See Appendix, p. 151.) While no such "eternity structure" or "speaking monument" is visibly posited by Wordsworth, the adjacence of such a convention to the elision of the human intermediary in "Yew-Trees" suggests that the poet has subsumed or refined an archaic genre, and created in its stead a composite "descriptive" sketch which still expresses feelings or features essential to the older genre. This displacement from mythic into what is often called meditative or descriptive verse is a Wordsworthian characteristic and if explored would tell us something about poetic as well as human time: that is, about the relation of Wordsworth's poetry to archaic forms, whether these involve religious ideas or superstitions, concepts of genre, venerable devices such as personification, or poetic diction generally.

All figuration, Wordsworth held, must be grounded in feeling, in a recoverable emotion which would justify the apparently archaic form and explain its persistence. A purely formal interpretation could link Wordsworth's impersonality here to his interest in the ballad as a "Relique of Ancient English Poetry." "There is a Yew-tree" might be construed as a variant of "There is a Thorn: It looks so old. . . ." Ballad and Yew-tree are homologous: reliques, English, part of the poetry of nature. The poet's respect for local tradition (much of the information in the first dozen lines may come from that source) could also be linked to this interest in ballads. But what feeling allows the form to survive, and creates in "Yew-Trees" a mutant ballad, "descriptive" rather than "lyrical"?

Now Wordsworth is obviously not a Polonius when it comes to genres. Rather, his feeling for the Yew-tree, in its historic actuality or as a totemic figure in literary discourse, revives the truth of that *imaginative transference* which is at the root of opposite yet related devices essential to poetry: impersonation (personification, animistic metaphor), on the one hand, and impersonal constructions eliding narrator or human intermediary on the other. Negation of self is, in both, accompanied by a magnified sense of the other which leads to mythic, archaic, or spectral symbols. The yews make a ghost of the speaker.

This feeling of ghostliness is, possibly, an imaginative need rather than the direct precipitate of a yew-tree experience: what matters is Wordsworth's inward grounding of an idea of ghostliness that motivates elision of self-reference. The archaic or literary forms subsumed by Wordsworth are the literal spooks of Gothic ballad or tale, and the etiolated personifications endemic to poetic diction. In a poet like Collins these urbane and demonic types of ghostly personification blend uneasily. In a poet like Shelley they also blend uneasily. Wordsworth's poetic reflection, however, centers not on figures of speech alone but also on speech as a figure: that is, on the relation between spectral feeling and poetic voice. The "riddling" quality which Riffaterre attaches to the dramatic intrusion of archaic personification resides in the modality of poetic speech itself—at least from the moment we ask, who is speaking?

Trees do not "speak" to Wordsworth any more than to us. They are mute, like the gods are mute; yet "the speaking face of nature" is as understandable a metaphor as "the still, sad music of humanity." An act of listening precedes or is constitutive of the naturalized oracular voice we hear in Wordsworth's poem. Although no listener appears till the end of "Yew-Trees," he is there all the time, as the poet-medium who "listens" to nature, to the trees, to local tradition, to his own ominous or sensitive imagination—to "Nothing that is not there and the nothing that is."

III

Riffaterre overlooks the problem of voice or of the poet as intermediary. Is this a simple flaw or is it connected with the "impersonality" of the structural method? His remark that "the narrator's thoughts, the ghosts, take his place," localizes an effect which is all-pervasive, though reaching a telltale climax with the personficiations of lines 25ff. The poet's extroverted use of personification is taken too literally and his use of elision not literally enough. It seems like a mistake anyone might make. But it could be motivated by a misleading idea on how poems "develop": as if the end of a poem must show a thematic or semantic increment over its beginning. This too is a common assumption. What makes the mistake suspicious is that it involves concepts of voice and time, and these precisely are what the structural method cannot handle except (as here) by reducing them to a semantic-thematic drift. Wordsworth's lyric, moreover, conspires with this kind of eternity-structuring because it records how the sense of human time is phantomized by the ancient yews. Their span of years compared to ours leads us into thoughts of eternity.

Riffaterre refers to the experience of phantomization, but in a strange and limiting way. "The yew is not described in relation to the tree of that name, but as an image of an existence closer to Eternity than ours." A wedge is driven by such an interpretation between name and thing as surely as in Platonic theories of mimesis. The yews become, in fact, a kind of Idea ("image of an existence closer to Eternity"), and the poem a way of approaching it by an ideal, that is, nonreferential use of words. The authenticity of poetry as a temporal art is diminished by importing an unprogressive (Platonic) or too easily progressive (semantic-thematic) concept of development.

Though the structural approach claims to deal with the representation of reality as a "verbal construct in which meaning is achieved by reference from words to words, not to things," it does not guarantee an understanding of words as a temporal medium. The method, moreover, elides the status of poetry as mediation by emphasizing the status of language as a determining—and vis-à-vis the reader—deterministic medium. The subjectivity of both author and reader is reduced by the concept of a "reading" that "allows the reader no freedom of choice in the understanding of descriptive details." All these details, Riffaterre goes on, "converge and concur irresistibly toward the one single significance, once the sequence has started moving—all function as structural variants of that obsessive, rapidly overwhelming semantic variant."

Yet do things roll on so roundly and irresistibly here? It might be argued instead that the merging of casual deictic phrasing ("There is a Yew-tree") and oracular pronouncement ("There is a Yew-tree") creates a peculiarly Wordsworthian tone, hovering between pompous cliché and sublime simplicity. This counterpoint of understatement and overstatement is found even in the general development of the poem, where the initial, understated figure (the impersonal construction) leads into an overstated figure (the strong personifications). The thought ghosts of the poet become ghost thoughts. This "Gothic" reversal, of course, never literally takes place, it merely threatens to take place: the poem evokes a borderline situation where voice is environed by ghostly pressures yet maintains an in-betweenness. The in-between character of the Wordsworthian narrative voice can be interpreted in several, nonexclusive ways: as indicating a tension between mutism and oracular eloquence, or self-depletion (the self phantomized by a sublime experience) and self-redemption (through identification with the sublime), and so forth. Coming closer to Wordsworth's own terms, one could emphasize a split between humanizing and eternizing movements of thought: the poet, haunted by the "unimaginable touch of Time," puts himself or a surrogate beyond the "touch of earthly years."[7]

If there is no irresistible sequence, there is also no "starter" or "system component which triggers the sequence" except the poem's first phrase. But any first-term theory makes one suspicious, and suggests in its begetter a sin against time. "Thought hath no beginning," Wordsworth wrote: we are always in the midst, or several beginnings exist among which we must choose. My personal way of linking the poem to a dominant theme or "overwhelming variant" would be to bring to bear a series of juxtapositions which might (1) encompass the mode of the poem by transforming "speaking monument" to "speaking tree" (sounding boughs / sounding bows) and "conscious (oracular) cave"; and (2) analyze the problematic situation of consciousness itself. Consciousness is problematic in these verses because it is *absent* as a representamen (there is no "I"), problematic elsewhere in Wordsworth because it is *present* as an embarrassed, garrulous, naive, or egotistical voice.

If the absence of self-reference points to a "ghostliness" in the self, the presence of strong personification points to a "ghostliness" in fictional or rhetorical language. The "riddle" of the poem turns on the relation of imagination to rhetoric, on the one hand, and of imagination to human time and personal identity on the other. The riddle brings the simple content of "Yew-Trees" as a poem about oracular places once more into view.

Yews are identified with the oracular by their longevity and funerary character. In so subtly eliding the human intermediary, Wordsworth evokes a state of consciousness directed toward a quasi-eternal object and proceeding from a quasi-eternal repose. What is that state, however, if not an imagined kind of death? Where could the speech, which is the poem, come from if not from a mind that has outlived itself: a posthumous mind which reposes in that funerary bower of yews? By a proleptic act of imagination, then, the poet speaks to us from the grave. He provides us with a speech monument, a funerary inscription, a meditation as exemplary as "Tintern Abbey" on what may survive.

Foreseeing always runs the danger of death-seeing. Think of Thomas Gray's "Ode on a Distant Prospect of Eton College" with its ghostly personifications. Wordsworth's poem, like Gray's, recalls the sixth book of *The Aeneid*, which vividly pictures the gates of hell beset by a swarm of evil personifications—and in their midst an opaque elm, its branches full of clinging dreams. "Yew-Trees" emerges into a more soothing prospect, perhaps even into the "peace which passeth understanding."[8] As in Virgil, however, the prophetic threshold is shadowed by a threshold peril: the mind of the poet could disappear into that dark wood of dreams.

IV

It is strange to think of "Yew-Trees" as a ghostly ballad. Yet voice in Wordsworth is often a "wandering utterance,"[9] an echo existing before as well as after the poem which gives it a home. What he names the "ghostly language of the ancient earth"[10] is transmitted not by nature alone but also by "wandering" stories that attach themselves to this or that place, inciting nature poetry, or "localized romance." These stories seem to have an impersonal existence; and we are reminded that literary structuralism gained its inaugural success with Propp's analysis of such wandering legends or ballads.

The anonymous or impersonal status of these narratives suggests that they are, like the yews, a kind of triumph over time. They reveal constants which survive all intermixture and accretion. Narrative is the field of combination which foregrounds, by repetition, these constants; yet in the ballads of Wordsworth narrative is vulnerable, as if voice were more ghostly than any story could show or as if time no longer had time. The wonder-wandering of romance or the temporal spatiousness of storytelling is reduced, even punctured, by an urgency I have elsewhere called apocalyptic, but which generally presents itself as a breaking or undoing or interruption of the narrative line.

There is, virtually, no narrative in "Yew-Trees." The question is less what interrupts the narrative line than how so static a poem makes time and keeps moving. It is no problem for Riffaterre. His structuralism puts language where the subjectivity or consciousness of the poet might be: words are analyzed into kernel statements and chains of derivation. A poem conjugates itself by sequences of words correlatively grammatical and semantic. So all the details in lines 16 to 18 are said to be "but a grammatical expansion of the meaning of the word 'growth' which is in itself only a generalization of 'trunk.'"

Riffaterre's phraseology is not beyond question. Why "expansion" rather than "repetition"? Is grammar always expansive? Is he insinuating a generous metaphor, which views language as a tree of life, branching out into lollipops of words? I am not so sure that Wordsworth's yews are such a tree of life. The relation of these yews to grammar—to articulate speech or writing—is uncertain. So the very first phrase of the poem has an absoluteness which the rest of the sentence qualifies without modifying. Speech seems always about to stop. Every clause or addition, even past the full stop of line 8, is but an appositive to "There is a Yew-tree." The same holds true of the second subject phrase—"those fraternal Four of Borrowdale." What follows has something of the accretive development of a cult hymn, and more should be said about the cultic stutter of this so-called descriptive poetry. Riffaterre's brilliant observation that "in the midst of its own darkness" reverses a characteristic representation of epiphany is used only to reveal a sequence culminating in the "natural temple" theme.

The progression of Wordsworth's poem (noted by Riffaterre) toward a final perspective that alleviates the burden of the mystery is, it seems to me, a halting one, and as precarious as that final perspective itself. To ascribe an auto-motive potential to the language of poetry demystifies it prematurely and fails to weigh the relation of cultic and grammatical.

A canceled ending[11] fortifies our sense that Wordsworth's description is partially inspired by cultic forms. The duplicitous character of his verbal style—the blending of under- and overstatement—allows a number of double readings: cultic-descriptive, cultic-grammatical, descriptive-grammatical. Because Wordsworth's symbols are underdetermined *topoi* ("kernels" in Riffaterre's phrase), they can be expanded in the way he shows, but they may also be viewed as dream-like and overdetermined *places* (fixations) impeding real consecutiveness and narrative flow. "There is a Yew-tree" seems as simple and understated an opening as "There was a Boy," but it could also be a minimalist's epiphany, or an elegiac anticipation of the disappearance from earth of such natural temples.

A reading which recovers the strange interplay of cultic feeling and modern self-consciousness will also recover the precarious subjectivity of the poet. Consider the phenomenon of centroversion in Wordsworth: how his mind circles and haunts a particular place until released into an emancipatory idea of Nature. The yews, in this light, are *omphaloi*: boundary images, or signs of a liminal situation, a cultic and charged threshold.[12] As we follow the poet's words we are kept moving along a border between natural and supernatural ideas; and there is no guarantee he might not go over the line into a dark and discontinous fantasy.

"Nor uninformed with Phantasy, and looks / That threaten the profane"— he could go over the line right there. His description of the Borrowdale yews does more than evoke a natural temple. "Phantasy," hypostatized this way, is already a spooky personification: a kind of snake or guardian monster of the grove. To reduce line 19 to topos or figure diminishes the phenomenality of words. We cannot exclude the possibility that "the forms / Of Nature have a passion in themselves,"[13] though Wordsworth's hint of that is characteristically defensive ("Nor uninformed...").

Yet even the negatives have a quasi-narrative function. They protract the poem, and cue us to the vulnerability of a thinker who is extending so "heavy" a thought that it tends to collapse his medium. The verbal shape of "Uninformed" is especially interesting. *Un / in* presses on the root word *form*, all the more so if the context makes *un* and *um* converge. ("Uninformed" is preceded by *Um*fraville, circ*um*ference, and followed by *um*brage, *un*rejoicing, *un*disturbed.) The impression is subtle: read, for example, "Nor unformed with Phantasy," and nearly the same meaning obtains. The *in* and *un* struggle to come together as one intense meaning, while *um* presents itself as a stronger or heavier *un*. The final verse's reduplicative onomatopoeia liquefies this pattern (absorbing the vowel plus *r* effect from the "Nor...o'er...or" sequence), as if the convergence of *n* and *m* into some mutist sound *nm, nn,* or *mm,* had been overcome, though "inmost" echoes the danger.

Such verses are "produced too slowly." There are several other impediments to easy progression. They are felt more, it is true, in lines 19ff. "Nor uninformed with Phantasy," helped by the preceding image of convolution, definitely turns the poem away from efficiently linked commonplaces. Even the latter, however, did not get far from an absolute phrase or concept. Each new phrase in lines 1-18 touches back to "There is a Yew-tree" through apposition or some lingering, contiguous device of this sort. No strong main verbs join the three sentences which make up the entire poem—perhaps two sentences, since line 9 does not really introduce a new subject or verb, so that the period at the end of line 8 is more like a semicolon. Line 9, in fact, could easily have come immediately after line 1 or line 3, so close are we still to the original theme. The impression can arise that Wordsworth would have liked to anticipate and close with the simple exclamation "This solitary Tree!"

After line 19 dashes multiply, phrases accumulate, and we approach an enumeration which is near-chaotic (near-ecstatic), yet carefully reticulated by an abundance of particles. On the one hand, pillared shade, sable roof, ghostly shapes, Death the Skeleton, natural temple, United worship, etc.; on the other, upon, by, beneath, of, as if, for, with, etc. "United worship" (31) may not be an adjective-noun phrase, but it could be, so weak are the preceding verbs and so forceful the pull of the noun phrases. Other obstacles to an easy manner of proceeding are such tmetic insertions as "undisturbed" (30), weak joining words, "o'er / With" (29-30) followed by "or in" (31), and the occasional sense that one word is the scrambled echo of another: "noontide" (26), "united" (31).

"United" is, in fact, the most intriguing case. Its equivocal syntax has been mentioned; but in sound, too, there is an equivocation. The *un* sequence may lead to a momentary and illusory reading of it as *un-ited*. ("Umbrage," in a previous line, if we are sensitive to the *un / um* morpheme, may split into a punning compound, "shadow-age," an undersense supported by the more obvious pun in "pining."[14] The reader, of course, resolves the riddle word *un-ited* by the proper, forward movement. But once the word has been slowed or foregrounded in this way, a new, less commonsensical deciphering may suggest itself. It again brings the poem to a halt or condenses it as one riddling phrase. *United* could be read *U*nited, that is, *Yew*nited (Yewnighted).

V

Make not your rosaries of yew-berries

Keats, *Ode on Melancholy*

Slowing the reader makes him aware that the forms of language, like those of nature, "have a passion in themselves." A snake lies coiled within "Phantasy." The slowing of reading also makes him aware of time. Like language, time is more than a medium. There seems to be no way to force its growth or to subdue it to the predictable. Time has the erratic motion of a snake coiled up.[15] There is something treacherous in the flow of time or of words which makes Wordsworth exceedingly cautious. Though English is not a jungle, Wordsworth is more in the tropics than Huxley would have us believe.

Wordsworth's "yewnity," a dream word disturbing further the not undisturbed realism of the poem, has the dark appeal of its double or compound character. Half-perceived, half-created by the reader, it is a centaur shape guiding him to a new understanding of how words and things, signifier and signified, connect. It suggests the possibility of a strangely mimetic or organic literary form, of a language of nature: here is a kernel out of which, however unconsciously— by vegetable genius—the poem grows. "Yewnity" suggests a model for analysis imitating the branchings of tree or flower from a deeply nurtured, perhaps covert, point:

So from the root
Springs lighter the green stalk, from thence the leaves
More aery, last the bright consummate flow'r....
. . . flow'rs and thir fruit
Man's nourishment, by gradual scale sublim'd....

(*Paradise Lost* V, 479-83)

Paradigm Lost, something echoes in us. For the yew standing in the midst of its own darkness is the opposite of a heliotrope. A melantropic or nightshade plant, it evokes a persephonic kind of nourishment and the role of darkness in the growth of the mind—especially the poet's mind:

> Vallombre's groves
> Entering, we fed the soul with darkness...
>
> I called on Darkness....
>
> Visionary power
> Attends the motions of the viewless winds,
> Embodied in the mystery of words:
> There, darkness makes abode, and all the host
> Of shadowy things work endless changes....
>
> There I beheld the emblem of a mind
> That feeds upon infinity, that broods
> Over the dark abyss, intent to hear
> Its voices....[16]

At this point the reader becomes uncertain. He is asked to view darkness as an element of growth. But what darkness is meant? That which surrounds Milton, his night labor? Or is it a solitariness bordering on solipsism? Or a visionary dreariness close to psychotic dejection: ghostly, apocalyptic thoughts; some morbid or empathic or self-emptying identification? In short, a counter-Enlightenment sense of what nurtures the inspired or demonic artist?

"Yewnity" evokes a drive for fellowship with essence which can be as draining as a vampire. "My heart aches, and a drowsy numbness pains / My sense...." The sympathetic imagination may darken into "horrid sympathy." There could be depletion, loss of self, loss of control. The post-Petrarchan love poem is not the only locus of this ambivalent ecstasy, this absence / presence vacillation. Even Coleridge's perpetual quest to hold the one and the many in the palm of his mind, by such semigreek, semimonstrous wordages as "Esemplastic" and "Unitrine," brings us into the realm of sudden reversals. What if in "Unitrine" the word-drugged mind suddenly hears "urine"?

Consider a characteristic observation from Coleridge's *Notebooks*: "Fancy and Sleep *stream* on; and (instead of outward Forms and Sounds, the Sanctifiers, the Strengtheners!) they connect with them motions of the blood and nerves, and images forced into the mind by the feelings that arise out of the position & state of the Body and its different members...Thank Heaven! however / Sleep has never desecrated the images, or supposed Presences, of those I love and revere."[17] The yews, in this darkness visible, are like Virgil's elm full of a difficult, even obscene shadow life. The poem, however, is by Wordsworth, not Coleridge: why view it, then, through the focus of a quack linguistic compound, "yewnity"? Or why not stress, as a benightmared Coleridge does, the "outward Forms and Sounds, the Sanctifiers, the Strengtheners!"?

A reader's responsibility is not easily defined. He must decide how much darkness is to be developed. It is always a matter of "yewnity" versus "unity," whoever wrote the poem. For a "yewnifying" critic darkness is of the essence: the persephonic food cannot be separated from the bright cereal. In some interpreters, of course, there are three parts of light to one of darkness, as in the Persephone myth itself. Only one season is given to Hades. Some interpreters are more evangelical still, and reduce the part of darkness to that which allows the light to shine or the grain to die in order to ripen. Others are more willing to be badnewsmen. No one can remove the reader's responsibility entirely: in this, to each his own conscience. But Wordsworth's poem, taken as a model, suggests that the relation between dark and light or heliotropic and melantropic readings, is only precariously "unificent." In fact, to deny imagination its darker food, to seek and make it a "Shape all light," is to wish imagination away.

Darkness, as I use it here, is a metaphor, though justified not only by "Yew-Trees" but also by an entire group of poems that have melancholy for their subject. More precisely, their subject is the curious link between melancholy and imagination. The group accompanies the friendship of Wordsworth and Coleridge in the seminal period of 1797-1804. The theme of melancholy was, of course, a topical one, and survives into the "Despondency Corrected" section of Wordsworth's *The Excursion*. The profiles of poetical character and gloomy egotist seemed to merge; and whatever the cause of the perceived link between them—between imagination and melancholy—Wordsworth thought that Nature might temper and even undo it. The one myth he allowed himself was that Nature could turn the "self-haunting spirit" outward and make it excursive once more. Yeats said that acquaintance with Chaucer's poetry had redeemed his imagination from abstraction, from a void which was the breeding place of visionary thoughts. So Nature, in Wordsworth, is an antivisionary or anti-self-consciousness principle. One impulse from nature—"one soft impulse saved from vacancy"—may turn the imaginative mind from sterile self-regard or a fruitless brooding on its own abyss.

Coleridge participated in this myth of Nature and may have helped to elaborate it. Yet he never could internalize those strengthening and steadying "outward Forms." "I may not hope from outward forms to win / The passion and the life, whose fountains are within," as he wrote in April 1802, in what was to become the "Dejection Ode." Where are those fountains in yet another April, that of 1798?

> No cloud, no relique of the sunken day
> Distinguishes the West, no long thin slip
> Of sullen light, no obscure trembling hues.[18]

Life seems as shrunk or sunk as in Donne's "Nocturnal upon St. Lucy's Day." Yet the poet sees the night filled with invigorating and sanctifying forms. He clears the nightingale of the melancholy attributed to it by "penseroso" man.

"In Nature there is nothing melancholy." The nightingale is set, with moon and star, against the night: it is a wakeful, clear, "allegro" ("Like tipsy Joy that reels with tossing head") presence. So also, in his own tree poem of 1799, "This Lime-tree Bower my Prison," he looks to those "outward Forms" for a support accidentally or fatefully denied him. He imagines others enjoying them while he sits darkling.

Wordsworth, interestingly enough, had anticipated his friend in a poem that could have been called "This Yew-Tree Bower a Prison":

> Nay, Traveller! rest. This lonely Yew-tree stands
> Far from all human dwelling. . . .
>
>   Who he was
> That piled these stones and with the mossy sod
> First covered o'er, and taught this aged Tree
> Now wild, to bend its arms in circling shade,
> I well remember. . . .
>
>   Stranger! these gloomy boughs
> Had charms for him; and here he loved to sit,
> His only visitants a straggling sheep,
> The stone-chat, or the glancing sand-piper. . . .
>   and so, lost Man!
>
> On visionary views would fancy feed,
> Till his eye streamed with tears. In this deep vale
> He died,—this seat his only monument.

"Lines Left upon a Seat in a Yew-tree"[19] seems to have been communicated to Coleridge by Charles Lamb, and may have directly inspired "This Lime-tree Bower." The antimelancholy group of poems can be said to begin with it, unless we count Coleridge's early "To the Nightingale" (1795), superseded by his famous "conversation poem" of 1798. The relation between the two poets is not a simple one, whether in 1797, when these verses were composed, or in 1803/04 when "Yew-Trees" may have been conceived, or in 1815 when Coleridge begins the *Biographia Literaria*, partly in reaction to Wordsworth's *Collected Poems*, which printed "Yew-Trees" for the first time in a section entitled "Poems of the Imagination." We don't know how Coleridge read "Yew-Trees" except for the fact that he cited it in the *Biographia Literaria* (chapter 22) as instancing that "imaginative power" in which "[Wordsworth] stands nearest of all modern writers to Shakespeare and Milton; and yet in a kind perfectly unborrowed and his own."

The drive toward unity, then, includes the relation between the two poets. Yet within that drive there is a difference. Wordsworth's yews are certainly outward forms, and set a limit to nightmare. In fact, the power of the Wordsworthian mode, as Coleridge describes it in the *Biographia*, is precisely in its ability to create an aura of the supernatural without distorting the outward, natural forms.[20] Wordsworth does not couple with the dark as Coleridge seems forced to do in his night terrors and poems like "The Ancient Mariner," which *stream on*.[21] He goes slowly—too slowly, sometimes; an obverse distortion is then produced which tells us that here, too, time is out of joint. And while Wordsworth's trees remain trees, unmetamorphosed by myth or imagination, they are not purely "outward Forms," "Sanctifiers," "Strengtheners." The four of Borrowdale, which are several-in-one like the poem's phantom personifications, suggest a near-vampiristic pressure of unification. Does that pressure come from an oneiric or theurgic or sexual-organic source? Can we go further still and see in this *yewnity* the "express resemblance" of the power called Imagination by Wordsworth and the romantics?

VI

It would be hard to think of a more striking symbol for *in eins Bildung*, Coleridge's false etymologizing of *imagination*, or rather of its German equivalent, *Einbildungskraft*. Wordsworth himself, in his Preface of 1815, cites with approval Charles Lamb's definition of imagination as that power which "draws all things to one; which makes things animate or inanimate, beings with their attributes, subjects with their accessaries, take one colour and serve to one effect." But it is Coleridge who cannot leave the concept or the word alone. Not uncharacteristically, he dissolves the word into strange roots and derivations, as if it had to be resynthesized with the help of German or Greek. "Eisenoplasy, or esenoplastic Power.... 'Esemplastic. The word is not in Johnson, nor have I met with it elsewhere.' Neither have I. I have constructed it myself from the Greek words, εἰς ἕν πλάττειν, to shape into one...."[22] The natural forms of language, under this pressure of reconstruction, project new and distorted shapes, perhaps oneiric, perhaps metaphysical. It is with words as with things: Coleridge "streams" beyond their natural form. There is an "uttermost"[23] quality to his etymological word chains and definitions.

This learned or playful yet always compulsive manipulation of words is linked by Coleridge's *Notebooks* to his quest for unity in all areas of life, including the most personal. His concern with imagination reflects directly his concern with Wordsworth's quality of life and mind. Wishing to be unified—atoned—with the Wordsworth household, he devises magical and quasi-theological emblems which suggest the possibility of his inclusion (See his 1805 notebook entry reproduced on pp. 144-45[24]). The "one life" he always seeks requires here an "in eins Bildung" of four-(five)-in one. From such *Notebook* entries it is easier to understand the pressure that made chapter 13 of the *Biographia*, grandly entitled "On the Imagination, or Esemplastic Power," deteriorate into fragments, or why he spars with Wordsworth over "poetic diction"—in some respects a magical technique rather than a natural language—or why he is so involved in panentheistic notions.[25]

Coleridge, of course, does not overlook the demonic side of this imaginative desire for unity, and especially not in his friend. He wants to be part of Wordsworth's "yewnity"—of his family tree—yet sees the moral cost. "There is a dark / Inscrutable workmanship," Wordsworth write in his poem on the Growth of a Poet's Mind, "that reconciles / Discordant elements, makes them cling together / In one society."[26] This growth into unity could be perceived as that of a selfish weed, absorbing the life around it, and actually creating the darkness it seems to change into life. After his quarrel with Wordsworth, never entirely made up, Coleridge becomes more sharply aware of the shadow side of his friend's character. While working on the *Biographia*, and laboring to differentiate himself from Wordsworth, he confides what he calls a "Gnostic Whisper" to his "white-faced Friend" and "negative Comforter"—that is, his notebook, which has effectively taken the place of his other, now uncomforting friend:

*In*firmities sunk under, the Conscious Soul mourning and disapproving, are less hindrances than *Anti*firmities—such as *Self*-ness = the $\epsilon\iota\delta\omega\lambda o\nu$ = το ον, $<$ = το εν χαι πᾶν : and *separative* instead of being, what it ought to be, at once *distinctive* and yet, at the same moment or rather act, *conjunctive, nay, unificent!* I will not refer to 'Αυστραλις; but to a *truly* great GENIUS, 'Αξιόλογος—Were *intellect* only in question, στς would rather groan under his manifold sins & sorrows, all either contained in or symbolized by, ΩΠΜ, than cherish that self-concentration of $<$ Αξ....

Community with nature; $+$ the Eye & Heart intuitive of *all* living yet *One* Life in all; $+$ the modifying Imagination, the true creative, εσενοπλασιχος, ενεργεια; $+$ robur intellectuale—Σεπτεντρ ιονίσμου ....[27]

2623 18.1
fı'

$$\left.\begin{array}{l} \text{William} \\ \text{Dorothy} \\ \text{Mary} \end{array}\right\} \text{Wordsworth}$$

$$\left.\begin{array}{l} \text{S. T.} \\ \text{Sara} \end{array}\right\} \text{Coleridge}$$

$<$ O blessed Flock! I the sole scabbed Sheep!
And even me they love, awake, asleep. $>$

$$W + D + M = \underline{W. + STC + SH} = \text{Ενοπεντας}$$

$<$ Well—and if it be Illusion—yet surely an Illusion, which acts at all times and in all moods and places, awake, asleep; sick, & in health;

alone, and in company; in sorrow and in Joy; present or absent; in
moments of self-condemnation and self-acquittal; o surely that Illusion
is hardly distinguishable, from Truth / *Reality* it assuredly is—and such
is the Illusion if Illusion it must be, that I am persuaded, I love
W.M.D.S. better than myself, & myself chiefly in them. >

2624 18.2

$f_1{}^v, f_2$

ΣAPA	Coleridge		W+M+D=W	Coleridge
William	Dorothy		William	Mary

Coleridge (like Hazlitt, Keats, and Shelley) is seeking to come to grips with the
extraordinary "self-ness" of Wordsworth, which seems to contradict the latter's
concept of the sympathetic imagination so influential on the younger romantics.
The conflict, in emblem form, is that of oak versus yew, of "robur intellectuale"
versus "yewnity." It continues a contrast between Milton and Shakespeare which
meant so much to an age seeking to define the "poetical character." Shelley
added to this Garden of Genius the mimosa or Sensitive Plant; while Keats's
notion of negative capability sought to reconcile the empathic or animistic verve
of imagination with skeptical robustness.

In "Yew-Trees" there is an imaginative merging with the trees, yet no liter-
alization of an archaic or superstitious figure occurs. To identify even formally
with such a figure—to become the voice of the yews— is to be no more than
Coelus' "region-whisper" in Keats: "I am but a voice. / My life is but the life of
winds and tides" (*Hyperion* I, 340). Poetry would regress to the Ovidian mode
and lose itself again in "Fable's dark abyss." Wordsworth modifies not only the
instinctual drive toward unity but even the imaginative drive toward such visionary figures as intimate the possibility of unity or metamorphosis, of a transformation *in allo genere.*

Yet the yews are not merely figures of discourse. They are yews. Wordsworth's
scruples concerning figuration, if only that, would make him an even drier pur-
itan of the imagination than he is. Words need saying only as much as the things

they stand for. If the poet is tempted to identify with the yews to the extent of becoming their voice, it means the trees are threatened.

What threatens them? And how far must a poet identify with them for the threat to be removed? If Wordsworth identifies with them, and they disappear nevertheless, what is left of him or to him? "And O, ye Fountains, Meadows, Hills, and Groves, / Forbode not any severing of our loves!"[28] We enter a perspective which links the poet to nature. His fate is bound up with that of the yews, a peculiar bond that must still be clarified.

VII

Thine arms have left thee....

William Cowper, *Yardley Oak*

The image of the yews changes as the poem develops. While the Lorton yew is provident of arms, the Borrowdale grove seems to sustain, if anything, only the "phantasy." To say "sustain" is not totally appropriate, for when the theme of nutriment is actually introduced in lines 24-25 ("festal purpose," "unrejoicing berries"), it points to a deadly or sacrificial rather than to a nurturing sustenance. Indeed, the "looks" of the trees are now like arms directed against the "profane" observer. Though pastoral, these yews are also martial, as if girding us for a warfare not dependent on war—for a spiritual combat associated perhaps with the "ghostly Shapes" now mentioned.

Milton had sought to revalue the theme of epic warfare by emptying it of what he mocked as "tilting furniture"; and there is a comparable emptying of ballad or lyric in Wordsworth, who writes without remarkable incidents, plot, or visionary artifice. Having removed self-reference from the poem, he at the end also distances the yews, as if they, too, were so much "furniture." A few ghostly abstractions remain, listening to far-away sounds. What sort of warfare is this?

What is being waged is peace rather than war. It is a peace that does not come easily here: the wise passiveness, the mighty heart lying still, the burden of the mystery lightened. A peace too much like death, we murmur. For the implied self-emptying is so great that it threatens to take nature with it. The "pillared shade," though better than a temple made of pillars—"Quam si repostus sub trabe citrea / Fulgeret auro, et Phidiaca manu"—still stands between us and unmediated vision.[29] The threat to the yews as emblems of the nearness of nature to eternity comes from within the very drive for "yewnity." Repose from that drive is the peace for which Wordsworth strives. It would mean atonement of the guilt of separation or selfness, and a stilling of his scrupling response to intimations of immortality: whether these come as inner moods or as sounds from a distant source. "Nay, Traveller! rest."

Wordsworth's earlier yew-tree poem, his first mature lyric, begins with that call for repose. But the resting is also an arresting of the mind, as the traveler is halted by a voice "left" in nature. Rest is not mere idling but heightened attention. The unidentified voice, itself an "impulse saved from vacancy," inscribes the unmarked object with a moral tale. Though this tale comes, as it were, from nature, and though it calls for rest, it reveals a dark, unnatural incident.

We are told of a man now dead who committed a kind of self-murder by sinning against the sweet air. He used nature to feed his soul with darkness. The theme of rest mingles ambiguously with that of arrest, death, and judgment as a proud man is described who could not forgive neglect and turned away from the world with "rash disdain." His *contemptus mundi* (48-49) entices us to an equal "scorn" which Wordsworth warns against (54-55). The poem is, as we have said, the first of those anatomies of melancholy seeking to liberate us from the "penseroso" spell of the imprisoned self-consciousness. Sitting in judgment on himself and the world, the solitary's feelings for the beauty of nature merely intensify his sense of reclusion. Such impulses as come to Wordsworth daily, or from the "pure source" evoked at the end of "Yew-Trees," fail to release him from his living tomb.

We see why the spiritual and historical complexity of romantic nature poetry is not satisfied by such positive assertions as Riffaterre's "Sensation is all—which is exactly what descriptive poetry is about." For sensation is all *and* nothing. How does one value "one soft impulse saved from vacancy," or a ghostly mood, or the evening sky's peculiar tint of green: "And still I gaze—and with how blank an eye!"[30] From Francis Jeffrey to Irving Babbitt, Wordsworth suffered the "rash disdain" he warned against. His *labor of the negative* (Hegel) was mistaken for self-inflating bombast or a crude nature worship.

Wordsworth does not subdue thought to sensation, or the meditative to the descriptive mode. His poetic labor undoes sensation as well as thought, or self-consciousness, or the visionary desire for absolutes. It is no accident that his first yew-tree poem opens with a call for rest and that the later lyric ends with a supernatural image of repose. For the negative labor presupposed and in part accomplished by these poems is extreme—even if, historically and socially considered, it may not appear to be labor at all. We are already in an era of industrialization where the work ethic prevails. The image of labor is changing, and the idea of the poetical character is in doubt. What "character" does one show by "resting," by entering the castle or garden of poetic indolence? "What benefit canst thou do, or all thy tribe, / To the great world? Thou art a dreaming thing, / A fever of thyself...."[31] The paradox of "negative capability" had to be founded.

The historical context emerges now with some clarity. Wordsworth's yew-tree poem was written with a sense of impending doom, so that the very phrase "There is a Yew-tree" (cf. the Immortality Ode's "There is a Tree, of many one") is a perpetuation wish rather than a descriptive statement. The equivalent of "Woodsman, spare that tree" or, perhaps, "Time, spare that tree," it expresses the poet's awareness that the age of trees is coming to a close, that the agrarian or agricultarian mode of life is threatened by a speeding up of the rhythm of events in the Industrial Revolution and the Napoleonic wars. The year in which the poem may have been composed brings the end of the Peace of Amiens, an illusory moment of repose.[32] "Nay, Warrior, rest." Those who might have read the poem then would have understood the quietly topical connection between that moment and Poitier, Crecy, Agincourt. Will the trees survive this storm as well, to shelter or inspire a future generation?

VIII

lente lente currite noctes equi
Marlowe, *Dr. Faustus*

If the yews make a ghost of the speaker, futurity plays a part in this phantomization. Wordsworth's prophetic fear is that the trees, despite their longevity, will disappear from the earth, becoming mere figures—archaisms, ghosts—in memory. Yet Wordsworth's resistance to overt prophecy is as strong and complex as our resistance, according to Freud, to the death wish. Perhaps, then, prophecy is a death wish. We think of the drama played out between God and prophet in the Book of Jonah. Wordsworth's "daring sympathies with power" during even the worst periods of the French Revolution troubled him deeply. The Wordsworthian reticence seems to avoid both death wish and self-fulfilling prophecy. He defers or "dates on" the doom he feels.

So the inner argument may well be: as the yews go, so goes the world. If the yews are a metonymy for quasi-eternal nature, is that nature still "life and food / For future years"? Or are the years to come endangered by a modern ghostliness, by an alienation of mind from rural nature in the wake of the industrial and revolutionary mentality? Wordsworth cannot conceive of a mind from which nature has faded, unless it is a mind approaching the Last Judgment. Yet, often enough, time appears to him so accelerated that "thoughts of more deep seclusion" verge on thoughts of apocalypse. This sense of acceleration and of concomitant ghostliness is clarified by comparing three moments in his biography, each five years or so apart.

In 1793 Wordsworth visits Tintern Abbey for the first time; in 1798 he revisits it and writes the poem; and in 1803/04 he begins "Yew-Trees." The poem of 1798 is similar in some respects to that of 1803/04: it shares, for example, the themes of time, repose under a dark tree, and waters "rolling from their mountain springs / With a soft inland murmur." The great difference is that in 1798 the insistence of nature in the poet's consciousness yields a hope that sets a limit to phantomization and so allows "repose." But when this "repose" recurs at the end of "Yew-Trees," it is close to denoting eternal rest. Fear, hope, silence, and foresight, which were living acts of mind and heart in "Tintern Abbey," are now phantoms similar to those surrounding the dead Adonais in Shelley's later elegy.

"Yew-Trees," in fact, imagines a repose *from* consciousness. But this would elide not only self-reference but also—as "mute repose"—speech itself. Speech, or effective rhetoric, speech as more than internal work, is questioned. While "Tintern Abbey" is a complex murmur still in touch with mountain spring or flood, in "Yew-Trees" it is as if Wordsworth were himself among the ghosts, listening to verses written only five years earlier—and how distant now! The square of the distance, one might say, that "Tintern Abbey" stands from its own source of five years past: from river, cliff, and haunting cataract experienced in 1793.

"The Cataracts blow their trumpets from the steep; / No more shall grief of mine the season wrong."[33] Present joy, present time, is being wronged by a grief not fully named, but which involves a fear for the future of nature. A repose is sought from an incumbent sense of duty, as if the burden of delaying the Last Judgement, when nature shall be no more, had devolved on this poet. "No more shall grief of mine the season wrong" is the pastoral "murmur" that replies here to a martial or apocalyptic "voice." What the cataracts intimate—whether they support Wordsworth's visionary fear or urge him to leave futurity to God— remains unclear. But they are, like poetry itself, a responsive voice. "A Voice shall speak, and what will be the Theme?"[34] Voice precedes theme, and may even define the future, that is, the future relation of imagination and nature. We are still in a responsive, rather than mute, universe. Poetry, though divided between seeing and foreseeing, or present and future, harmonizes as best it can words and time in a "timely utterance."[35]

IX

By this circuitous route, then, we return to the question of words and the rhetorical aspect of human life. The phenomenological perspective I have restored can be reconciled with a structuralist reading. But it integrates better, I would think, concepts of time, voice, presence, and history, with language.

Riffaterre proceeds from a methodological assumption that "words are all" to the conclusion that in descriptive poetry "sensation is all." This is a strange reversal, and suggests that behind some types of structural analysis there lurks a positivism of the word and a nostalgic materialism. Though one can be in sympathy with Riffaterre's debt to historical semantics—which traces back every *Bedeutungswandel* or change of meaning to a substantial idea—one misses the chastening and skeptical attitude toward meaning in Valéry and later semioticians. For them a text or its meaning is a residue, an abandoned series of transformations, an incomplete or frozen metamorphosis. Each interpreter is a new Ovid, translating the text into subtler surfaces until it appears utterly "devoured by forms" like Valéry's dancer or Shelley's cloud.

The figure of a great and venerable tree, "Survivor sole, and hardly such" (to quote from Cowper's remarkable "Yardley Oak," the nearest analogue to Wordsworth's poem), leads to similarly chastening but also to comforting thoughts. A constancy is pictured amid change, and with power to resist an extreme metamorphosis. The theme is still decay, but "magnificent decay."[36] Some ancient science of substance, therefore, might seem more appropriate here than a deconstructive "annihilating all that's made" to shadowy words. The hylic fiction serves to draw us closer to earth or to the material imagination.

Yet we remain, with respect to earth, in a state marked by an unresolved, powerful, yet calm ambivalence: a state Wordsworth called "wise passiveness" and Keats characterized as "negative capability." The danger of these trees becoming mere figures of speech, either because they are about to be destroyed or because they are about to lose their hold on the mind of man—this virtual danger may actually reinforce in the mature poet those early or premature intimations he describes in the Great Ode: "obstinate questionings / Of sense and outward things, / Fallings from us, vanishings. . . ." Though such nature-loss, such skirting of the "abyss of ideality," may augur a gain, and though Wordsworth engages in "Tintern Abbey" and elsewhere with the theme of loss and gain, he will not take an ultimate decision upon himself. On this issue there is vacillation rather than an authoritative resolution by means of visionary or poetic voice. "Milton! England hath need of thee," yet Wordsworth refused to be Milton on the matter of nature's ultimate importance to the life of the mind.

He delays, in fact, rather than hastens a decision: he intervenes to the extent of being the first poet to grant nature due process. Greatness and scrupulousness combine to make a difficult poetry hardly recognized as such even today. It is in many ways the most ghostly poetry ever written: one in which speech itself is near to fading out, like echo, or the voice of genius that dies with the tree it inhabits. The oracular voice is muted to become, as in "Yew-Trees," words that speak "of nothing more than what we are," words that do not tilt the balance against nature. Yet these words may give too much to nature, if they must be, in time to come, and for good or bad, a homeless or disembodied utterance. If nature as we know it must die, or change utterly, then poetry as we know it must die, or change utterly. This extreme calculus of words, and this internal, obstinate questioning of every ghostly or glorious mood, is what all readers feel in Wordsworth, though they may not be happy with it if they expect from poetry a decisive rhetoric or a seductive animation.

APPENDIX

I. Anonymous, "An Inscription: Quercus loquitur"

> O YE!
> WHO by retirement to these sacred groves
> Impregnate fancy, and on thought divine
> Build harmony—If sudden glow your breast
> With inspiration, and the rapt'rous song
> Bursts from a mind unconscious whence it sprang:
>   —Know that the sisters of these hallow'd haunts.
> Dryad or Hamadryad, tho' no more
> From Jove to man prophetick truths they sing;
> Are still attendant on the lonely bard,
> Who step by step these silent woods among
> Wanders contemplative, lifting the soul
> From lower cares, by every whisp'ring breeze
> Tun'd to poetick mood; and fill the mind
> With truths oracular, themselves of old
> Deign'd utter from the Dodonean shrine.

From Dodsley, *A Collection of Poems by Several Hands,*
4th ed. (1755).

II. Wordsworth, "Address From the Spirit of Cockermouth Castle" (1835)

> "Thou look'st upon me, and dost fondly think,
> Poet! that, stricken as both are by years,
> We, differing once so much, are now Compeers,
> Prepared, when each has stood his time, to sink
> Into the dust. Erewhile a sterner link
> United us; when thou, in boyish play
> Entering my dungeon, didst become a prey
> To soul-appalling darkness. Not a blink
> Of light was there;—and thus did I, thy Tutor,
> Make thy young thoughts acquainted with the grave;
> While thou wert chasing the winged butterfly
> Through my green courts; or climbing, a bold suitor,
> Up to the flowers whose golden progeny
> Still round my shattered brow in beauty wave."

10
"Timely Utterance" Once More

"It would be not only interesting but also useful to know what the 'timely utterance' was," Lionel Trilling wrote in 1941. He eventually does "hazard a guess."[1] Time has not diminished our fascination with the phrase: the guessing continues, while Trilling's interpretation has become part of the poem's aura and entered the consciousness of many readers. Just as we find a ring of cosmic junk around planets, so it is with interpretive solutions stabilized by the gravitational field of a well-known poem. Moreover, Trilling's critical style is itself of interest. To "hazard a guess" indicates a modest attitude (he does not speak as a specialist, rather as an educated, reflective reader) but also, perhaps, a subdued sense of venture. For Wordsworth's diction is a riddle as well as a puzzle, and we answer it at the risk of appearing foolish, of exposing our superficial views on language and life.[2]

"Timely utterance," of course, is not the only crux in Wordsworth's Ode, nor the only mystery-phrase singled out by readers. There is the bombast (Coleridge's term) of stanza 8, addressed to the Child as Prophet and Philosopher; there is the delicate vatic vagueness of "fields of sleep"; there is, at the end, "thoughts that do often lie too deep for tears."

These cruxes—and there are others—all share a problem of reference: we do not know what the "timely utterance" was: "fields of sleep" is a periphrasis that should yield a proper name, perhaps of a place as mythic as the Elysian fields ("fields of light," cf. *Aeneid* VI, 640); the sublime words that describe the infant seem really to describe some other, more fitting, subject; and who knows what the deep thoughts are about.

Let me clarify, in a preliminary way, this problem of reference. Those deep thoughts: their occasion is clear (the simplest thing, the meanest flower), and their emotional impact also is clear. But where precisely do they lie, where is "too deep for tears"? Is it, to quote a moving sonnet in which Wordsworth mourns the loss of his daughter Catherine, that "spot which no vicissitude can find"?[3] Or is the obverse suggested, that they are *not* thoughts of loss, mortality or the grave, but arise from a still deeper level, from under or beyond the grave? But what can *that* mean? Or is Wordsworth adjuring himself not to cry, not to give in to a pathos permitted even to Aeneas ("Sunt lacrymae rerum. . ." *Aeneid* I, 468), as he forbids mourning despite nature's valedictory intimations:

> And O, ye Fountains, Meadows, Hills and Groves,
> Forbode not any severing of our loves!

I multiply questions because I suspect that a simple solution, or stabilizing specificity, cannot be found. Yet the nonspecific quality of such verses does not harm them. It acts somewhat like formal perspective, in which an abstract reference-point allows the imaginative construction of naturalistic space. For, with the partial exception of stanza 8 on the sublime Child, we remain very much in a familiar world. Wordsworth extends, it is true, the boundary of natural events, yet never crosses it decisively into another region. Plato's doctrine of anamnesis or pre-existence is made to support ordinary feelings, to give them a memorable frame, not to justify fantastic speculation. The Ode's closing sentiment even limits the kind of thoughtful brooding (the "philosophic mind") that is its very concern: there is neither analytic nor visionary excess.

The more we press toward reference, the more a Wordsworthian thought-limit or boundary appears. One is tempted to ask, and without constraining an answer: are the thoughts secretly apocalyptic? Or so gravely sentimental that they border on a crazy sort of concreteness, as mind passes from the "meanest" sign to the sublimest natural laws via an elided corpse? (For one could imagine the poet thinking: This flower at my feet may be nourished by the putrefaction of the dead, who are remembered unto life in this way.[4])

> The cloud of mortal destiny,
> Others will front it fearlessly—
> But who, like him, will put it by?

Wordsworth's poetry has the strength to absorb thoughts that might unbalance the mind. "Dim sadness, and blind thoughts," he calls them in "Resolution and Independence," "I knew not, nor could name." The "burthen of the mystery" is acknowledged and lightened. Alas, the "burthen of the mystery" is another one of those strange phrases, strong yet vague. I turn now to what occasioned these preliminary reflections: "timely utterance."

II

The context is not as much help as it might be.

> To me alone there came a thought of grief:
> A timely utterance gave that thought relief. . .

The thought is almost as unspecific as what gives it relief. Perhaps it does not have to be specific, since the stanza's first verses suggest that what mattered was the contrast of thought and season. To me alone, among all beings, there came this untoward thought, like an untimely echo. Hence, after it is dispelled, Wordsworth vows: "No more shall grief of mine the season wrong." Only "seasonable sweets" (Keats) from now on. One possibility for interpretation, therefore, is that he was interested in expressing a relation, or a broken then restored relation, rather than the precise detail of this single experience. The broken relation between his heart and the "heart of May" is always to be repaired. There may even be a repetition of that relational structure:

> The cataracts blow their trumpets from the steep;
> No more shall grief of mine the season wrong;
> I hear the Echoes through the mountains throng;
> The Winds come to me from the fields of sleep. . .

Two types of utterance are presented in asyndetic sequence: one comes from nature, and seems to heighten, like a punctuation from above, the timely utterance (indeed, there is a possibility that it was the timely utterance); and one comes from within the poet, as if to answer or echo nature (relation having been restored) and so to confirm, even structurally, that the disturbing fancy has passed. This echo-structure is made literal by the next line. "I hear the Echoes from the mountain throng." Together with "The Winds come to me from the fields of sleep," it suggests an extension of sensibility, some inner horizon opening up, as the poet hears into the distance. What is heard is not just waterfall or winds (whatever their message) but the principle of echo itself. Hence the echoes "throng"; they are suddenly everywhere; as thick as sheep at folding time. The stanza as a whole evokes a *correspondence* of breezes, sounds, feelings, one that has absorbed discordant elements (cf. 1850 *Prelude* I, 85, 96ff., 340-50). Its culmination is the hallooing of "Shout round me, let me hear thy shouts, thou happy Shepherd-boy!"

The movement of empathy here is so strong that we almost feel the apostrophe as a self-address, as if the poet were that "Child of Joy." His flock, as in Shelley's "Adonais," is composed of "quick Dreams, / The passion-winged Ministers of thought." Though we are moving toward the opposite of a pastoral elegy, the double form or echo-aspect of this provisional climax ("Shout. . .shout") may be modifying as well as intensifying. Is not the cry optative rather than indicative in mood, an utterance that *projects* an utterance, so that it is hard to tell the spontaneous from the forced joy? The "let me hear" repeats as a variant the "shout round me," yet it also points inward: it seems to appeal for a sound so strong that the poet cannot but hear ("I hear, I hear . . . with joy I hear" is delayed to the next stanza, and is immediately counterpointed: "But there's a Tree, of many, one . . . ") An inward and meeting echo, a reciprocal response, is not assured even now.

III

Broken column, broken tower, broken . . . response. The theme of lost Hellenic grace or harmony is not relevant except as it is also more than Hellenic and recalls the "echo" formula of a poetry at once pastoral and elegiac:

> All as the sheepe, such was the shepeheards looke

Spenser writes in "January," the first eclogue of the *Shepheardes Calender*. And

> 'Thou barrein ground, whom winters wrath hath wasted,
> Art made a myrrhour to behold my plight . . .'

This correspondence of season with mood, or of nature with human feelings, is the simplest form of the echo-principle in pastoral verse. Echo is something more than a figure of speech:

> Now lay those sorrowful complaints aside,
> And having all your heads with girland crownd,
> Helpe me mine owne loves prayses to resound;
> Ne let the same of any be envide:
> So Orpheus did for his owne bride:
> So I unto my selfe alone wil sing;
> The woods shall to me answer, and my eccho ring.

Spenser gives himself away in an *Epithalamion* of his own making: his poetry participates in the marriage, it weds the world, the word, to his desire, or more exactly to the *timing* which builds his rime, and which can call for silence ("And cease till then our tymely joyes to sing: / The woods no more us answer, nor our eccho ring") as well as responsive sound. In this sense poetry is itself the "timely utterance"—not Spenser's *Epithalamion* as such, nor "Resolution and Independence" (or a part of it, as Trilling and Barzun suggest[5]), or any other specific set of verses.

Yet what is meant by *poetry* cannot be formalized, as I have seemed to suggest, in terms of generic features. I might like to claim that "timely utterance" opens every poetic form to the incursion of pastoral;[6] and Wordsworth himself gives some purchases on such a view:

> The Poets, in their elegies and songs
> Lamenting the departed, call the groves,
> They call upon the hills and streams to mourn,
> And senseless rocks; nor idly; for they speak,
> In these their invocations, with a voice
> Obedient to the strong creative power
> Of human passion.
>
> *(The Excursion* I, 475-81)

Yet what matters is neither the pastoral setting nor the overt, figurative expression of sympathy ("Sympathies there are," Wordsworth continues, "More tranquil, yet perhaps of kindred birth, / That steal upon the meditative mind, / And grow with thought"). What matters is the sense of a *bond* between mind and nature, of a *responsiveness* that overcomes the difference of speech and muteness, or articulate and inarticulate utterance.

> Far and wide the clouds were touched,
> And in their silent faces could he read
> Unutterable love.
>
> . . . . . .
>
> . . . In the mountains did he *feel* his faith.
> All things, responsive to the writing, there
> Breathed immortality, revolving life,
> And greatness still revolving; infinite
>
> *(The Excursion* I, 203-5, 226-29)

The capacity for "timely utterance" in this timeless, mute, or unutterable situation maintains the bond, and justifies the poetry. "The strong creative power / Of human passion" is equivalent to poetry in this respect. "Passion" often has, for Wordsworth, the sense of passionate speech that identifies with "mute, insensate things." "My heart leaps up"—an "extempore" lyric whose final lines come to serve as an epigraph to the Intimations Ode, and which has been nominated by some scholars as the "timely utterance"—is about this bond. The poem is remarkable as an utterance, as a speech act that falls somewhere between vow and passionate wish:

> My heart leaps up when I behold
> A rainbow in the sky:

> So was it when my life began;
> So is it now I am a man:
> So be it when I shall grow old,
>   Or let me die!

That "Or let me die!" is a true "fit of passion," one of those Wordsworthian moments where feeling seems to overflow and be in excess of its occasion. It is, one might say, untimely.

Yet we feel its emotional truth, and it becomes timely again once we recall another utterance, that of God when he makes the rainbow a sign of His bond:

> I have set My bow in the cloud, and it shall be a token of a covenant between Me and the earth. And it shall come to pass, when I bring clouds over the earth, and the bow is seen in the cloud, that I will remember My covenant, which is between Me and you and every living creature of all flesh; and the waters shall no more become a flood to destroy all flesh.

> (Genesis 9:13-16)

If Wordsworth's vow recalls that primal vow, it is a response that says: This is *my* bond, *my* way of binding each day to each and continuing in time. Cut the link of nature to human feelings and the bond is broken. Once dead to nature, I might as well die. Poetry is a marriage-covenant with nature, a "spousal verse" even more demanding of "dew" response than Spenser's *Epithalamion*.

IV

To utter things in a timely way is the ideal situation, of course; yet Wordsworth usually represents the ideal in its wishful or miscarried form. The words *tempus* and *tempest* are related; and the *Prelude's* opening episode already suggests a problem. The "correspondent breeze" is said to have become "A tempest, a redundant energy / Vexing its own creation (I, 37ff). There is a disproportion or discord between the "gentle breeze" of the poem's first verse and this tempestuous, self-forcing power. The *untimely* is never far away (cf. I, 94-105).

But our own solution may have been untimely, that is, premature. Even should "timely utterance" be an inspired periphrasis for poetry, and exclude the promoting of a particular poem or passage, we continue to think of poetry as a *manifold* of utterances that is *one* only if the idea of vocation is adduced: if poetry is also "poesy." The utterances are not only qualified by being timely (either vis-à-vis others or oneself); they are unified by being timely. That is their essential quality, or the predicate pointing to a predicament. A reader alerted by the Vergilian motto of the Ode ("paulo majora canamus") would recognize the question of poetic growth and maturation: of the *career* of the poet. Is there a future for Wordsworth as poet, or for poetry itself? Has the time for poetry, as "timely utterance," passed?

Moreover, the Ode's vacillating strain, its blend of humble and prophetic tones, recalls Milton's stylized hesitation in *Lycidas*: poetry is conceived of as a precarious venture, that may be prematurely launched, untimely tried by "forc'd fingers rude." It is Milton who linked poetry's timeliness explicitly to a vocation that was imperious, prophetic, dangerous. If not now, when?

The "Now" that begins stanza 3 of Wordsworth's Ode may therefore be more than a pivoting or idle word. Its place in time, as well as its syntactical position, is not easily fixed. It is like the anchor of hope. Its prepositional and propositional components fuse into an absolute construction. The word stands outside the events it qualifies: like a symbol in mathematics it could refer to every phrase that follows. The sequence of tenses in stanza 3 shifts from present to past to present, as everything tends toward that "Now." Coming to it, after two reflective and chiefly elegiac stanzas, it is as if a person were to draw a deep breath, then to exhale it, signaling a new start. The present, or this very utterance, cancels what has been. "Now" is in its virtuality the temporal word *par excellence*.

To make so ordinary a word extraordinary may be self-defeating in terms of the diction of poetry. Yet poetic language, it could be argued, is ordinary language in its always residual or always future promise. "Now," as common as herded sheep, is also remarkable as the index for "A Presence which is not to be put by" (*Intimations Ode*, 120). A passage-word, it intimates the possibility— not the fact—of a decisive turning point, something about to be, or about to be... uttered. Within the flow of language it is an open-vowelled *nunc stans*, a fleeting epiphanic sound. And the transition from "thought of grief" to "relief," which it introduces, and then, in the next stanza, to "blessing," comes through drinking in a surround of sounds: the utterance itself, the cataracts, echoes, winds, and the first clear vocative of the poem, "Shout round me...." It is as if Wordsworth had been released into voice as well as blessing, into a voice that is a blessing.

> Ye blessed Creatures, I have heard the call
> Ye to each other make...

> (St. IV)

It is a moment remarkably similar to the removal of the curse from the Ancient Mariner in Coleridge's poem; there is the same feeling of relief, the creatures (*res creatae*) are acknowledged and blessed. Coleridge, however, separates blessing and utterance, as if timely utterance were not, or not yet, possible.

> O happy living things! no tongue
> Their beauty might declare:

A spring of love gushed from my heart,
And I blessed them unaware.

Yet in Wordsworth too there may be a hesitation of the tongue, some impedi-
ment to the coincidence of voice and blessing. It emerges when we ask whether
the action of stanza 4 takes place in real or fantasied time. "Ye blessed Creatures,
I have heard the call / Ye to each other make; I see / The heavens laugh with
you...." need not be a descriptive statement about what is happening then and
there. It could be an anticipatory and envisioning response to "Shout round me,
let me hear thy shouts...." A wish-fulfillment, then, a proleptic extension of
the poet's own vocative, his pausal "Now." The "I have heard" may refer to the
past ("There was a time") or it may have come so close to the moment of speaking that it is a confirmatory "Roger." Wordsworth does not actually say that *he*
is laughing with the creatures; but as he looks round once more, repeating the
"turning" described in the opening stanzas, he sees and hears the things he said
he could no more.

The reader, of course, no less wishful than the poet, would like to assume that
the thought of grief has passed and that the birds and beasts did in fact sing and
bound, and that only the discordant heart of the poet had to be tuned. But the
"Now" remains slightly apart, hyper-referential, or just plain *hyper*. It is a
wishing-word. The music of Wordsworth's Ode is so elaborate that it untunes the
timely-happy connection between heaven and nature, as between heart and
nature, a connection the poet is always reestablishing. His poem is the most complex Music Ode in English, conveying and absorbing the difference between voice
and blessing, words and wishes, being and being-in-time.

V

All things, responsive to the writing
Wordsworth

I have offered a mildly deconstuctive reading: one that discloses in words "a
'spirit' peculiar to their nature as words" (Kenneth Burke). Such a reading refuses
to substitute ideas for words, especially since in the empiricist tradition after
Locke ideas are taken to be a faint replica of images, which are themselves directly
referable to sense-experience. One way of bringing out the spirit peculiar to
words, and so, paradoxically, making them material—emphasizing the letter in
the spirit—is to evoke their intertexual echoes. Ideas may be simple, but words
are always complex. Yet the construction of an intertextual field is disconcerting
as well as enriching because intertexual concordance produces a reality-discord,
an overlay or distancing of the referential function of speech, of the word-thing,
word-experience relation. Even though the *fact* of correspondence between
language and experience is not in question (there is a complex answerability of

the one to the other), the *theory* of correspondence remains a problem. I want to conclude my remarks by suggesting that intertextual awareness follows from the character of words, and that it does not divorce us from dearly beloved experience, or Wordsworth's "the world, which is the world of all of us."

"There was a time" (l. 1) immediately introduces the motif of time in a colloquial and inconspicuous way. Yet as the poem proceeds, the expression begins to border on myth. It becomes reminiscent of the *illo tempore*, the "in those days," of mythical thought. Wordsworth locates that mythical epoch at the barely scrutable edge of everyone's memory of childhood. During this numinous time, a "celestial light" invests natural objects, although later we learn also about darker moments, "Blank misgivings of a Creature/Moving about in worlds not realized" (Ode, 144-45). The darkness and the light are intervolved, as in a Grasmere storm. But the metaphor of light predominates, and the poet's loss is described in terms of it.

The third stanza deepens as well as qualifies that sense of loss. The "to me alone" of line 22 points to an event closer to augury than subjective feeling; it singles the poet out. He haruspicates himself. His inability to respond fully to nature, what does it mean? Was the vanished natural light perhaps an inner and now failing light, not *given* from outside but rather *bestowed* from within by imagination?

That gleam, moreover, whatever its source, seems preternatural. It suggests that the bond between nature and imagination is precarious from the outset, with imagination seeking to wed itself to nature, in order to become poetry rather than prophecy. That is certainly how it seemed to Blake when he read the Ode. He was deeply moved by it, but denounced the "natural man" in Wordsworth always rising up, as he put it, against the imaginative man.

Those aquainted with Wordsworth know that a simple turn of thought can trigger a radical turning about of his mind and release a near-apocalyptic sense of isolation. Blake is right in the sense that even when the final mood-swing or "*envoi*" of the Ode ends ominously,

> And O, ye Fountains, Meadows, Hills, and Groves,
> Forebode not any severing of our loves!

(187-88)

Wordsworth pretends that the portent comes from nature rather than from himself. He will not acknowledge that the bond with nature—more psychic than epistemic—is broken. "I could wish my days to be/Bound each to each by natural piety."

"I *could* wish"? How strangely tentative that sounds! The wish hesitates, I suspect, because its very success, its potential fulfillment, might go against nature by confirming the omnipotence of wishful thought. A similar scruple may hover over stanza 3 and the "timely utterance" that allows the ode to turn upward instead of spiraling downward or breaking off. The very discretion of the phrase protects it from being construed as a wish, or any sort of direct—imperative—speech-act.

"Timely utterance," then, does not pose only a problem of reference. The indirect phrasing involves signifier as well as signified: the poet's attitude toward a higher mode of speech, whether wishful or prophetic. Wordsworth's expression is guarded: he does actually wish; rather, he "could wish" that the bond with nature should continue, and that the mutability suggested by "There was a time" should not bode an end to time itself, a discontinuity between *illo tempore* and his present or future state. The "timely utterance" meets that anxiety about time; and as "utterance" it suggests that someone else has made a wish for the poet and so relieved him of the responsibility. It is as if a thought had been taken out of his heart and uttered. The structure is similar to that of the famous dedication scene in *The Prelude*, which makes him aware of his calling as poet. "I made no vows, but vows/Were then made for me; bond unknown to me/Was given. . ." (V, 534—36).[7] In the Ode, too, we do not know who utters what. Even if the utterance took place within the poet, it was not his but some other voice. A "discours de l'Autre" (Jacques Lacan) takes away the burden of wishful or visionary speech. There exists, in fact, one such Discourse of the Other that is *timely* and *bonding*, and even joins the theme of speaking to that of giving light:

And God said, Let there be light: and God divided the light from the darkness. And God called the light Day, and the darkness he called Night. And there was evening and there was morning, one day.

These are "timely" words indeed: they create time, they establish it beyond all misgiving. What is founded, moreover, bonds a reponsive nature (or what is to be nature) to an utterance, and God to his own work, for he acknowledges by direct acts of naming and blessing what has been called into being.

I am tempted, at last, to make an assertion and identify the "timely utterance." "Let there be light: and there was light" utters itself in the poet's mind as a proof-text, that is, not only as a deeply subjective wish for the return of the light whose loss was lamented in the first two stanzas, but also as that wish in the form of God's first words, His "Let there be."

I have taken one phrase as my starting point and made many angels dance on it. These revels would be in vain if Wordsworth's Ode were not involved in the question of voice as well as light: in what connection there still might be between poetry and prophecy. "A Voice to Light gave Being," Wordsworth writes in a later Great Ode, alluding to fiat or logos. Yet there is a fear lest poetic voice, in its very power, may call on darkness, and become decreative rather than creative and so a "counter-spirit" or parody of the "divine I AM." Then the prophetic or poetic voice could serve, however involuntarily, the cause of cursing, not of blessing, and wish for an end, a dissolution of work and world. The utterance that surprised Wordsworth is, from one perspective, an archetypal instance of wish-fulfillment or omnipotence of thoughts. Yet from another perspective it is an exemplary instance of poetry as a creative speech-act that leads to natural piety rather than to apocalyptic solipsism or transcendence.

Wordsworth's most felicitious poetry merges wishing, reponding, and blessing: merges, in fact, a first timely utterance, the fiat, and a second timely utterance, the covenant. If, in stanza 3 of his Ode, the sounding cataracts and the "timely utterance" are echo-aspects of each other, it is because what was founded must be founded a second time, on the flood; just as the light that was has to be lit again, now. The Covenant is a second creation confirming the first; while the rainbow as a timely sign recalls an utterance that could make the poet's heart leap up. The Intimations Ode is the third of this series. It is the poet's response, his covenant-sign, his own "timely utterance," incorporating mutely—as silent light—the divine *davar*, that is, the text on which my own intertextual leaping comes to rest.

11
The Poetics of Prophecy

In our honorific or sophomoric moods, we like to think that poets are prophets. At least that certain great poets have something of the audacity and intensity—the strong speech—of Old Testament prophets who claimed that the word of God came to them. "The words of Jeremiah, the son of Hilkiah. . . To whom the word of the Lord came in the days of Josiah. . ." It is hard to understand even this introductory passage, for the word for "words," *divre* in Hebrew, indicates something closer to "acts" or "word events," while what the King James version translates as "to whom the word of the Lord came," which hypostatizes the Word, as if it had a being of its own, or were consubstantial with what we know of God, is in the original simply *hajah devar-adonai elav*, "the God-word was to him." We don't know, in short, what is going on; yet through a long tradition of translation and interpretation we feel we know. Similarly, when Wordsworth tells us that around his twenty-third year he "received" certain "convictions," which included the thought that despite his humbler subject matter he could stand beside the "men of old," we seek gropingly to make sense of that conviction. "Poets, even as Prophets," Wordsworth writes,

> each with each
> Connected in a mighty scheme of truth,
> Have each his own peculiar faculty,
> Heaven's gift, a sense that fits him to perceive
> Objects unseen before. . .
> An insight that in some sort he possesses,
> A privilege whereby a work of his,

Proceeding from a source of untaught things
Creative and enduring, may become
A power like one of Nature's.

(1850 *Prelude* XIII, 301-12)

In the earlier (1805) version of *The Prelude* "insight" is "influx," which relates more closely to a belief in inspiration, or a flow (of words) the poet participates in yet does not control: "An influx, that in some sort I possess'd."

I will somewhat neglect in what follows one difference, rather obvious, between poet and prophet. A prophet is to us, and perhaps to himself, mainly a *voice*—as God himself seems to him primarily a voice. Even when he does God in many voices, they are not felt to stand in an equivocal relation to each other: each voice is absolute, and vacillation produces vibrancy rather than ambiguity. In this sense there is no "poetics of prophecy"; there is simply a voice breaking forth, a quasivolcanic eruption, and sometimes its opposite, the "still, small voice" heard after the thunder of Sinai. I will try to come to grips with that difference between poet and prophet later on; here I should only note that, being of the era of Wordsworth rather than of Jeremiah, I must look back from the poet's rather than from the prophet's perspective, while acknowledging that the very concept of poetry may be used by Wordsworth to reflect on—and often to defer—the claim that he has a prophetic gift.

There is another passage in *The Prelude* that explores the relation between poet and prophet. Wordsworth had been to France during the Revolution, had followed that cataclysmic movement in hope, had seen it degenerate into internecine politics and aggressive war. Yet despite the discrediting of revolutionary ideals, something of his faith survived, and not only faith but, as he strangely put it, "daring sympathies with power." In brief, he saw those terrible events in France as necessary and even divinely sanctioned. To explain his mood Wordsworth writes a confessional passage that also gives his most exact understanding of prophecy:

But as the ancient Prophets, borne aloft
In vision, yet constrained by natural laws
With them to take a troubled human heart,
Wanted not consolations, nor a creed
Of reconcilement, then when they denounced,
On towns and cities, wallowing in the abyss
Of their offences, punishment to come;
Or saw, like other men, with bodily eyes,
Before them, in some desolated place,
The wrath consummate and the threat fulfilled;
So, with devout humility be it said,

So, did a portion of that spirit fall
On me uplifted from the vantage-ground
Of pity and sorrow to a state of being
That through the time's exceeding fierceness saw
Glimpses of retribution, terrible,
And in the order of sublime behests:
But, even if that were not, amid the awe
Of unintelligible chastisement,
Not only acquiescences of faith
Survived, but daring sympathies with power,
Motions not treacherous or profane, else why
Within the folds of no ungentle breast
Their dread vibration to this hour prolonged?
Wild blasts of music thus could find their way
Into the midst of turbulent events;
So that worst tempests might be listened to.

(1850 *Prelude* X, 437-63)

This eloquent statement has many complexities; but it is clear that though Wordsworth felt himself "uplifted from the vantage-ground / Of pity and sorrow," he did not leave them behind in this moment of sublime vision and terrible purification. It is certainly a remarkable feature of a prophet like Jeremiah that "borne aloft / In vision" he yet takes with him "a troubled human heart." Like Jonah, he tries to evade the commission, though not, like Jonah, by running away but rather by claiming he is not of age when it comes to speech ("Then said I, Ah, Lord GOD! behold, I cannot speak: for I am a child"). Jeremiah even accuses God, in bitterness of heart, of the very thing of which God accused Israel: of seducing the prophet, or of being unfaithful (Jeremiah 20:7ff.).

Wordsworth expresses most strongly a further, related aspect of prophetical psychology: the ambivalent sympathy shown by the prophet for the powerful and terrible thing he envisions. This sympathy operates even when he tries to avert what must be, or to find a "creed of reconcilement." The poet's problem vis-à-vis the Revolution was not, principally, that he had to come to terms with crimes committed in the name of the Revolution or of liberty. For at the end of the passage from which I have quoted he indicates that there had been a rebound of faith, a persuasion that grew in him that the Revolution itself was not to blame, but rather "a terrific reservoir of guilt / And ignorance filled up from age to age" had "burst and spread in deluge through the land." The real problem was his entanglement in a certain order of sensations which endured to the very time of writing: he owns to "daring sympathies with power," "motions," whose "dread vibration" is "to this hour prolonged," and whose harmonizing effect in the midst of the turbulence he characterized by the oxymoron "Wild blasts of music."

We understand perfectly well that what is involved in Wordsworth's sympathy with power is not, or not simply, a sublime kind of *Schadenfreude*. And that no amount of talk about the pleasure given by tragedy, through "cathartic" identification, would do more than uncover the same problem in a related area. The seduction power exerts, when seen as an act of God or Nature, lies within common experience. It does not of itself distinguish poets or prophets. What is out of the ordinary here is the "dread vibration": a term close to music, as well as one that conveys the lasting resonance of earlier feelings. How did Wordsworth's experience of sympathy with power accrue a metaphor made overt in "wild blasts of music"?

The tradition that depicts inspired poetry as a wild sort of natural music ("Homer the great Thunderer, [and] the voice that roars along the bed of Jewish Song") circumscribes rather than explains these metaphors. When we take them to be more than commonplaces of high poetry we notice that they sometimes evoke the force of wind and water as blended sound (cf. "The stationary blasts of waterfalls," 1850 *Prelude* VI, 626), a sound with power to draw the psyche in, as if the psyche also were an instrument or element, and had to mingle responsively with some overwhelming, massive unity. Despite the poet's imagery of violence, the ideal of harmony, at least on the level of sound, is not given up. The soul as a gigantic if reluctant aeolian harp is implicitly evoked.

How strangely this impulse to harmony is linked with violent feelings can be shown by one of Wordsworth's similes. Similes are, of course, a formal way of bringing together, or harmonizing, different areas of experience. From Coleridge to the New Critics the discussion of formal poetics has often focused on the valorized distinction between fancy and imagination, or on the way difference is reconciled. Shortly before his reflection on the ancient prophets, and when he is still describing the indiscriminate carnage unleashed by Robespierre, Wordsworth had recourse to a strange pseudo-Homeric simile comparing the tempo of killings to a child activating a toy windmill:

> though the air
> Do of itself blow fresh, and make the vanes
> Spin in his eyesight, *that* contents him not,
> But, with the plaything at arm's length, he sets
> His front against the blast, and runs amain,
> That it may whirl the faster.
>
> (1850 *Prelude* X, 369-74)

An aeolian toy is used, explicitly now, to image a sublime and terrible order of events. The instrument is given to the wind, so that it may go faster; yet this childish sport is set in an ominous context. The innocent wish to have something go fast reflects on the child whose mimicry (as in the Intimations Ode) suggests his haste to enter the very world where that haste has just shown itself in heinous form. Though there is something incongruous in the simile, there is also something fitting: or at least a drive toward fitting together incongruous passions of childhood and adulthood; and may this drive not express the dark "workmanship that reconciles / Discordant elements" by a mysterious, quasi-musical "harmony" (1850 *Prelude* I, 340ff.)? Here the reconciling music, by which the mind is built up, is already something of a "wild blast"; and when we think of the passage on prophecy to follow, on Wordsworth's "daring sympathies with power," we realize that what is involved in these various instances—lust for carnage, vertigo-sport, the child's impatience to grow up, the poet's fits of words, and the prophet's sympathy with the foreseen event, however terrible—is an anticipatory relation to time, a hastening of futurity.

The music metaphor, associated with wind and water sound, occurs in yet another context close to apocalyptic feelings. (By "apocalyptic" I always mean quite specifically an anticipatory, proleptic relation to time, intensified to the point where there is at once desire for and dread of the end being hastened. There is a potential inner turning against time, and against nature insofar as it participates in the temporal order.) Wordsworth's dream in *Prelude* V of the Arab saving stone and shell from the encroaching flood, also identified as the two principal branches of humane learning, mathematics and literature, is given an explicitly apocalyptic frame. The poet is meditating on books "that aspire to an unconquerable life," human creations that must perish nevertheless. Quoting from a Shakespeare sonnet on the theme of time, he reflects that we "weep to have" what we may lose: the weeping represents both the vain effort and the proleptic regret, so that the very joy of possessing lies close to tears, or thoughts deeper than tears. Only one detail of the ensuing dream need concern us. It comes when the Arab asks the dreamer to hold the shell (poetry) to his ear. "I did so," says the dreamer,

> And heard that instant in an unknown tongue,
> Which yet I understood, articulate sounds,
> A loud prophetic blast of harmony;
> An Ode, in passion uttered, which foretold
> Destruction to the children of the earth
> By deluge, now at hand
>
> (1850 *Prelude* V, 93-98)

A "blast of harmony" is not only a more paradoxical, more acute version of the metaphor in "blast of music," but we recognize it as an appropriate figure for the shouting poetry also called prophecy. In the lines that follow, Wordsworth stresses the dual function of such poetry: it has power to exhilarate and to soothe the human heart. But this is a gloss that conventionalizes the paradox in "blast of harmony" and does not touch the reality of the figure.

Our task is to understand the reality of figures, or more precisely, the reality of "blast of harmony," when applied to prophecy, or prophetic poetry. I will suggest, on the basis of this figure, that there is a poetics of prophecy; and I will study it by reading closely two episodes in *The Prelude* entirely within the secular sphere: the "spot of time" alluding to the death of the poet's father, and the ascent of Snowdon. After that a transition to the prophetic books, and to Jeremiah in particular, may lie open.

II

The death of Wordsworth's father is not attended by unusual circumstances. As Claudius says in a play we shall refer to again: a "common theme / Is death of fathers." Yet it is precisely the commonplace that releases in this case the "dread vibration." The thirteen-year-old schoolboy is impatient to return home for the Christmas holidays, and climbs a crag overlooking two highways to see whether he can spot the horses that should be coming. From that bare, wind-blown crag he watches intensely, and shortly after he returns home his father dies. That is all: a moment of intense, impatient watching, and then, ten days later, the death. Two things without connection except contiguity in time come together in the boy, who feels an emotion that perpetuates "down to this very time" the sights and sounds he experienced waiting for the horses. Here is Wordsworth's account in full:

> There rose a crag,
> That, from the meeting-point of two highways
> Ascending, overlooked them both, far stretched;
> Thither, uncertain on which road to fix
> My expectation, thither I repaired,
> Scout-like, and gained the summit; 'twas a day
> Tempestuous, dark, and wild, and on the grass
> I sate half-sheltered by a naked wall;
> Upon my right hand couched a single sheep,
> Upon my left a blasted hawthorn stood;
> With those companions at my side, I watched,
> Straining my eyes intensely, as the mist
> Gave intermitting prospect of the copse
> And plain beneath. Ere we to school returned,—
> That dreary time,—ere we had been ten days
> Sojourners in my father's house, he died,

And I and my three brothers, orphans then,
Followed his body to the grave. The event,
With all the sorrow that it brought, appeared
A chastisement; and when I called to mind
That day so lately past, when from the crag
I looked in such anxiety of hope;
With trite reflections of morality,
Yet in the deepest passion, I bowed low
To God, Who thus corrected my desires;
And, afterwards, the wind and sleety rain,
And all the business of the elements,
The single sheep, and the one blasted tree,
And the bleak music from that old stone wall,
The noise of wood and water, and the mist
That on the line of each of those two roads
Advanced in such indisputable shapes;
All these were kindred spectacles and sounds
To which I oft repaired, and thence would drink,
As at a fountain; and on winter nights,
Down to this very time, when storm and rain
Beat on my roof, or, haply, at noon-day,
While in a grove I walk, whose lofty trees,
Laden with summer's thickest foliage, rock
In a strong wind, some working of the spirit,
Some inward agitations thence are brought,
Whate'er their office.

(1850 *Prelude* XII, 292-333)

The secular and naturalistic frame of what is recorded remains intact. Yet the experience is comparable in more than its aura to what motivates prophecy. Though there is no intervention of vision or voice, there is something like a special, burdened relation to time. Wordsworth called the episode a "spot of time," to indicate that it stood out, spotlike, in his consciousness of time, that it merged sensation of place and sensation of time (so that time was *placed*), even that it allowed him to physically perceive or "spot" time.

The boy on the summit, overlooking the meeting point of two highways, and stationed between something immobile on his right hand and his left, is, as it were, at the center of a stark clock. Yet the question, How long? if it rises within him, remains mute. It certainly does not surface with the ghostly, prophetic dimension that invests it later. At this point there is simply a boy's impatient hope, "anxiety of hope," as the poet calls it (313), a straining of eye and mind that corresponds to the "far-stretched" perspective of the roads. But the father's death, which supervenes as an "event" (309), converts that moment of hope into an ominous, even murderous anticipation.

In retrospect, then, a perfectly ordinary mood is seen to involve a sin against time. The boy's "anxiety of hope," his wish for time to pass (both the "dreary time" of school and now of watching and waiting) seems to find retributive fulfillment when the father's life is cut short ten days later. The aftermath points to something unconscious in the first instance but manifest and punishing now. The child feels that his "desires" have been "corrected" by God. What desires could they be except fits of extreme—apocalyptic—impatience, brought on by the very patience or dreary sufferance of nature, of sheep and blasted tree? That the boy bowed low to God, who corrected his desires, evokes a human and orthodox version of nature's own passion.

A similar correction may be the subject of "A slumber did my spirit seal," where a milder sin against time, the delusion that the loved one is a "thing" exempt from the touch of years, is revealed when she dies and becomes a 'thing" in fact. The fulfillment of the hope corrects it, as in certain fairy tales. In Wordsworth, hope or delusion always involves the hypnotic elision of time by an imagination drawn toward the "bleak music" of nature—of a powerfully inarticulate nature.

Yet in both representations, that of the death of the father and that of the death of the beloved, there is no hint of anything that would compel the mind to link the two terms, hope against time and its peculiar fulfillment. The link remains inarticulate, like nature itself. A first memory is interpreted by a second: the "event" clarifies an ordinary emotion by suggesting its apocalyptic vigor. But the apocalyptic mode, as Martin Buber remarked, is not the prophetic. Wordsworth's spots of time are said to renew time rather than to hasten its end. A wish for the end to come, for time to pass absolutely, cannot explain what brought the two happenings together, causally, superstitiously, or by a *vaticinum ex eventu*.

Perhaps the apocalyptic wish so compressed the element of time that something like a "gravitation" effect was produced, whereby unrelated incidents fell toward each other. It is, in any case, this process of conjuncture or binding that is mysterious. Not only for the reader but for Wordsworth himself. A more explicit revelation of the binding power had occurred after the death of the poet's mother. Wordsworth's "For now a trouble came into my mind / From unknown causes" (1850 *Prelude* II, 276-77) refers to an expectation that when his mother died the world would collapse. Instead it remains intact and attractive.

> I was left alone
> Seeking the visible world, nor knowing why.
> The props of my affection were removed,

> And yet the building stood, as if sustained
> By its own spirit!
>
> (1850 *Prelude* II, 277-81)

What he had previously named, describing the relationship between mother and infant, "the gravitation and the filial bond," continues to operate without the mother. This event contrary to expectation is the "trouble"; and the "unknown causes" allude to the gravitation, or glue or binding, that mysteriously sustains nature, and draws the child to it in the mother's absence. Even loss binds; and a paradox emerges which focuses on the fixative rather than fixating power of catastrophe, on the nourishing and reparative quality of the "trouble." Wordsworth, too benevolent perhaps, suggests that time itself is being repaired: that the pressure of eternity on thought (the parent's death) creates an "eternity of thought" (1850 *Prelude* I, 402). The survivor knows that the burden of the mystery can be borne, that there is time for thought.

Whether or not, then, we understand Wordsworth's experience fully the "spots of time" describe a trauma, a lesion in the fabric of time, or more precisely, the trouble this lesion produces and which shows itself as an extreme consciousness of time. Not only is there an untimely death in the case of the father, but it follows too fast on the boy's return home. As in *Hamlet*, "The time is out of joint. O cursed spite / That ever I was born to set it right!" The righting of the injury somehow falls to the poet. "Future restoration" (1850 *Prelude* XII, 286), perhaps in the double sense of a restoration of the future as well as of a restoration still to come, is the task he sets himself.[1]

Prophecy, then, would seem to be anti-apocalyptic in seeking a "future restoration," or time for thought. But time, in Wordsworth, is also language, or what the Intimations Ode calls "timely utterance." That phrase contains both threat and promise. It suggests the urgent pressure that gives rise to speech; it also suggests that an animate response, and a harmonious one, is possible, as in Milton's "answerable style," or the pastoral cliché of woods and waters mourning, rejoicing or echoing in timely fashion the poet's mode. Ruskin referred to it as the pathetic fallacy but Abraham Heschel will make pathos, in that large sense, the very characteristic of prophetic language.

More radically still "timely utterance" means an utterance, such as prophecy, or prophetic poetry, which founds or repairs time. The prophet utters time in its ambiguity: as the undesired mediation, which prevents fusion, but also destruction. It prevents fusion by intruding the voice of the poet, his troubled heart, his fear of or flight from "power"; it prevents destruction by delaying God's decree or personally mediating it. Wordsworth speaks scrupulous words despite his sympathy with power and his attraction to the muteness or closure forseen. By intertextual bonding, by words within words or words against words, he reminds us one more time of time.

We cannot evade the fact that the anxious waiting and the father's death are joined by what can only be called a "blast of harmony." The two moments are harmonized, but the copula is poetic as well as prophetic. For the conjunction of these contiguous yet disparate happenings into a "kindred" form is due to a "working of the spirit" that must be equated with poetry itself. While in the boy of thirteen the process of joining may have been instinctual, the poet recollects the past event as still working itself out; the incident demonstrated so forceful a visiting of imaginative power that later thought is never free of it. What is remarkable in this type-incident—and so remarkable that it keeps "working" on the mind "to this very time"—is not only the "coadunation," as Coleridge would have said, or "In-Eins-Bildung" (his false etymology for the German *Einbild-ungskraft,* or imagination), but also that it is a "blast," that the workmanship reconciling the discordant elements anticipates a final, awesome unification. Hope is always "anxious" in that it foresees not just unity but also the power needed to achieve unity, to blast things into that state. The fear, then, that mingles with apocalyptic hope also stills it, or brings it close to "that peace / Which passeth understanding" (1850 *Prelude* XIV, 126-27), because of the uncertain, terrible nature of this final bonding, which evokes in the episode on the crag a bleak and bleating music and images of stunned, warped, blasted, inarticulate being.

III

I turn to the climactic episode of *The Prelude*, the ascent of Snowdon in Book XIV. Disregarding all but its barest structure, we see that it again presents a sequence of two moments curiously harmonized. The theme of time enters *as elided* when the moon breaks through the mist and into the absorbed mind of the climber. "Nor was time given to ask or learn the cause, / For instantly a light upon the turf / Fell like a flash..." (XIV, 37-39). This moment of prevenient light is followed as suddenly by a wild blast of music: the roar of waters through a rift in the mist. The second act or "event" is here an actual sound, separated off from sight and almost hypostatized as a sound. It is quite literally a "blast of harmony": "The roar of waters...roaring with one voice."

The appearance of the moon out of the mist is not, however, as unmotivated as might appear. It realizes an unuttered wish, "Let there be light," as the poet climbs through the darkness to "see the sun rise." Spotting the moon fulfills his hope in an unexpected way, which also foreshortens time. The mind of the poet is disoriented; but then time is lengthened as the sight of the moonstruck scene takes over in a kind of silent harmonization. If my hypothesis is correct, there is something truly magical here. The effect ("And there was light") utters the cause—that is, utters the scriptural text ("Let there be light") lodging as desire in the poet. Silence emits a "sound of harmony" (XIV, 98-99) analogous to the music of the spheres. Not the poet but heaven itself declares the glory, the "And there was light" as "night unto night showeth knowledge." Wordsworth seems to behold visibly the "timely utterance" with which Genesis begins—the very harmony between cause and effect, between fiat and actualizing response—and this spectacle seems to be so ghostly a projection of nature itself (rather than of his own excited mind) that he claims it was "given to spirits of the night" and only by chance to the three human spectators (XIV, 63-65).

Yet if the first act of the vision proper proves deceptive, because its motivation, which is a scriptural text, or the authority of that text, or the poet's desire to recapture that fiat power, remains silent and inward, the second act, which is the rising of the voice of the waters, also proves deceptive, even as it falsifies the first. The sound of the waters (though apparently unheard) must have been there all along, so that what is shown up by the vision's second act is a premature harmonizing of the landscape by the majestic moon: by that time-subduing object all sublime. Time also becomes a function of the desire for harmony as imagination now foreshortens and now enthrones the passing moment, or, to quote one of many variants, "so moulds, exalts, indues, combines, / Impregnates, separates, adds, takes away / And makes one object sway another so..." In the poet's commentary there is a further attempt at harmonizing, when moon and roaring waters are typified as correlative acts, the possessions of a mind

> That feeds upon infinity, that broods
> Over the dark abyss, intent to hear
> Its voices issuing forth to silent light
> In one continuous stream
>
> (XIV, 71-74)

An image of communion and continuity is projected which the syntax partially subverts, for "its" remains ambiguous, and we cannot say for sure whether the voices belong to the dark abyss or the heavenly mind. What remains of this rich confusion are partial and contradictory structures of unification, which meet us "at every turn" in the "narrow rent" of the text, and add up less to a "chorus of infinity" than again to a "blast of harmony."

IV

For prophet as for poet the ideal is "timely utterance," yet what we actually receive is a "blast of harmony." In Jeremiah a double pressure is exerted, of time on the prophet and of the prophet on time. The urgency of "timely utterance" cuts both ways. Moreover, while the prophet's words must harmonize with events, before or after the event, the word itself is viewed as an event that must harmonize with itself, or with its imputed source in God and the prophets. A passage such as Jeremiah 23:9-11 describes the impact of the God-word in terms that not only are conventionally ecstatic but also suggest the difficulty of reading the signs of authority properly, and distinguishing true from false prophet. "Adultery" seems to have moved into the word-event itself.

> Concerning the prophets:
> My heart is broken within me,
> all my bones shake;
> I am like a drunken man,
> like man overcome by wine,
> because of the LORD
> and because of his holy words.
> For the land is full of adulterers;
> because of the curse the land mourns. . . .

The time frame becomes very complex, then. On an obvious level the God-word as threat or promise is interpreted and reinterpreted in the light of history, so that Jeremiah's pronouncements are immediately set in their time. "The words of Jeremiah, the son of Hilkiah. . . to whom the word of the Lord came in the days of Josiah. . ." The ending *jah*, meaning "God," reveals from within these destined names the pressure for riming events with God. Jeremiah's prophecies are political suasions having to do with Israel's precarious position between Babylon on one border and Egypt on the other in the years before the destruction of Jerusalem by Nebuchadnezzar. The very survival of Israel is in question; and the prophet is perforce a political analyst as well as a divine spokesman. He speaks at risk not only in the hearing of God but also in that of Pashur, who beat him and put him in the stocks (20:1-4), in that of so-called friends who whisper "Denounce him to Pashur," and in that of King Zedekiah, the son of Josiah, king of Judah, who sends Pashur (the same or another) to Jeremiah, saying, "Inquire of the Lord for us" about Nebuchadnezzar, king of Babylon (21:1-3).

On another level, however, since the book of Jeremiah knows that the outcome is "the captivity of Jerusalem" (1:3), a question arises as to the later force of such prophecy. Near the onset of Jeremiah's career a manuscript of what may have been a version of Deuteronomy was found, and a dedication ceremony took place which pledged Judah once more to the covenant. The issue of the covenant—whether it is broken, or can ever be broken—and the part played in this issue by the survival of a book such a Jeremiah's own is another aspect of the prophet's utterance. Can one praise God yet curse onself as the bearer of his word (20:13-14)? Or can Judah follow God into the wilderness once more, showing the same devotion as when it was a bride (2:2)? "I utter what was only in view of what will be. . . . What is realized in my history is not the past definite of what was, since it is no more, or even the present perfect of what has been in what I am, but the future anterior of what I shall have been for what I am in the process of becoming." That is Jacques Lacan on the function of language.

Indeed, the contradictions that beset "timely utterance" are so great that a reversal occurs which discloses one of the founding metaphors of literature. When Jacques Lacan writes that "symbols. . .envelop the life of man in a network so total that they join together, before he comes into the world, those who are going to engender him 'by flesh and blood'; so total that they bring to his birth, along with the gifts of the stars, if not with the gifts of the fairies, the shape of his destiny; so total that they give the words that will make him faithful or renegade, the law of the acts that will follow him right to the very place where he *is* not yet and even beyond his death; and so total that through them his end finds its meaning in the last judgement, where the Word absolves his being or condemns it," he is still elaborating Jeremiah 1:4. "Now the word of the LORD came to me saying, 'Before I formed you in the womb I knew you, and before you were born I consecrated you; I appointed you a prophet to the nations.'" This predestination by the word and unto the word—the "imperative of the Word," as Lacan also calls it, in a shorthand that alludes to the later tradition of the Logos—is then reinforced by Jeremiah 1:11-12. "And the word of the LORD came to me saying, 'Jeremiah, what do you see?' And I said, 'I see a rod of almond.' Then the LORD said to me, 'You have seen well, for I am watching over my word to perform it.'"

Here the pun of "rod of almond" (*makel shaqued*) and "[I am] watching" (*shoqued*) is more, surely, than a mnemonic or overdetermined linguistic device: it is a rebus that suggests the actualizing or performative relationship between words and things implied by the admonition: "I am watching over my word to perform it." The admonition is addressed to the prophet, in whose care the word is, and through him to the nation; while the very image of the rod of almond projects not only a reconciliation of contraries, of punishment (rod) and pastoral peace (almond), but the entire problem of timely utterance, since the almond tree blossoms unseasonably early and is as exposed to blasting as is the prophet, who seeks to avoid premature speech: "Ah, Lord God! Behold, I do not know how to speak, for I am only a child."

The forcible harmonizing of *shaqued* and *shoqued*, the pressure of that pun, or the emblematic abuse of a pastoral image, alerts us to the difficult pathos of prophetic speech. What does "watching over the word" involve? The prophets are politically and psychically in such a pressure-cooker situation ("I see a boiling pot," Jeremiah 1:13) that a powerful contamination occurs. Their words cannot always be distinguished from those of God in terms of who is speaking. The prophet identifies now with God and now with his people; moreover, his only way of arguing with the Lord is through words and figures given by the latter. Lacan would say that there is an inevitable inmixing of the Discourse of the Other. Jeremiah argues with God in God's language; and such scripture formulas as "according to thy word" recall this confused and indeterminate situation.

When, in famous lyric verses, Jeremiah admits that he cannot speak without shouting, and what he shouts is "violence and destruction" (20:8), it is as if the God-word itself had suffered a crisis of reference. For this typical warning is now directed not against Israel but against God: it refers to the condition of the prophet who feels betrayed as well as endangered. Jeremiah's hymn begins: "O Lord, you seduced me, and I was seduced," where "seduce," *pittiytani*, can mean both sexual enticement and spiritual deception—as by false prophets. No wonder that at the end of this hymn, the most formal and personal in the entire book, there is a surprising and unmotivated turn from blessing ("Sing to the LORD: praise the LORD") to cursing ("Cursed be the day on which I was born!" 20:13-18). However conventional such a curse may be, and we find a famous instance in Job, it cannot but be read in conjunction with "Before I formed you in the womb I knew you." Jeremiah's "Cursed be the day" is a Caliban moment: God has taught the prophet to speak, and so to curse; or it is a Hamlet moment, the prophet being "cursed" by his election to set the time right. But more important, the curse is the word itself, the violence done by it to the prophet. He feels it in his heart and bones as a burning fire (20:9). The word that knew him before he was conceived has displaced father and mother as begetter: when he curses his birth his word really curses the word. Jeremiah is not given time to develop; he is hurled untimely into the word. The words of the prophet and the words of God can be one only through that "blast of harmony" of which Wordsworth's dream still gives an inkling.

V

When even an intelligent contemporary discussion of "The Prophets as Poets" talks of a "symphony of the effective word" and "the gradual union of person and word," and sees prophecy advancing historically from "word as pointer to word as the thing itself," it adopts metaphors as solutions. The animating fiat spoken by God in the book of Genesis, which founds the harmonious correspondence of creative principle (word) and created product (thing), is literalized by a leap of faith on the part of the intelligent contemporary reader.

Yet with some exceptions—Wolfgang Binder and Peter Szondi on the language of Hölderlin, Erich Auerbach on Dante and figural typology, Northrop Frye on Blake, M.H. Abrams and E.S. Shaffer on the Romantics, Stanley Cavell on Thoreau—it is not the literary critics but the biblical scholars who have raised the issue of secularization (or, what affinity is there between secular and sacred word?) to a level where it is more than a problem in commuting: how to get from there to here, or vice versa. Since Ambrose and Augustine, and again since the Romantic era, biblical criticism has developed together with literary criticism; and still we are only beginning to appreciate their mutual concerns.

It is no accident that the career of Northrop Frye has promised to culminate in an Anatomy of the Bible, or in a summa of structural principles that could harmonize the two bodies of the logos: scripture and literature. By labeling an essay "The Poetics of Prophecy," I may seem to be going in the same direction, and I certainly wish to; yet I think that the relationship between *poetics* and *prophetics* cannot be so easily accommodated. The work of detail, or close reading, ever remains, and quite possibly as a task without an ending. Even when we seek to climb to a prospect where secular and sacred hermeneutics meet on some windy crag, we continue to face a number of unresolved questions that at once plague and animate the thinking critic.

One question is the status of figures. They seem to persist in language as indefeasible sedimentations or as recurrent necessity, long after the megaphone of prophetic style. Moreover, because of the priority and survival of "primitive" or "oriental" figuration, such distinctions as Coleridge's between fancy and imagination tend to become the problem they were meant to resolve. Strong figurative expression does not reconcile particular and universal, or show the translucence of the universal in the concrete: there is such stress and strain that even when theorists value one mode of imaginative embodiment over another— as symbol over allegory or metaphysical wit—they admit the persistence and sometimes explosive concurrence of the archaic or depreciated form.

Another important question is the status of written texts in the life of society or the life of the mind. Almost every tradition influenced by Christianity has aspired to a spiritualization of the word, its transformation and even disappearance as it passes from "word as pointer to word as thing itself." A logocentric or incarnationist thesis of this kind haunts the fringes of most studies of literature, and explains the welcome accorded at present to semiotic counterperspectives. Textual reality, obviously, is more complex, undecidable, and lasting than any such dogma; and the dogma itself is merely inferred from historically ramified texts.

A last question concerns intertextuality. From the perspective of scripture intertextuality is related to canon formation, or the process of authority by which the bibles (*biblia*) we call the Bible were unified. The impact of scripture on literature includes the concept of (1) peremptory or preemptive texts and (2) interpreters who find the unifying principle that could join books into a canon of classics. From a secular perspective these books, whether classified as literature or as scripture, have force but no authority; and to bring them together into some sort of canon is the coup of the critic, who harmonizes them by the force of his own text. His work reveals not their canonicity but rather their intertextuality; and the most suggestive theory along these lines has been that of Harold Bloom.

The impact, according to him, of a preemptive poem on a later one is always "revisionary": the one lives the other's death, deviating its meaning, diverting its strength, creating an inescapable orbit. "Revisionary" suggests, therefore, a relationship of force: again, a blast of harmony rather than a natural or authoritative unification.

For a reason not entirely clear to me, Bloom wishes to establish English poetry after Milton as a Milton satellite. Milton becomes a scripture substitute with the impressive and oppressive influence of scripture itself. Later poets must harmonize with Milton, willingly or unwillingly: even their deviations are explained by attempts to escape the Milton orbit. Yet I have shown that Wordsworth may imitate a scripture text ("Let there be light") with a power of deviousness that is totally un-Miltonic. Milton and Nature, Wordsworth saw, were not the same. His return to scripture is not to its precise verbal content, though it is an implicit content (Genesis, light, voice) that infuses the texture of the vision on Snowdon. The form of the fiat, however, predominates over its content; and what we are given to see is not scripture reenacted or imaginatively revised—new testamented—but the unuttered fiat in its silent yet all-subduing aspect. What Wordsworth names and represents as Nature is the fiat power working tacitly and harmoniously, reconciling discordant elements, building up the mind and perhaps the cosmos itself.

Snowdon's Miltonic echoes, therefore, which recapitulate a portion of the story of creation as retold in the seventh book of *Paradise Lost*, are allusions whose status is as hard to gauge as those to *Hamlet* in the "spot of time" referring to the father's death. The converging highways, moreover, in that spot of time could lead the contemporary reader (perhaps via Freud) to Oedipus, so that a question arises on the relation of revisionary to hermeneutic perspectives, making the intertextual map more tricky still. Yet Wordsworth's vision, natural rather than textual in its apparent motivation, can still be called revisionary because a prior and seminal text may be hypothetically reconstituted.

The act of reconstitution, however, now includes the reader in a specific and definable way. The *poet* as reader is shown to have discovered from within himself, and so recreated, a scripture text. The *interpreter* as reader has shown the capacity of a "secular" text to yield a "sacred" intuition by a literary act of understanding that cannot be divided into those categories. On the level of interpretation, therefore, we move toward what Schleiermacher called *Verstehen*, on the basis of which a hermeneutic is projected that seeks to transcend the dichotomizing of religious and nonreligious modes of understanding and of earlier (prophetic) and later (poetic-visionary) texts.

VI

Returning a last time to Wordsworth: much remains to be said concerning the "gravitation and the filial bond" that links earlier visionary texts to his own. The reader, in any case, also moves in a certain gravitational field; and I have kept myself from being pulled toward a Freudian explanation of the nexus between the boy's "anxiety of hope" and the guilty, affective inscription on his mind of a natural scene. My only finding is that should a God-word precede in Wordsworth, it is rarely foregrounded, but tends to be part of the poem's ground as an inarticulate, homeless or ghostly, sound. It becomes, to use one of his own expressions, an "inland murmur."

In the second act of Snowdon this sound comes out of the deep and is suddenly the very subject, the "Imagination of the whole" (1805 *Prelude* XIII, 65). Though the text behind that sound cannot be specified, it is most probably the word within the word, the Word that was in the Beginning (John 1:1), and which uttered as from chaos, "Let there be light." In Milton the first words of the "Omnific Word" are "Silence, ye troubl'd Waves, and thou Deep, peace" (*Paradise Lost* VII, 216), a proto-fiat Wordsworth may have absorbed into his vision of silence followed by his more radical vision of the power in sound.

When the poet writes, "The sounding cataract haunted me like a passion" ("Tintern Abbey"), there is again no sense of a proof text of any kind. We recognize a congruity of theme between this waterfall and the "roar of waters" heard on Snowdon, and perhaps associate both with Psalm 42: "Deep calls unto deep at the thunder of thy cataracts." Such allusions may exist, but they are "tidings" born on the wave of natural experience. Yet a prophetic text does enter once more in the way we have learned to understand. The word "passion," by being deprived of specific reference, turns back on itself, as if it contained a muted or mutilated meaning. By a path more devious than I can trace, the reader recovers for "passion" its etymological sense of "passio"—and the word begins to embrace the pathos of prophetic speech, or a suffering idiom that is strongly inarticulate or musical, like the "earnest expectation of the creature...subjected...in hope" of which Paul writes in Romans (8:19-20), like sheep, blasted tree, and the boy who waits with them, and the barely speaking figures that inhabit the poet's imagination. The event, in Wordsworth, is the word of connection itself, a word event (the poem) that would repair the bond between human hopes and a mutely remonstrant nature, "subjected in hope."

"Do you know the language of the old belief?" asks Robert Duncan. "The wild boar too / turns a human face." Today the hope in such a turning includes the very possibility of using such language. A mighty scheme not of truth but of troth—of trusting the old language, its pathos, its animism, its fallacious figures— is what connects poet and prophet. When Wordsworth apostrophizes nature at the end of the Intimations Ode, he still writes in the old language, yet how precariously, as he turns toward what is turning away:

> And O, ye Fountains, Meadows, Hills and Groves,
> Forebode not any severing of our loves!

BIBLIOGRAPHICAL NOTE

The locus classicus of Coleridgean poetics is found in Chapters 13 and 14 of the *Biographia Literaria* (1818), "On the Imagination, or Esemplastic Power," etc. *Aids to Reflection* (1824), and a mass of miscellaneous lectures and readings contain many subtle and varying attempts to distinguish between symbolical and allegorical, analogous and metaphorical language, and so forth. Coleridge's reflections on the subject of style and unity are much more intricate than my general comment suggests; see, for one example, "On Style," reprinted in *Coleridge's Miscellaneous Criticism*, ed. T.M. Raysor (Cambridge, Mass., 1936), pp. 214-17. Yet even there German-type speculation is mixed with practical and preacherly admonition. The major German influence in regard to art, revelation, and the question of unity (or "identity philosophy") was, of course, Schelling. Martin Buber's distinction between apocalyptic and prophetic is made in "Prophecy, Apocalyptic, and the Historical Hour," in *On the Bible* (New York, 1968). For Abraham Heschel on pathos, see *The Prophets* (New York, 1962). The intelligent contemporary discussion on prophets as poets is in David Robertson's chapter of that title in *The Old Testament and the Literary Critic* (Philadelphia, 1977). Robertson acknowledges his debt to Gerhard von Rad's *Old Testament Theology*, vol. 2. To the literary scholars mentioned in my essay, I should add Paul de Man's and Angus Fletcher's work on the theory of allegory; Walter Benjamin's seminal reconsideration of baroque allegory in *The Origin of German Tragic Drama* (originally published in 1928); and articles by Robert W. Funk on the parable in the New Testament and in Kafka. Frank Kermode is also working on the parable and has begun publishing on the idea of canon formation. Elinor Shaffer's *Kubla Khan and the Fall of Jerusalem* (Cambridge, England, 1976) links up more specifically than Basil Willey movements in Bible criticism and considerations of literary form. Her chapter entitled "The Visionary Character" is especially valuable in summarizing the movement of thought whereby poets, critics, and theologians came to consider Holy Writ as composed of different poetic and narrative genres, and faced the question of how to value nonapostolic (generally "apocalyptic" rather than "prophetic") visionariness. My quotations from Jacques Lacan can be found in *Ecrits: A Selection* (New York, 1977), pp. 68 and 86. The issue of secularization in literary history is central to M.H. Abrams' *Natural Supernaturalism* (1971) and has elicited, in the Anglo-American domain, many partial theories from Matthew Arnold to Daniel Bell. Stanley Cavell's *The Senses of Walden* (1971) reveals a Wordsworthian type of underwriting in Thoreau, and one so consistent in its allusions to earlier epics and scriptures that *Walden* begins to emerge as a sacred book.

12
Elation in Hegel and Wordsworth

Let me confess that I have used "elation" in the past to render the Hegelian word "Aufhebung," which is usually translated "sublation." By this sleight of terms I suggest, against Hegel's own tendency in the last section of the *Phenomenology*, which passes from "Religion in the Form of Art" via "revealed Religion" to "Absolute Knowing," that the basic move in his dialectic is, even here, *aesthetic*—without defining that elusive word. My procedure of associating an unclear term, "Aufhebung" ("elation"), with an obscure concept (the "aesthetic") will not seem promising at first. My experiences are not those of a trained philosopher but of a reader fascinated by a phenomenon to which the name "aesthetic" was assigned only in the eighteenth century; a phenomenon, nevertheless, that is as clear in its effect if unclear in its structure and properties as the enchanted quark in the system of what physicists call "weak reactions."

I begin with the last paragraph (808) of Hegel's *Phenomenology*.[1] The self has to penetrate and digest (these are Hegel's own words) the entire wealth of its substance. That substance is equivalent to its history, its Being in Time; yet to fulfill its history by knowing what it is, the self must, says Hegel, "abandon its outer existence and give its form over to recollection." Even so, "sunk in the night of its self-consciousness," that is, submerged in this moment of ultimate recollection, its vanished existence is not only preserved but also "aufgehoben," raised to a higher level; and in the enjoyment of this new existence, of this brave new world born out of the fullness of knowledge, the mind starts fresh as if all that preceded were lost, and it had learned nothing from previous incarnations ("Geister"). Yet they are preserved through internalization (*Er-innerung*);

preserved, that is, not as a block of positive knowledge but as our very substance. Now we see through history, not with it; as Blake said we see through the eye, not with it; and history reveals itself as a marathon of spirits, each relieving and supporting the other, and exhibiting as a totality—then comes a crucial phrase— "the raising up of the spirit's depth, or its dilation," "das Aufheben seiner Tiefe, oder seine *Ausdehnung*."

Does "Aufheben" relate to "Aufhebung"? Does the ponderous machine of the dialectic verge on a levity close to levitation, not in the mystical sense, but in what I am tempted to call the aesthetic sense, when thoughts become perceptions—true hallucinations with the lucidity of pristine eye and ear? Is "das aus dem Wissen neugeborene. . . [die] Unmittelbarkeit," close to the Apollonian convergence of appearance ("Schein") and radiance ("Schein"), which Nietzsche saw as the aesthetic foundation of Greek thought, despite the obstinate bass of Dionysos? "Alles Tiefe soll hinauf," all depth must rise—like the sun sucks the depth of the sea to its height—is Zarathoustra's version of absolute knowing, in the chapter mockingly entitled "On Immaculate Knowledge" ("Von der unbefleckten Erkenntniss"). And Wallace Stevens:

> The philosopher's man alone still walks in dew,
> Still by the sea-side mutters milky lines
> Concerning an immaculate imagery.
>
> "Asides on the Oboe"

Hegel's elation of the deep is a powerful metaphor. In context it describes a final "negativity," though "kenosis" is the better word, since it renders the point at which self resting in itself goes out again and accepts this outward-bound movement as its identity. Hegel speaks with a pathos that evokes the human difficulty of letting go of self, of plowing it back into the ground of an action which is exalted by its apparent fading. The figure he uses refers, in its pathos, not only to the structure of Christian revelation ("Offenbarung") based on Christ's "kenosis" but is more generally apocalyptic: this depth must be Plutonian or Neptunian, depth of earth or sea, rising up not to destroy so much as to reveal what lies hidden; or to destroy by the mere fact of revealing. There is an "immaculate disclosure," to quote Stevens again, "of the secret no more obscured."

The impression left by the ending of the *Phenomenology*, then, is less of earth-shaking violence than of a quasinatural shift in perception. Night is illuminated rather than utterly replaced; the stars stay bright rather than fading into day. Even the immense labor of the spirit we call world history, whose depth is glimpsed, at every moment in time, only superficially, is now seen as easily as a surface: it has dilated our eyes or itself, it is as ungravid as light, light as light. The unclear burden of traumatic, divisive, or indigest knowledge falls away. The myth of depth falls away. This elation, this lightening of the very notion of substance, rather than its denial or continued heavy elaboration, is what may allow us to change Hegel's aesthetic phenomenology into a phenomenological aesthetics.

Too many quotable passages could intrude at this point to confirm how characteristically elation is associated with lightness or the lifting of burdens. It is a "blessed mood / In which the burthen of the mystery. . . . Is lightened." So Wordsworth; and to him I turn to make my case that elation should be considered as an aesthetic sort of logic.

In a sonnet "Composed by the Side of Grasmere Lake" in the year the *Phenomenology* was completed (1807), the poet describes the quiet waters of a lake as they reflect the starry sky:

> Clouds, lingering yet, extend in solid bars
> Through the grey west; and lo! these waters, steeled
> By breezeless air to smoothest polish yield
> A vivid repetition of the stars;
> Jove, Venus, and the ruddy crest of Mars
> Amid his fellows beauteously revealed
> At happy distance from earth's groaning field,
> Where ruthless mortals wage incessant wars.
> Is it a mirror?—or the nether Sphere
> Opening to view the abyss in which she feeds
> Her own calm fires?—But list! a voice is near;
> Great Pan himself low-whispering through the reeds,
> 'Be thankful, thou; for, if unholy deeds
> Ravage the world, tranquillity is here!'

The raising up of the deep (9-11) is conveyed by an image at once pastoral and apocalyptic. In that nether Sphere the vulcanic fires are unlike those presently ravaging Europe. The abyss is a Milky Way, self-nourished and calm. The nether Sphere, moreover, discloses the abyss to *our* view or to *its own* view. Perhaps the distinction is too fine, but it suggests that, because of the wars, the Sphere has become obscure to itself, unsure about its destiny or motive (feeding sources), and so looks within. Wordsworth goes through the looking glass to create an uncanny image of Nature turned reflective. For all is not well in a world at war, which might engulf Jena and even distant and peaceful Grasmere. The sounds of war threaten the consolations of philosophy and the subsistence of a pastoral refuge. The question becomes, how deep must we forage to find a countervailing force; and whether that force from the deep can come from mind acting on itself, disclosing and preserving its own "fires." The mind cannot deny history, in the present shape of Napoleon, who said that "Politics is fate;" but what then is the fate of mind in such an era, which is our era too?

Wordsworth's Grasmere sonnet ends with a divine whisper: "Tranquillity is here." Those words are not completely reassuring. Though we recognize that

Pan's message is the opposite of "panic," it does not enter the flow of thought as naturally as the two questions that constitute the surmise of lines 9-11. To many readers it may seem like a wishful conclusion. The "here," moreover, is more restless than it should be. [2] Its primary locus is Grasmere, where the poet is composing or in a "composed" state of mind. But there are other foci of tranquillity. We recall the skygods previously invoked "at happy distance from earth's groaning field." We also recall the "calm fires." The effect of this spreading "here" is that tranquillity is not "here," except in hope or by a fanciful movement akin to hope.

The pastoral poet who looks at the lingering clouds, as night approaches and the stars come out, is reading signs, as the farmer does in Virgil's *Georgics* or as Coleridge does in the weather-wise opening of his Dejection Ode. The weather includes, of course, what the gods have in store politically (we are in the midst of the Napoleonic wars), and the future of imagination itself, which acts in this ominous, premonitory way. The appearance of Pan, though somewhat mechanical (contrast Proteus rising from the sea in the earlier sonnet, "The World is too much with us") is not just tranquillizing. Though peace is desired—not least as a stilling of the foreboding mind—this Pan, like the more dramatic Proteus, suggests an imaginative need: the need to conjure up a figure of salvation.

That figure is personified in another sonnet ("London 1802") by invoking Milton. His patriotic and passionate sonnets were a discovery for Wordsworth, who had been disdainful of the sonnet form as well as struggling to reconcile his pastoral identity with the encroaching sounds of war, that is, with a martial and public voice. The Grasmere sonnet is Miltonic in a modified, even subversive way. A capacity to be moved by the Classical imagination, to use it even while fighting it, is what Milton impressed, indelibly, on English verse; and in this sonnet, I believe, Milton's acknowledgment of the heroic Classical temper is given a new if subdued political twist. For the resurgence of Classical imagery in Wordsworth after 1801 may express not only the Classical spirit transplanted to England, with Milton as exemplar, but also a sense of what joins the warring nations, a sense of the Latinity which France and England have in common as cultures. The "here" in "Tranquillity is here" could refer then to the comfort, the nourishment, found in a certain imaginative mode: "here" in a conscientious classicism on English soil, parallel to the conscientious catholicism on English soil which the Church of England aspired to. These gentle, whispering breezes, these calm fires, should suffice a mind tempted by violent stimulants. Pan stands for a heroic *peace* in a world given to violence and apocalyptic fancies. An unterrible beauty is born, an *English* classicism.

Hegel and Wordsworth have entered an epoch in which philosophy forms an alliance with art in order to resist the political appropriation of mind. Only such an alliance, already adumbrated in Schiller's *Letters on Aesthetic Education* (1795), could restore contemplation as the "green belt" of an increasingly industrialized, action-oriented, and deprivatized world. If the characteristic of action is to insist on a specific end, on change rather than interpretation, and to consume itself in achieving this end, it does not have to respect the inertial force of the past or try to sublate it. Though it may have to respect the past provisionally to gain its purpose, action ideologizes interpretation and keeps moving relentlessly toward an all-consuming point which is the new regime, the new order. The alliance philosophy can make with art, through what we have learned to call the "aesthetic," is always characterized, therefore, by a structure of postponement; the doubting or delaying of closure, the insistence on remainders or of a return of the past, and—more problematically—on a concept of elation that embraces both the reality of history and freedom of mind. The elated consciousness, however, may differ from the manic only by a precarious margin. While elation is never regression in the service of politics but rather a change of what is known into *Anschauung*, since the same condition underlies both states of mind what delivers us from politicization or the slavery of an exclusively practical thinking can be sucked into the opposing (manic) orbit.

The issue I raise is focused by the complexities of Hegel's last paragraph, its problems with closure. The dialectic, even in this ultimate moment, seems restless. Tranquillity is not here. Where Hegel sees a last term, identified with spirit itself, and sublating the entire labor of history, I can see only the aesthetic principle that has kept him moving toward this juncture, and which is like Wordsworth's self-feeding abyss, or the nourishment alluded to in Hegel's final citation from Schiller's poem on friendship. It depicts God as without friend or equal, therefore having to create spirits ('Geister'), so that he can mirror Himself in them. "From the cup of this vast realm of spirits / Foams forth to Him the Infinite." The cup overflows, of itself as it were, made drunk by its own essence; it seems, once more, an image of the deep elated, yet it remains a source of nourishment as in Wordsworth's sonnet. That Hegel's philosophical tract ends with a literary allusion may be conventional enough; but that the figure is a figure of nourishment suggests that figuration itself can nourish. The *Phenomenology*, at any rate, does not shut like the trap-door in a logical demonstration: its closure is of a different kind.

When I assert, therefore, that the movement of Hegel's prose is recognizably aesthetic, I refer to that rich difficulty of closing in a dialectic that leads to and postpones a final resolution. The dialectic approaches the condition of music as Suzanne Langer describes that medium:

Articulation is its life, but not assertion; expressiveness, not expression. The actual functioning of meaning, which calls for permanent contents, is not fulfilled; for the *assignment* of one rather than another possible meaning to each form is never explicitly made.[3]

For Hegel, we would only have to substitute "is made, and then taken away, or sublated." Donald Davie has suggested that the poet—I would add the aesthetic philosopher—decides the sense and brings the period to a close, not because he is now prepared to commit himself to an assertion but rather to find an equivalent for music's "reorientation in each new resolution to harmony." "The whole play of literal meaning, in fact, is a Swedish drill," adds Davie, "in which nothing is being lifted, transported, or set down, though the muscles tense, knot, and relax."[4] My only quarrel is that this image trivializes the concept of elation just as I.A. Richards, wishing to deny the specificity of an aesthetic state of mind, evades it by his vision of an expanded empirical psychology. Commenting on "the widespread increase in the aptitude of the average mind for self-dissolving introspection, the generally heightened awareness of the goings on of our own minds, merely as *goings on*, not as transitions from one well-known and linguistically recognized moral or intellectual condition to another," he suggests that this change is shown most clearly in "such prose as Mr. Joyce's or Mrs. Woolf's [which] is a dilution (or better, an expansion, 'like gold to aery thinnesse beate') of a use of words that has in most ages been within the range of poetry."[5]

Where Richards says dilution I would substitute dilation, the word closest to Hegel's *Ausdehnung*. With dilation or dilution we are not far from dissolution; and so the question of closure, through art or logic, intensifies itself. We too are faced with the "undisciplined revelry" or "stupor of consciousness and wild stammering utterance" which constitute the pseudo-infinity, the "schlechte Unendlichkeit" Hegel tried to put behind him in every transition and decisively in that from the Religion of Art to Absolute Knowing. From my point of view he succeeds only in putting the issue *before* us; and in the second part of this essay I would like to examine the relation of closure to elation in both the literary and the philosophical work of art.

Geoffrey Hill has said that "the technical perfecting of a poem is an act of atonement, in the radical etymological sense,—an act of at-one-ment. . . a bringing into concord, a reconciling, a uniting in harmony."[6] He also quotes Yeats from a letter to Dorothy Wellesley that "a poem comes right with a click like a closing box." The transition from technical perfection, the "click," to feelings of atonement, is not unproblematic. Logical closure may be technical, like that click; but artistic closure, except for a general sense of the right words in the right place is not punctual. In significant art there is instead a sensitivity to premature closure, one that delays or multiplies endings and creates limits that prove liminal. Despite the rigor of certain schools (the Chicago Aristotelians, for example, schematized the relation between formal devices and effects) no consensus has been achieved on how to effect affect. Genre theory can at most talk of intended effects, or the matching of particular literary devices with a particular expectation: what Wordsworth called the "contract" between writer and audience. But Wordsworth also said it was the prerogative of the creative writer to break this contract. Art seems to play a larger sense of closure against its punctual forms, including logical form. But what does "a larger sense of closure" mean?

Take Wordsworth's well-known lyric of eight lines, one of the "Lucy" poems, which has been explicated so many times without its meaning being fully determined:

> A slumber did my spirit seal;
> I had no human fears:
> She seemed a thing that could not feel
> The touch of earthly years.
>
> No motion has she now, no force;
> She neither hears nor sees;
> Rolled round in earth's diurnal course,
> With rocks, and stones, and trees.

It does not matter whether you interpret the second stanza (especially its last line) as tending toward affirmation, or resignation, or a grief verging on bitterness. The tonal assignment of one rather than another possible meaning, to repeat Suzanne Langer on musical form, is curiously open or beside the point. Yet the lyric does not quite support Langer's general position, that "Articulation is its life, but not assertion," because the poem is composed of a series of short and definitive statements, very like assertions. You could still claim that the poem's life is not in the assertions but somewhere else: but where then? What would articulation mean in that case? Articulation is not anti-assertive here; indeed the sense of closure is so strong that it thematizes itself in the very first line.

Nevertheless, is not the harmony or aesthetic effect of the poem greater than this local conciseness; is not the sense of closure broader and deeper than our admiration for a perfect technical construct? The poem is surely something else than a fine box, a well-wrought coffin.

That it is a kind of epitaph is relevant, of course. We recognize, even if genre is not insisted on, that Wordsworth's style is laconic, even lapidary. There may be a mimetic or formal motive related to the ideal of epitaphic poetry. But the motive may also be, in a precise way, meta-epitaphic. The poem, first of all, marks the closure of a life that has never opened up: Lucy is likened in other poems to a hidden flower or the evening star. Setting overshadows rising, and her mode of existence is inherently inward, westering. I will suppose then, that Wordsworth was at some level giving expression to the traditional epitaphic wish: Let the earth rest lightly on the deceased. If so, his conversion of this epitaphic formula is so complete that to trace the process of conversion might seem gratuitous. The formula, a trite if deeply grounded figure of speech, has been catalyzed out of existence. Here it is the formula itself, or better, the adjusted words of the mourner that lie lightly on the girl and everyone who is a mourner.

I come back, then, to the "aesthetic" sense of a burden lifted, rather than denied. A heavy element is made lighter. One may still feel that the term "elation" is inappropriate in this context; yet elation is, as a mood, the very subject of the first stanza. For the mood described is love or desire when it *eternizes* the loved person, when it makes her a star-like being that "could not feel / The touch of earthly years." This *naive* elation, this spontaneous movement of the spirit upward, is reversed in the downturn or cata-strophe of the second stanza. Yet this stanza does not close out the illusion; it preserves it within the elegiac form. The illusion is elated, in our use of the word: "aufgehoben" seems the proper term. For the girl is still, and all the more, what she seemed to be: beyond touch, like a star, if the earth in its daily motion is a planetary and erring rather than a fixed star, and if all on this star of earth must partake of its sublunar, mortal, temporal nature.

Closure then cannot be reduced to a technical feature, to conciseness. Wordsworth discloses the link between elation as a mood (euphoria, denial of mortality, eternizing) and elation as a style of thought. But if elation is a fallacy brought on by passion, then what is "Aufhebung"? As a form of logic we would have to call it elative or ecstatic. *Erinnerung*, Hegel writes in a passage already referred to, preserves the experience of yesterday, the experience of previous generations ("Geister") so inwardly that it seems to be forgotten; not a part of *us* but of a *substance* in which we participate. That is the burden of the second part of Wordsworth's *Er-innerung*, his tranquil recollection.

Note also what happens to the medium of the words. Genre analysis cannot do more than recuperate formulas or figures associated with epitaphs. Yet a previous poem in the same cycle, "Strange fits of passion," relates the same experience in a form that has no link to the epitaph. It is a pseudo-ballad, mocking that genre's supernatural symbolism and sentimental or surrealistic plot. Between that poem and this a purification has occurred. Genre stands between writer and reader as an obstacle, a false mediation: it is cleared away, and we are left with the barest story, unobtrusive figures of speech, and a diction that is at once sparse and natural.

The form of dealing with death is now drawn as if directly from language rather than from the epitaph tradition. There is a new immediacy ("Unmittelbarkeit"). Tradition and history enter only in the same ghostly way as in Hegel, as an elation of "depth of Spirit." Since the subject is a death, we can also talk of purification; though as a spiritual and verbal, not a ritual process. Through purified words we glimpse the nature of all words. Words, better by far than air or earth, are the elated monument.[7]

To sum up: In Wordsworth's lyric the specific gravity of words is weighed in the balance of each stanza; and this balance is as much a judgment on speech in the context of our mortality as it is a meaningful response to the individual death. At the limit of the medium of words, and close to silence, what has been purged is not concreteness, or the empirical sphere of the emotions—shock, disillusion, trauma, recognition, grief, atonement—what has been purged is a series of flashy schematisms and false or partial mediations: artificial plot, inflated consolatory rhetoric, the coercive absolutes of logic or faith.

A question remains. Why is closure needed at all? Because the realm of the dead—the "Geisterreich"—is not tranquil. Lucy haunts the poet as a virginal figure, an unconsummated force of life: she must have shape, if only in this tomb or crypt of words. There is the poet's guilt in living on, or living a life the other has not had. The poet as lover may even have created the distance that kept the beloved at a distance. She was, as she is now, untouchable. "A slumber did my spirit seal": the seal is like a hymen over consciousness.

Yet Lucy may be everyone whose spiritual or imaginative potential is unrealized; whose is not? The poet as poet is haunted by the restless ghost, the unconsummated spirit of others, by their inarticulate or virtual mode of being. Life has foreclosed them, and art makes restitution through an elated, unclosured form of mourning that evokes "unknown modes of being," and resists premature burial—the empty abyss of the Absolute, Hegel says at one point (*Phenomenology*, 803), which coercive plot, rhetorical formalism and religious ritual impose. Aesthetics helps art to sustain itself in the face of these absolutes that without wanting to know it are moved by the very thing they bury: a fit or dream of passion that defies mortality, that leaps over the grave or even moon in its longing for an "object all sublime."

I now face a traffic jam of thoughts. The anthropologist in me is interested in how closure and elation might enter rites of burial and purification. The psychoanalyst in me wonders what role the "lost object" plays in mourning: an object that can be as evasive as musical meaning. The philosopher of language remembers how many utopian or racially motivated theories of language-purification have been put forward. The student of religious experience notes the prevalence of ecstasy in ancient religion and modern revivals; but even if he believes with Hegel that "The tables of the gods provide no spiritual food and drink, and in his games and festivals man no longer recovers the joyful consciousness of his unity with the divine," or further that "The words of the Muse now lack the power of the Spirit, for the Spirit has gained its certainty of itself from the crushing of gods and men" (*Phenomenology*, 752), both art and religion remain alive, and he must deal with their persistence. Do they still purify, or counteract, the dream-life in us, its uncontrollable momentum? Do they draw it into the light, so that its pollution of living forms can be checked?

It is difficult, in short, to separate off Aesthetics as a field of inquiry, one based on distinctive features disclosed in experience by our experience of art. The claim for Aesthetics as such a field, or the only claim I can make, is that in conjunction with art it develops interpretive powers that bring us closer to all types of experience, not in their immediacy but in their mediatedness. Every work of art, from this point of view, is a criticism of life in terms of a criticism of mediations: of conventions, schematisms, institutions, of art itself, and the way we think or talk about it.

This expansion of Aesthetics as a critique is not as unmanageable as it may seem. For, quite obviously, students of Aesthetics will want to establish priorities; and their training will predispose them to begin with traditional inquiries into the distinctive features of the different art media. What relationship is there between media and meditations? Is one medium purer or of more value than another? How do we understand the cathartic power of media, vis-à-vis themselves or vis-à-vis mediations they criticize? Are art media continuous, like different epochs of the mediatory process in the *Phenomenology*?

I come somewhat reluctantly to the issue of purity. Purity, more than presence, is the metaphysical category proper. It raises the question whether we can live without symbols, atonements, or idols that mask as mediations. Wallace Stevens' famous lines on "the first idea" suggest that the artist is always improvising "Notes"—musical *Zettel*—"Toward a Supreme Fiction," toward the fictive image of a world where time and nature have purified themselves:

> How clean the sun when seen in its idea
> Washed in the remotest cleanliness of a heaven
> That has expelled us and our images.

Not only does this suggest that meanings are excrementitous, or that we always wish to return, like Hegel, to the sensory freshness of things, their recovered immediacy; it could also point to a more radical appreciation of that "Nirvana Principle" I have renamed elation.

Taking a lyric of eight lines and filtering the *Phenomenology* through its needle-like focus may seem to confirm the desperate straits of the would-be aesthetician. But experiences do exist that have such focusing power. Here and there every thinker's work refines itself into aphorisms that keep us going and make us tolerate analysis, however elaborate, as a form of mediation. When Freud says "The end [i.e., aim] of life is death," he states the economy of human life in words so denuded that, as in Wordsworth's lyric, our feelings interpret the words rather than the words our feelings. Speech that reaches this degree of brevity and focus does not wish to exist except as a sort of epitaph, the articulation of an ethics of the dust, or a last line of resistance to the law it pronounces. Pascal's *pensées* are also like that.

I wish to conclude with a suspicious yet inevitable thought on the character of aesthetic elation. Emerson, in one of those terrible moments of optimism to which he is subject, writes to Carlyle in the context of the latter's recently published *Sartor Resartus*. *Sartor* is an uncleanly book, a rag-bag philosophy, conceived, Carlyle jokes, among the Old Clothes shops of London, where Teufelsdrökh pursues his Hegelian-Schellingean *Naturphilosophie*, converting every phenomenon into a ghostly solicitation from the "Geisterreich" Hegel wishes to lay or elate. "There is a part of ethics," Emerson remarks ". . . which possesses all attraction to me; to wit, the compensations of the Universe, the equality and the coexistence of action and reaction, that all prayers are granted, that every debt is paid. And the skill with which the great All maketh clean work as it goes along, leaves no rag, consumes its smoke."[8]

Every text, however, is itself a residue. The work of purification cannot consume the evidence of its labors: what it leaves behind, in Hegel, is nothing less than history itself in the form of Hegel's own text. "What remains, today, for us, here and now, of Hegel?" is how Jacques Derrida begins his reflections on textuality in *Glas*. No law can obliterate or cancel the bond of textuality. Not even the economic or psychic law of exchange suggested by modern semiotics. "Each column" Derrida writes, alluding to the two columns on his printed page, as well as to the monumentalism of art, "Each column moves itself onward with unmovable self-sufficiency and yet the element of contagion, the infinite circulation of general equivalence relates each phrase, each word, each truncated piece of writing, to every other, within each column, and, from column to column, *what has remained* [is] infinitely calculable." There is always a remainder that cannot be purged, whatever violence of intellect we apply.

Elation, then, even as aesthetic principle, is still in the realm of ecstatic longings, or the quest for purity. The hypnotic trance or slumber that sealed Wordsworth's spirit, and which made him a sleepwalker in "Strange fits of passion," is not unlike the "benign stupor" or "blank dream" that is a clinical symptom of psychotic elation. The latter can alternate with a melancholic low—a fearful sense of unreality, "Fallings from us, vanishings; / Blank misgivings of a Creature / Moving about in worlds not realised" (*Intimations Ode*). Psychotic elation or mania has been interpreted by Bertram Lewin as "a living-out of the fantasy of being dead," or as a somnambulic repetition of the infant's sleep at the breast. It may be accompanied by strong oral desires, by the grandiose absorption of "food for thought." But, as Lewin, our best scholar of the elations has remarked: "The metaphysics here is a little difficult."[9]

Hegel's dialectic, his "labor of the negative," must be compared as well as contrasted with "denial" in the technical psychoanalytic sense: a defense mechanism that plays a central role in elation. The end of all this labor is, if not a blank dream, then an internal coming to rest—an ingesting, an *Erinnerung* of nothing less than All. Yet Hegel's self-elating spirit cannot find rest in itself alone:

it continually negates its inwardness as well, as if it could come to rest only in an object. Wordsworth notes a similar conflict in his early development. His eye "Could find no surface where [its] power might sleep"; both ocean and sky, "spangled with kindred multitudes of stars" "spake perpetual logic to [his] soul" (1850 *Prelude* III, 158ff.). Between that relentless, sleepless state, and a desired repose that is constantly negated in view of a higher repose (as in Hegel's dialectic), there must be a relation. "Sleep and death," Lewin remarks, "may be presented as a happy 'being devoured' or they may be avoided by a supervigil." In Hegel the supervigil, the sleeplessness or even deathlessness of consciousness, coexists with a "maternal yearning" or the "pure 'pathos' of substance." Closure, whether represented as sleep, death, or ecstasy, is elated by a moving principle that claims to be logical even if it is aesthetic.

In his chapter on Classical art in the *Lectures on Aesthetics*[10] Hegel refers to the end of the *Odyssey* (Book 24, 41-63), where Agamemnon meets Achilles in the Underworld and describes the latter's death-rites. According to Agamemnon, after performing the lustration ceremonies the Acheans hear coming from the sea an unearthly wailing that would have panicked them had not Nestor interpreted it. "'The mother,'" says Nestor, "'is emerging from the sea together with her immortal nymphs to behold her dead son.' And fear left the high-spirited Acheans." It left them, adds Hegel, because now they understood: the immortal mother, as mourner, comes toward her son Achilles in human form. Though a goddess, her eye and ear encounter only human form and measure; Achilles is her son and she, like the Greeks, is full of grief. "Around you," continues Agamemnon, addressing Achilles, "stood the daughters of the Ancient of the Sea, lamenting, and putting ambrosial garments on you; the Muses too, all nine of them, alternating in beautiful song, lamented; and no Achean was seen who did not weep, so did the clear-voiced chant move everyone."

Let my essay come to rest on this mention of the Muses. At the end of the *Odyssey*, if not as such at the end of Hegel's *Phenomenology*, they emerge from the sea, an emanation of the deep. As they come, an unearthly sound is converted into human shape and melody. They appear even in the "Geisterreich" of the dead, which yearns for an elation of its own.

13
Wordsworth Before Heidegger

> The poets were there before me.
>
> Freud

I am a language being; nothing in language is alien to me, not even Heidegger's German. It is true that most translations of Heidegger's work are rejected by English as if they were failed transplants. Yet the effort to English Heidegger may be similar to that which characterizes his own project of translating Being into Time by a special diction that takes time. The tightness of that diction is remarkable: a Milky Way of constellated sound that we try to space out. The mind needs more air for even such simple sentences as "Das Dasein entwirft als Verstehen sein Sein auf Möglichkeiten" ("As understanding, Dasein projects its Being upon possibilities," *Being and Time*, para. 32).[1] Compound nouns accompany verbs and prepositions that make us aware of the compounding in a prose that moves assonantally between noun elements and non-noun elements: *sein Sein* is a conspicuous example.

Exquisite parodies have appeared of this impersonal, reduplicative style, one that haunts the very ear eager to shake it off. The coup de dés which, according to Mallarmé, every thought emits is here played with thunderstones rolled by Wotan and the Nordic gods—though Heidegger, of course, would like to regard German as akin to Greek. The effect is, in any case, that of discovering the properties of language not through the microscopic techniques of the linguists but through a telescope. Since Being is what is nearest to us, that very nearness, in its pristine or occulted form, is the problem. To understand Being we must find a distance which is at once analytic and organic: a vantage point that does not remove us from time or language or alienate them further into object relations.

So Heidegger takes time. To read him is to renounce not only the six or sixty drachma course of the Sophists, that is, the culture industry or learning as mere technique. It is also to renounce hope for novelty. Leave behind all news, you who enter the book called *Being and Time*.

Why read—read Heidegger—then? Because the scrupulous form of reading we call interpretation discloses the fact that our increasingly furious search for news misunderstands the relation of Being and Time. We think that because time eludes us, except as clock-time or as the ready-made and ready-to-hand, there is no present, no parousia. The frustration of holding fast the being of time, our being in time—which Augustine described in well-known passages of his *Confessions*—spurs human consciousness to ever greater efforts to catch up on news, or to recuperate history, or to redeem a scarecrow vacuity by means of metaphysics.

Heidegger's analysis of time-greed, *Neugier* or curiosity (*Time and Being*, para. 36), and its relation to chatter and ambiguity, traces our difficult desire to have Being disclosed from within secular life. It puts into relief the degraded evangelical link between words and news, a cupidity often satirized by literary keepers of the language as a social phenomenon without ontological implications.

So in *The Spectator* of August 8, 1712, Pope and Addison poke fun at their countrymen's "general thirst after News" raised to fresh heights after the recent war. "Notwithstanding the Multitude of Annotations, Explanations, Reflections, and various Readings which it passes through, our Time lies heavy on our Hands till the Arrival of a fresh Mail." Our authors propose, therefore, a daily Paper containing all the most remarkable occurrences in every little place within ten Miles from London, or within range of the Penny Post. "Correspondencies" established in several localities would furnish "Intelligence" as follows:

> "'Letters from *Brompton* advise, that the Widow *Blight* had received several visits from *John Mildew*, which affords great Speculations in those Parts....
> Letters from *Paddington* bring little more, than that *Will Squeak*, the Sow-gelder, passed through that Place, the 5th Instant.'"

After Heidegger—with powerful anticipations in Nietzsche's critique of the will to knowledge and in religious scruples concerning *curiositas*—questions are raised once more about the very concept of a secular modernity (*Neuzeit*) and its self-legitimation through speculative or scientific news.[2] Heidegger himself, of course, had to come to terms with a great, counter-evangelical idea: Nietzsche's affirmation of repetition, the idea of the eternal return, a joyful, yet totally non-recuperative testing of soul.

Time is certainly a ghost we defend against: the nagging, unremitting sense that we have missed something, overlooked something, lost something, not fore-seen something. But what is missing? What *is* it? Or, what is *it*? Heidegger shows that we cannot even answer a question of this format without evading the defini-tion of the "it is" in the definition. These punctual definitions are too often quasi-ocular schemes to fix the truth of Being in Time. We are greedy for the spoils of pointing. But such categorical grammars, such constricting visibilities, are false modes of totalization that gain us meaning at the expense of the meaning of Being.

Heidegger emphasizes, therefore, that intellectual seeing comes via speaking; the logos is an "apophantic" sound or utterance (para. 7B). The philosopher should seek this logos, a language of knowledge that is ontic without ceasing to be temporal, and phenomenological rather than ocular in its analysis of entities. "The task of *liberating* grammar from logic" is how Heidegger puts it at one point (para. 34); and he anticipates a necessary "harshness of expression" com-plicated by the "minuteness of detail" with which his concepts will be articulated (para. 7C). Heidegger's language of knowledge, then, would be like exegesis raised to a higher power; extra-colloquial yet shared and exchanged without the taint of bookishness. It is a form of close reading or close writing that apprehends what Heidegger calls the closeness rather than closure of Being. Words expound time; time manifests itself in the being words have, which is also our being. No news, no gospel, will do more, for the time being.

I realize that in making a case for Heidegger I may not be making a case for him but for *Dichtung*: the writer's freedom to break the covenant with ordinary language, one that was made *for* him rather than *by* him. Heidegger's diction thickens like the air when omens are thought to be present. It is, and has re-mained, a stumbling block. His style in German is as troublesome as the corre-lative problem of capturing that style in English. Can we *translate* Heidegger: can Heidegger be Englished, but also can he be Germaned? What meaning is in the violence he does to the vernacular, even while disclosing the "thereness" of un-theorized existential structures? It is the sort of violence we *might* accept in an oracular or hermetic poet, or a translator who is recovering an arcane diction. (Around this time, for example, Buber and Rosenzweig translate the Hebrew Bible into a pseudolect as remarkable in its harshness as Pope's *Homer* in its con-densed elegance.)

Let me state the issues involved in this problem of translatability: whether we can speak Being; whether that language of knowledge about Being can be found by the recovery of a "natural," vividly rhetorical, now alienated, speech; what sort of recall of it is possible through reading and writing; and whether the pro-fessional separation of philosopher and poet, *Denker* and *Dichter*, may not have led to a falsification of that language and a deformation of humanistic scholar-ship. These questions, answerable or not, have a power and dignity of their own.

My essay proceeds as follows: first, a description of Heidegger's language of knowledge in relation to the missing or "unknown" language of Being; then a close reading of parts of Wordsworth's *Intimation Ode*, a poem that also raises the provocative issue of a forgotten mode of Being, and how to speak it. By this juxtaposition I hope to accomplish my aim of drawing Heidegger into an English text-milieu; in short, of translating him.

"Our question as to whether Being will remain a mere vapor (*Dunst*) for us or become the destiny of the West," Heidegger writes, "is anything but an exaggeration and a rhetorical figure." And a paragraph later in *An Introduction to Metaphysics*: "We are merely holding fast, establishing something which has not yet been thought through, for which we still have no locus."[3] These are very different sentences. The first, despite the author's disclaimer, is highly rhetorical; it is hard for us now to respond to such stupefying phrases as "the destiny of the West." The second seems almost understated; we need the original version to realize how a rhetorical element again peers through. The sentence is a reflection on the word *fest-stellen* (holding fast, but related in German to "representing," *Vorstellen*, as well as *Stelle*, assigned or specific place), and it alludes to a whole range of discriminated, interactive synonyms that refer to place, standing, understanding (*Verstehen*). The uneasy correspondence of style and theme in Heidegger—uneasy, because we cannot claim that style is the dress or embodiment of thought where charged words fracture our classical notions of style—this uneasy, failing correspondence suggests that a meaning is always slipping away which words cannot emplace but can merely insist on. Hence Heidegger will say, further on in his book: "Genuine interpretation (*eigentliche Auslegung*) must point out what no longer stands (*dasteht*) in the words but is said nevertheless. Necessarily, then, interpretation must use violence."

Violence is always disconcerting: we suspect a psychological reason even when an author like Heidegger rules psychologism out. How can we determine, moreover, whether Heidegger's violence restores rather than alienates colloquiality? He does not differ from past thinkers who have doubted the capacity of ordinary language to carry the truth, or to facilitate a "correspondence." Their attack on natural language led many to chose Latin or even some sort of artificial, mathematical *mathesis*: Heidegger himself is determined to go behind Latin, back to mistranslated Greek sources, which he wishes—like Hölderlin—to graft onto German. Or is it to translate the other way, and achieve a Greek form of German?[4] But what do we make of this transvestite language, this extreme doubt directed against ordinary speech so as to disclose the extraordinary character of ordinary life? Do we not simply reach a deeper ambiguity, as this hyperbolic movement toward Greek produces an amphibolic German?

Two different kinds of violence may be observed in Heidegger's relation to words. One is rhetorical in the sense of aiming to open and coerce the mind through the ear; and the other is deconstructive, or translative, as when Heidegger operates on the historical body of discourse to retrieve what that knows yet cannot speak. Deconstruction is a mode of questioning, but it *asserts* the question, and therefore comes close to extracting a confession by a sort of language-torture. While rhetorical violence amplifies ordinary language, suggesting a return to the pristine power in it, to an occulted virtue, philosophical or deconstructive violence goes further. It suggests, in Heidegger, though not in Derrida, that there is an absolute diction whose being and meaning coincide; and Heidegger's prose is "on the way" to such a diction. Its deconstructive translation of German reverses the *translatio* or westerly gradient of the transmission of culture. Heidegger goes East, and reorients, for example, such terms for interpretation as *Erörterung*, to which he gives the etymological value of *Ort*, meaning place, but also place of origin, from *ortus*, a rising, as of the sun. Interpretation makes the question of Being rise (fall) into place. Heidegger removes the film of familiarity from a basic term and restores the rule of metaphor; but more than that, he intends us to rethink the very activity of interpretation, how we misuse hermeneutics (interpretation theory) to limit a disturbance of the peace provoked in language by the great or difficult work of thought.

The violence of overpersuasive rhetoric is felt above all in certain of Heidegger's writings early in the Nazi period. The book I have been quoting was originally a lecture delivered in 1935. Discussing the vaporized state of the word *Sein*, Heidegger allows himself an aggressive commonplace about the degradation of words in the contemporary world. Language, he says, is "worn out and used up, an indispensable but masterless and arbitrarily employed means of communication, as indifferent as a means of public transport, as a streetcar which everyone can enter or leave." And he goes on to a related commonplace. "The organizations, whose aim is the purification (*Reinigung*) of language and its defense against a progressive barbarization (*Verhunzung*), deserve our respect."

An ominous turn, surely, for what in Mallarmé's program to "purify the words of the tribe" is devoid of overt political pathos. Is Heidegger using "purification" with racial overtones in the Germany of 1935, or obversely, is his word "barbarization" really a double-edged expression directed against the Nazis?

Similarly, when in the notorious *Rektorratsrede* of 1933 Heidegger enunciates Nazi clichés, but then calls for the self-determination (*Selbstbehauptung*) of the University, what are we to think? Is it double talk, or is there an authentic double register? The Nazi ear would have been uneasily content; but for others the talk might have sounded like a call for resistance in the form of a reappropriation of the politicized and misused terms. One more example: the important essay on "The Origin of the Work of Art" must have been conscious of the rhetoric all around it: the Nazi party presented itself as a worker's party: a right-wing, national labor movement (NSDAP), in opposition to "international," "communistic" socialism. It cannot be an accident that Heidegger emphasized in this essay, contemporaneous with the 1935 lecture on metaphysics, the work-character of the *Kunstwerk*. I will quote just one passage, from the *Introduction to Metaphysics*: "The work of art is a work not primarily because it is wrought (*gewirkt*) or tooled, but because it brings about (*er-wirkt*) being in the participant; it brings about the phenomenon in which the emerging power, *physis*, comes to shine. It is through the mode of being of the work of art that everything else appears and is found; is first confirmed and made accessible, explicable, and understandable as being or not being."

The two kinds of violence against words I have mentioned can be matched with Heidegger's understanding of equivocation. I have already discussed his equivocal rhetoric; more effective by far, and ultimately more problematic, is his use of equivocation in the service of a fundamental, even fundamentalist, language-project. He harnesses sound, or the formalized power of paranomasia, to disclose a groundlessness in all contemporary modes of inquiry. Words, including the word Being itself, have lost, he claims, their *Nennkraft* or naming force, not simply because of attrition but because the question of Being itself has been driven underground. "The destroyed relation to Being as such is the actual reason for our general misrelation to language." There has to be a reappropriation of language so that it can become an *Ereignis* once more, a language-event. This reappropriation does not produce a personal or assertive style, however, but a radically impersonal discourse: wherever Being under-stands language, wherever Being is the subject, language destabilizes meaning, and we lose our standing or place (*ver-stehen*, with the prefix *ver-* assuming negative force) as language itself becomes the speaker. "Die Sprache spricht." This is Heidegger's theory of impersonality that has its analogues in Anglo-American poetics from the 1920s on, and in recent French attacks on ego-psychology. To quote a typical statement by Jacques Lacan: "I am not a poet but a poem. A poem that is being written, even if it looks like a subject."

Heidegger, then, is not a radical nihilist but a radical fundamentalist. His disqualifying of the truth of contemporary languages of knowledge recreates the simulacrum of a diction that speaks truth. His project bears comparison, in its very difference, with that of E. R. Curtius, whose great book on topoi, also written in this time of trial, was reminding Germany of Latin culture and the Romance languages, though seeking to place rather than purge German literature. Heidegger recollects what to him is a truer and more absolute foundation: pre-Hellenic Greek art and pre-Socratic thinking. It is a paradox, though, that his uncompromising cultural radicalism, which rejects accommodation in its drive for a "cure of the ground," and which, with a real advance in theory, frees hermeneutics from theological or classicist versions of the principle of accommodation—that this radicalism can sometimes lead to a crisis-rhetoric leaving him open to the barbaric simplifiers of his time.

Art passes a Last Judgment on us, said William Blake; so Heidegger's language will pass a Last Judgment on him. His ambitious critique of Western systems of ontology and their scientific grammars produces a textual footwork that is deft, fascinating, yet *nearly groundless*: it is based, willy-nilly, on an exegetical and stumbling mass of speculative etymologies, on forcible collocations of Greek and German fragments, or passages made into fragments. My judgment is that, whatever Heidegger's intent, this curious dance over the abyss, on the unstable tightrope of fragmented texts, proclaims rather than repairs the schism between knowledge and being, or logos and physis. Against brutal ideologies of their reconnection, against a *Blut und Boden* "violence from without," the philosopher presses back with an acknowledged "violence from within" in the form of a highly inflected language. To be blunt: it is as if Heidegger were saying, having experienced Nazi rhetoric: this is the language of Being trying to break through, this is its call, *Ruf, Aufruf*. But its terrible pathos must be deconstructed by a scrupulous, interpretive counterviolence. A critique or subversion of rhetoric is not enough; that would be like sandbagging the sea; what must be opened to view, and what explains if it does not justify Heidegger's own rhetoric, is the difficulty of finding a standpoint from which the meaning of Being can reveal itself once more in language, in the being of the words themselves.

No wonder, then, Heidegger's philosophy becomes *Dichtung*, a text with literary allure. Words seem to recapture their priority to ideas and meanings, to logical, political or semantic positivisms. One almost comes to believe there are no meanings as such: that meanings are the alienated products or consumer goods of philosophy. Heidegger's constructions always contain a deconstruction: violence done to a settled boundary or received meaning. Nothing new is gained, except an indeterminacy as to the locus of meaning, or a sense of the text itself as the place of revelation, a clearing (*Lichtung*) from which language, or Being itself, speaks.

It is strange, however, that we should have to thread the detour of a text in order to know ourselves. The theological solution for this is that God and God's word (the Bible) are closer to me than myself—nothing else, all other things (*Seiendes*) falling into the void and vanity of secularism. This is not Heidegger's answer. Yet his analysis continues to move in the area of what Zwingli's German names *zuzugs zu* (*Gott*). Whether or not Heidegger is actually influenced by German mystics or preachers, by their powerfully anaphoric and reiterative style, he explores that kind of prepositional and reduplicative language. He sensitizes us to a valorized void which he calls the "forestructure" of understanding. This void is not, as in the Judeo-Christian tradition, a nothing out of which a something comes. There is always something (*existentialia*); what appears to be nothing is what is forgotten or neglected or exists actively in the mode of presupposition. It must be recognized *as* something through understanding potentiated by interpretation.

So Heidegger discloses the prepositional values of a discourse which we have sentenced to a purely propositional mode. He is always prepositioning us. The concept of forestructure is part of his attempt to liberate *Rede* (discourse) from logical or assertive types of propositional truth and to reconstruct a genuine language of Being. "I am condemned to assertion," Roland Barthes once lamented, as if he were caught in German rather than French. Even French was not modal, not musical enough.

The unknown language, then, involves anamnesis in the form of deconstruction. From Plato's *Meno* and *Phaedo* on there have been arguments that knowledge is prestructured: that to understand we must already have understood. But when, and where; in what transcendent place or time? The Platonic concept of recollection is perhaps necessarily contaminated by myth: it is allied with the idea of pre-existence, of a heavenly academy, or seminary of souls, that precedes our fall into time and a mysterious forgetfulness of the prior life. It may be, then, that the lost or unknown language of Being survives vestigially as the language of myth; and in Ernst Cassirer's work on *The Philosophy of Symbolic Forms*, especially the second volume (1925), with its chapters on the mythical concepts of time and space, Heidegger could have found anticipations of his own interest in the fragmentary intuitions of the pre-Socratics and how they are related to a *Seinsvergessenheit* (forgetfulness of Being) that creeps into the very lineaments of Greek science, as into Plato's emphasis on Being rather than nonbeing. What Heidegger does is, first, to take the metaphysical topic of nonbeing seriously again, but as a *question* which he revives not only on the level of philosophy (handed down institutionally) but also as it appears from within daily experience, and so could be the focus of phenomenological description[5]; second, he rejects what to him is a vulgar humanism, one that explains Plato's concern with being or at least with *Seiendes*—secular life and its laws—as a benevolent strengthening of the reality-principle in the face of mythic or superstitious thought; third, he does not fall back into a study of myth, either philosophical (Cassirer) or scholarly (the great tradition of Usener and others on which Cassirer draws), but he insists instead on the reality of the question of nonbeing in life and mislanguaged thought. Lastly, Heidegger identifies the paradox of understanding with the problem of the hermeneutic circle, and claims that we necessarily come to the question of Being through that circle, because it discloses a *be-fore*, the preconceptual and projective realm that phenomenology had been trying to describe. "Vor—in jenes Nächste, das wir ständig übereilen, das uns jedesmal neu befremdet, wenn wir es erblicken." ("Forwards—into that which is nearest us, which we constantly and hastily pass by, which, each time that we do catch a glimpse of it, seems strange in a new way.") He discloses that *Vor-struktur*, describing brilliantly how our sense of time is distorted by the inauthenticities we fall into when we do not realize that understanding is already, as understanding, in touch with existence, and does not have to seek its life in stronger or more exotic realities than itself.

Heidegger demythologizes and descientizes philosophy, returning thought to its primordial alliance with a nonmythological *poesis*. To think Being (*Denken*) and to speak Being (*Dichten*) is to acknowledge rigorously the sentience of nonbeing by analyzing why and in what form Being is questionable. Mythology may be a more imaginative grammar than metaphysical ontologies, yet it too must be overcome, so that we can think what is thinkable and not create a false vacuum in which conceptions breed that seek to fill the vacuum—political religions, as Eric Voegelin called them, that cover up the sense of nonbeing, that concretize dreams of mastery or self-presence in the form of technological schemes that will devastate life on earth even more.

> Throughout all his poetic life Wordsworth was preoccupied by the idea, the sentiment, by the problem, of being. All experiences, all emotions lead to it. He was haunted by the mysterious fact that he existed.
>
> Lionel Trilling

I turn to Wordsworth because to "translate" Heidegger we must choose a text at home in the English literary tradition. Wordsworth's *Being and Time* is, as it were, his "Ode: Intimations of Immortality from Recollections of Early Childhood."[6] What makes the comparison ponderable is the part played in both Heidegger and Wordsworth by Plato's myth of recollection in relation to our forgetfulness of Being. Perhaps nowhere else in English is the sentiment of nonbeing so powerfully addressed as in Wordsworth's ode: addressed from within secular experience, in a vacillating style that ranges from the near-bathos of

> Turn whereso'er I may
> By night or day
> The things which I have seen I now can see no more
>
> (7-9)

to the sublimity of

> Fallings from us, vanishings;
> Blank misgivings of a Creature
> Moving about in worlds not realized
>
> (147-49)

Wordsworth may even give the impression of overvaluing such moments: however negative they are, they become for him "the fountain light of all our day . . . the masterlight of all our seeing." No more than intimations, they are declared to "Uphold us, cherish us, and make / Our noisy years seem moments in the being / Of the eternal silence."

The *Intimations Ode* discloses the motive for mythology and metaphysics, including Plato's anamnesis ("Our birth is but a sleep and a forgetting," is the well-known opening of stanza 5), by articulating a contradiction in human development. There is no point, not even birth or death, where existence and essence come together, where we can say "Now" in an absolute sense, where we can claim to have stood in time as on "being's height." Anamnesis links experience to a point beyond experience and so, at once, qualifies and disqualifies the empirical memory. Wordsworth begins, "There was a time," but that pastness is unacceptable if it empties the present; unacceptable also if it propels us from a mythic point of origin toward a mythic future: a delusive or self-displacing horizon of hope. The poet depicts the flux and reflux of a mind aware of a loss that cannot be fixed precisely, a thinking which is always already a grieving, as if thought and grief had an immemorial connection. The quest for Being is acknowledged yet seen through, as Blake said he saw through the eye rather than with it. So the poet keeps turning in every direction, or stands on his understanding of the sentiment of nonbeing. The "thoughts that do often lie too deep for tears," with which he ends, mark a referent located beyond mourning or object-loss: beyond nature, possibly, but also beyond myth as a resting-place for the homeless imagination.

Most remarkable is the diction of the ode. Not only its restless character—wavering between the simplest, most natural phrasing and ritualistic or sublime declamation—but its conjunctive-disjunctive progression. From stanza to stanza, and sometimes within verse-lines, we feel that the continuity may not hold. I am thinking in particular of one such moment, where the sense of the words goes astray, or nonsense is uttered.

This momentary *discours de la folie* is stanza 8 on the Child as Philosopher and Prophet. The stanza proved too much even for Coleridge, who cited it in the *Biographia Literaria* (ch. 22) as an example of a peculiar Wordsworthian defect: bombast, or "thoughts and images too great for the subject." Coleridge identified this subject as the child addressed in those hyperbolic terms. But the subject here is what is in question. The stanza was provoked by Wordsworth's prior wonderment at the imitative zeal of young children, how eager they are to become adults, as if their "whole vocation / Were endless imitation" (107-8). Like an extempore reaction, there follows this problematic and incongruous apostrophe, these eruptive and disruptive exclamations, that subvert the link between Being and Nature, or the imitation of nature:

> Thou, whose exterior semblance doth belie
> Thy Soul's immensity;

Thou best Philosopher, who yet dost keep
Thy heritage, thou Eye among the blind,
That, deaf and silent, read'st the eternal deep,
Haunted for ever by the eternal mind,—
    Mighty Prophet! Seer blest!
    On whom those truths do rest,
Which we are toiling all our lives to find;
In darkness lost, the darkness of the grave;
Thou, over whom thy Immortality
Broods like the Day, a Master o'er a Slave,
A Presence which is not to be put by;
    To whom the grave
Is but a lonely bed without the sense or sight
    Of day or the warm light,
A place of thought where we in waiting lie;
Thou little Child, yet glorious in the might
Of heaven-born freedom on thy Being's height,
Why with such earnest pains dost thou provoke
The Years to bring the inevitable yoke,
Thus blindly with thy blessedness at strife?
Full soon thy Soul shall have her earthly freight,
And custom lie upon thee with a weight,
Heavy as frost, and deep almost as life!

                                  (109-29)

What underlies (*sub-jectum*) human development, and gives it integrity? That is the question. Is it not strange, then, that a vulnerable infant should be envisioned as that subject? And that this infant is so different from the child depicted in the previous stanza? The infant of stanza 8 is delivered from the "endlessness" of imitation yet delivered up to an overshadowing, sempiternal present. The poet calls into a void that cannot answer because it is *infans*, and he calls up something *infandum*, a mighty imp who is supposed to authenticate a brief if constitutive moment of Being-in-Time.

Too much, surely, rests on this hypostasis of the Child. The very word "rest" becomes charged with pun and paradox. The child is one on whom "those truths do rest / Which we are toiling all our lives to find" (115-16).[7] Moreover, even while on "Being's height," the auratic child is already *under* Being, even entombed by it. Immortality is said to brood on it "like the Day, a Master o'er a slave" (117-18). How like a grave this is, "a place of thought where we in waiting lie." Neonatal dream and tomb-like bed merge into a scene of timeless, speechless waiting presided over by an Eye as uncannily entitive as in a Quarles emblem or the Masonic symbol on a dollar bill. Temporality is elided, and a strange brooding, as in Genesis 1, is evoked: that of the haunted, self-haunted mind. *But whose mind?*

There is no subject here in the sense of ego: there is only an image of divine idiocy, of underconscious or moony (lunatic) absorption:

> Thou Eye among the blind
> That, deaf and silent, read'st the eternal deep,
> Haunted forever by the eternal mind,—
>
> (111-13)

This eye may be the moon, should a cosmic representation be involved. Or, God's eye in the position of the moon;[8] and the problem of reference or attribution (of finding a subject to which these properties may be ascribed) perplexes the reader who must decide what "deaf and silent" refer to, and whether it is the child that is haunted by the eternal mind, or whether it is the eternal deep, read by the child, that is so haunted. What a night-piece! The Abyss itself is put *en abîme*.

Wordsworth's language seems to corrode stable reference. Yet this stanza is the one place at which his ode allows itself an eternizing glance, or an *un-timely* utterance, a casting of language toward the sphere of the fixed stars. That this casting reaches no further than the moon—a border image between the pure stars and the sublunar world—and no further than the infant—a boundary image beyond which all possibility of beginning, or beginning again, is lost in speculation—anticipates an overcoming of the "subject" of philosophy and the advent of the "subject" of psychoanalysis, Freud's "His Majesty, the Child," or recollections from early childhood that cause the binds and blinds in human development.

The more the subject is in question, the more "interlunation" (a nice word of Shelley's) of meaning. Whether the "obstinate questions" (144) are ours or the poet's, we glimpse everywhere equivocation, or an instability of reference that works against the vocation of imitation. Not only conventional double entendres, such as "belie" in line 108. There are also more insidious questions about reading: why is hearing elided into the image of a "deaf and silent" reading? Does the sound *ear* break through nevertheless in "exterior" (108) and "Seer" (114)? Even the word "read'st" seems to contain that (scrambled) ear. It is not love of ingenuity that motivates these observations but the problem of resting anything on so spectral a diction. If this is the nearest Wordsworth comes to a language of Being, it remains as susceptible to internal injury as a child's psyche.

In a late comment on the Intimations Ode Wordsworth defends his use of Plato's myth. "Archimedes said that he could move the world if he had a point whereon to rest his machine. Who has not felt the same aspiration as regards the world of his own mind? . . . I took hold of the notion of pre-existence as having sufficient foundation in humanity.'' Under the pressure of finding this strange Archimedian lever, this ''point whereon to rest''—the subject evaporates, like the word ''Being'' in Heidegger's view, and what remains is the self-generating strength of a hyperbolic language movement, a *Thou* that echoes an equally ecstatic *Now*. This *Now*, as at the beginning of the Ode's third stanza (19) is like the *Thou* of the eighth stanza, an impotent yet fiat-like shout (see also line 35), the insistence through voice of a *nunc* or *punctum stans*; and it takes us through and beyond referential meaning to a wishful term that would conflate the notion of presence and origin. Wordsworth's ode culminates in these two moments of stasis or ec-stasis: Now, Thou.

Yet the *Now* of stanza 3 is reinscribed in syntax, in time, as a ''Now, that,'' even as the *Thou* of stanza 8 is a ''Thou, who.'' The ''Thou, who'' pattern is that of predication, and has a significant religious history. The ''Now, that'' leads to reflection rather than to predication, to ''Time'' rather than to ''Being.'' Both styles are exacerbated by a curious literary genre to which Wordsworth is indebted: Pseudo-Pindaric Odes that attempt to translate an *ousiatic* Greek in order to speak Being. These Odes, puzzles of literary history, are interesting epiphanic abortions. Whether we turn to Collins or Wordsworth or Hölderlin or Coleridge or Shelley, the pseudo-Greek Ode is a linguistic monster, sometimes merely a linguistic machine, to liberate or steal back a language that discloses Being. Ideally, every poem aspires to the condition of restoring language to its status as an Archimedean tool, a meta-instrument, fundamental and moving. The philosophical critique of instrumental reason is preceded by a poetical critique of instrumental language in the form of maieutic and divinatory poetry. Wordsworth before Heidegger. . . .

14
The Unremarkable Poet

> wreaths of smoke
> Sent up, in silence, from among the trees!
> With some uncertain notice. . . .
>> (Wordsworth, "Tintern Abbey")

I

It is a general proposition in semiological analysis that signs are not signs unless they become perceptible, and that their perceptibility as signs depends on a contrast set up within the signifying system. Some parts of the system are "marked" and some "unmarked"; this contrast shapes perceptibility, and there is a conventional rather than inherent relation between linguistic features and their marked / unmarked status. Now this matter of perceptibility (or noticeability) affects the reader as well as the writer: in remarking what has been written the reader may see a different set of contrasts than the writer. Doubtless there are limits to this process of remarking; yet we all know that what is merely a primrose to one person may be a wonderful and complex world to another.

It is interesting that for a long time Wordsworth's poetry seemed so natural to readers that many considered it not poetry so much as a form of prose. Even when the distinction between prose and poetry had been modified to the point of breaking down, Cleanth Brooks, who used "paradox" and "irony" to define what was specifically poetic in all language, said that Wordsworth's paradoxes were peculiarly unemphatic compared to those of an earlier Poetry of Wit. Yet one could still uncover them by close analysis. Michael Riffaterre, similarly, points out in a recent essay that "smokeless", describing London in the sonnet "Composed Upon Westminster Bridge, September 3, 1802,"

> All bright and glittering in the smokeless air,
>
> (8)

calls up, without stress, its opposite: it cancels yet preserves the commonplace image of the city as a dirty, crowded place. Through "smokeless" the "latent intertext surfaces into the text": the word is a "hostage from the sociolect" which "forces" readers to apprehend a stereotypical contrast between Edenic country-side and corrupt, rapidly industrializing city.

Like Brooks, Riffaterre is seeking to smoke out the technique of a subtle poet. One cannot deny that there are contrasts in this poem: it is a question of how and where they operate, and why we have trouble in spotting them or making them significant. (Wordsworth was thoroughly abused by Jeffrey and other critics of his time for imposing unremarkable sights or sentiments on his audience.) "Smokeless", like the contrast of "wear" and "bare", or "theatres" and "temples", in

> This City now doth, like a garment, wear
> The beauty of the morning; silent, bare
> Ships, towers, domes, theatres and temples lie
> Open unto the fields, and to the sky;
>
> (4-7)

or like the adjacency of majesty and intimacy, might and stillness, in

> Dear God! the very houses seem asleep;
> And all that mighty heart is lying still!
>
> (13-14)

can be made perceptible by careful readers, whether or not they back what they do with a theory of literary, as distinguished from non-literary, language. This gain in perceptibility, however, does not resolve but focuses the quiet action or special negativity of Wordsworth's style.

II

Rather than insisting on paradox or the cancelled presence of the opposite term, it would be better to acknowledge that contrast in Wordsworth points beyond the activity of pointing. "Smokeless" signals, as it were, the absence of a signal, and comes close to subtly thematizing Wordsworth's wish not to violate—by "poetic diction" or some other artifice—nature's own mode of expression. Nothing here is forced on our awareness: what halted the poet-spectator then, and what allows him to halt us now (via this sonnet-tribute), is precisely not characterized by the usual trappings of picturesqueness or sublimity. It was a moment—who could pass it by?—of the "poetry of earth" and does not need the heightening of rhetoric.

> Earth has not anything to show more fair:
> Dull would he be of soul who could pass by
> A sight so touching in its majesty...
>
> (1-3)

Yet the poet *is* passing by; and one of the contrasts, barely perceived, is between the curious specificity of the title with its temporal marker ("September 3, 1802"), and the poem's first culminating image of repose of will, also temporal in its association, however modified: "The river glideth at his own sweet will." Riffaterre might say that the structure here is the same as in "smokeless": a commonplace ("the river of time") is both cancelled and preserved. Yet Riffaterre passed this one by; and we are left, in any case, with an unstable rather than stable contrast, for we do not know how to interpret, even should we notice it, the relation of "passing by" to these temporal markers, whether stressed or unstressed.

To talk of reserve or indeterminacy would be to praise Wordsworth's style without understanding it. How can a poem put on so much pressure without the reader feeling pressured, without, for example, overconscious dictions, paraphrases, and cryptic veilings? Goethe said of Nature that its secrets were in the open. In Wordsworth, too, there is no masque that obliges us to question what Parsifal failed to question. We can let things pass by: even the theme of "passing by". A Wordsworth poem often has no point. As readers we respond to the mystery of his response. That the poem exists at all, that it emerges into "answerable style" has to be understood together with that style.

At a very basic level, then, the present sonnet is simply an extended lo! or behold!, though these markers remain subvisionary. Nature works rarely by signs and wonders, and what matters in any case is "soul" as Wordsworth calls it in line 2: the poet's, not only nature's, capacity for "timely utterance." This phrase, from the *Intimations Ode*, reinstates the Parsifal moment: there must be—as a moral obligation, even if self-assumed—a capacity for response in the poet. This responsibility is involved with voice, or poetry as the temporality of rhetoric, as the pulse-point in the "incumbent mystery of sense and soul." Telling the time (which may go wrong) is always a prophetic venture yet absolutely ordinary. The initiative, moreover, cannot be nature's alone; the poet anticipates what may be coming his way and has to reform (re-mark) an inarticulate or mute code. Whether or not there is a language of nature there is a language of the heart that goes out to nature; and this going out, or being called out, brings Wordsworth to the subject of nature-personification when he writes programmatically about poetics, as in the famous Preface to *Lyrical Ballads*.

The theme of time, then, does not settle into such conventional frames as transience, regret, seizing the moment. Instead, as at the beginning of *The Prelude* (Wordsworth's autobiographical epic), a "correspondent breeze" within him joins the "congenial" power of a "half-conscious" external breeze that brings a blessing or invitation from nature. So also the Westminster Bridge sonnet's many eulogistic terms (fair, touching, beauty, bright, beautifully, sweet) suggest a *temporal greeting* rather than something purely descriptive. It is as if nature herself were saying "Good morning" to the wayfarer.

The "telling", of course, is all on the poet's side; only the "show" is nature's. Yet Wordsworth is uneasy with the deictic (epideictic) mode: something more direct, approaching apostrophe or prayer, a naïve or commonplace and absolutely basic vocative swells up, like the supreme cliché "Dear God!" which climaxes the sonnet and is in the place of a point, had he written in the pointed style.

Comments like this take us from what Schleiermacher defined as the "grammatical" to the "divinatory" level of interpretation. This is where a certain risk comes in: where the interpreter has to anticipate the poem, in the direction it is going. We know from other celebrated episodes that splendid evenings or mornings are "trials of strength" for the poet. In the most famous dawn-scene of them all (*Prelude* IV) he becomes, without knowing it, a "dedicated spirit": that is, devoted to poetry. "I made no vows, but vows / Were then made for me." What kind of vow or utterance can we associate with the simple, descriptive verses of the Westminster Bridge sonnet?

The poet, I suggest, is met on the way by a natural sign, a "good morning". Yet his passing by gives it the virtual status of good-bye or farewell. We do not know the locus of that "Good-bye," whether it is from nature or from the responsive soul; we know only that promise and parting coincide as in the blessing: "God be with you." Some sort of timely utterance, *parole* or password, is offered from within the tacit, natural spectacle. ("Day unto day uttereth knowledge.") Yet there is no word except these verses. And whatever is heard (or seen rather than heard) culminates in a vision of repose:

> Never did sun more beautifully steep
> In his first splendour, valley, rock, or hill;
> Ne'er saw I, never felt, a calm so deep!
>
> (9-11)

III

Wordsworth, looking at a city, sees "something like the purity of one of nature's own grand spectacles," as his sister wrote in her journal. That is clear. Yet how far back in time does the "first splendour" reach? Wordsworth suggests not only an extraordinary coincidence of urban and natural perspectives but the vision of a pristine urban landscape. At the very point that factories and urbanization are threatening the rural character of English towns, Wordsworth glimpses a radiant city established, as it were, from the beginning of time. By a quiet cliché ("in his first splendour") the poet travels back to the dawn of creation, now recaptured or renewed. It is this elision of time—this repetition in and despite time—which is part of the calm he feels.

The curious vigor of Wordsworth's clichés (or unremarkable phrases) remains to be explored. They function faintly like the classical "constant epithet" in that they are tautological as well as autological. Yet this constancy, in Wordsworth's case, is temporal rather than antitemporal. It remains closely linked to the immediate if repeated experience of the poet who recalls them. There is something like Proust's involuntary memory, as an experience repeats itself, or gives the impression of repetition, even if in fact two or more incidents are conflated. The poet is faced by an illusion of time dissolving, of being able to travel back to the origin (to an *illo tempore* or "first splendour"), or traveling even now among "Powers and Presences." So it is possible to draw a wayside omen and silent blessing from the Westminster Bridge sonnet, or to re-mark the position of the poet-traveller as, prophetically, "telling time." A further temporal aspect is disclosed by the rhetorical movement of the sonnet's second part.

This "glides" from a glimpsed origin to a calm that suspends the flow of time and could imitate a final repose. There is nothing sinister in such convergence of origin and end. The effect is more like an unexpected bridging or a time-dissolve. In this and other poems, moreover, the traveler does not cross, like Coleridge's Mariner, the border of naturalistic perception into some other world. Yet "traveling" does reveal an indefinite figural extension. Though it remains secular it authorizes us to view even the self as a figure: acting within a larger drama or frame, acting out a fantasy-role that remains, however, completely in touch with the familiar world.

The withholding of fantasizing, even in the legitimate or formal mode of myth, is, of course, Wordsworth's distinction among the English Romantics. His yearning for those nourishing pagan myths is not in question; and he can write about it as in a famous passage of *The Excursion* and in his well-known sonnet conjuring up Proteus and Triton. But his strength, and perhaps limitation, lies in his refusal of romantic classicism's liberal attitude toward myth. Keats, who placed myth-making on the side of a generous and impersonal imagination, suspected that Wordsworth's great refusal was really in the service of the ego, and so denounced his style as the "egotistical sublime." The puzzling strength of it does indeed lie in this area: the poetry is occasional, the depicted experience usually quite ordinary, and the narrator, though quirky, no more than a passing observer or very sensitive tourist. Yet the fantasy within stirs like a coiled snake. The challenge is to define Wordsworth's interiority (or is it exteriority?) which has frustrated so many interpreters who have turned to vague concepts of the unconscious or subconscious.

The fantasy-content of the present sonnet is clear enough despite its character as a poetry of earth. The toll or touch of time—the mortal nature of earthly things[1]—is made unimaginable by a style of weightless clichés and timeless (un-pointed) contrasts. The deep calm, therefore, "seen" by the poet, could frighten us: such a heart, alive yet lying still, what response is it capable of? Does the poet desire a peace close to death after all?

A later sonnet, in a rare moment of surmise, depicts earth or the nether sphere "Opening to view the abyss in which she feeds / Her own calm fires." A *calm fire* is the carefully framed visionary oxymoron to which the present sonnet also tends. But if its imagery is wishful beyond the restlessness of wishing, there is another fantasy that removes from the poet the weight of "timely utterance," together with the risk of untimely—unnatural—prophecy. I have suggested that the sonnet is a reflection on an utterance of nature's: an omen that cannot be called an omen, an oracle that is not an oracle but simply a temporal greeting. The fantasy in this is not the experience itself but that the poet may feel he has the blessing, or that his journey, at least, is blessed. For what journey is it? Is he privileging by the inscribed date the act of composition rather than his first ex-perience of the prospect, or is there a conflation of his journey to Calais and back?[2] Or is he traveling another route altogether, that of his vocation as poet, which was assured in a previous dawn (1805 *Prelude* IV, 330ff.) but which must always be confirmed by such intimations? If that is so, we are suddenly in a biblical as well as vernacular world, "touching in its majesty" indeed. As with the resonance of "first splendour," the poet becomes a figure traveling mentally along switching or conflating tracks of time. How does he compose all this into a semblance of unity, and may the title-phrase "Composed..." connect with the calm he so strongly images?

IV

"Composed..." is utterly conventional, and occurs in many sonnets written during that journey of 1802. "Composed by the Sea-Side near Calais, August, 1802"; "Composed near Calais, on the Road Leading to Ardres, August 7, 1802"; "Composed in the Valley near Dover, on the Day of Landing." Tradi-tionally "composed in" or "upon" refers to drawing a picture (impression) on the spot, under the very influence of the scene. It is not really different from

"Lines written in" or "near" a certain place. The tradition of those poems, their inscription of time and place, is not innocent: the tradition evokes or re-animates a buried consciousness; it puts the genius of the writer into relation with genius or spirit of place—and again raises the question what sort of signing is going on, by nature, or by the undulled soul strong enough to meet or complete nature's message. Tradition can be used to sensitize as well as desensitize a formula, so that "Composed..." is not ruled out as a significant phrase.

It is, in fact, one of those clichés that pass by us in common usage, but draw a response from us in poetic language. Riffaterre, whose distinction I summarize here, insists on two kinds of perceptibility. Without the commonplace, or phrases from the sociolect, there could be no perceptibility; yet it is the literary intervention which moves the commonplace from indeterminate to determinate and meaningful status.[3] "Smokeless" needs the context of the elided sociolect with its simple contrast of Edenic countryside and corrupt city to gain the point and pathos it has.

"Composed..." is even more unassuming, and only the title foregrounds it. Titles belong, however, more than other parts of the literary work, to the sociolect. When a title is particularly long—longer than the poem itself in some epigrams—then of course we discern a playful or literary dimension. This is the case even in "Tintern Abbey," whose full title, "Lines Composed a Few Miles above Tintern Abbey, on Revisiting the Banks of the Wye during a Tour, July 13, 1798," seems over-elaborated. But the title of the Westminster Bridge sonnet does not draw attention to itself, except for the specified date, also present in some other poems.

The reader, then, can only value the word "Composed" by a general hermeneutic principle, namely, that in literature (as in Scripture) every word counts, whether or not that is apparent in the immediate context. According to this view it is not the individual poem that determines the meaning of indeterminate phrases but the poem as part of an intertextual corpus which the skilled interpreter supplies. Alternatively, the poet could be using everyday speech so effectively that it becomes scriptural, even without a hermeneutic principle ("poetry is like Scripture"). The poet undoes the separation of literary (hieratic) and common speech.

The first principle, transferred from sacred hermeneutics to secular occasions, may have a heuristic value, but it is clearly the second principle which points beyond theory to a fact Wordsworth was able to create. I do not mean that he programmatically views vernacular or colloquial expressions as having scriptural dignity. I am talking about poems, not programs or intentions. The natural sight, like the casual salutation (*"Good-morrow, Citizen,"* in the sonnet "Composed on the Road Leading to Ardres"), is amplified by means that reinstitute the temporality of rhetoric. "Composed," without separating itself from its ordinary language or traditional status, raises a question about the poem as a response in time: to this place, this moment, this journey. Is his destiny as poet linked in any way to his destination: traveling to Calais during the Peace of Amiens, meeting his natural daughter for the first time, and returning around 3 September?

Wordsworth undertook the trip during an armistice and in view of a momentous step: his plan to marry an Englishwoman that autumn. The sonnet may be about crossings and thresholds, yet no liminal anxiety is allowed to come through, and only the title indicates something via its mention of a bridge. It is the reader who has to take responsibility for heightening the common word, which is neither transformed nor reified.

Yet "Composed," however ordinary, contrasts in the body of the poem with an emotion which is not only recollected *in* tranquility but is an emotion *of* tranquility. The one self-reference, "Ne'er saw I, never felt, a calm so deep," depicts that tranquillity as it affects the person of the poet. The composed—composured—mind then produces, by a stunning natural transfer, a sublime personification, first of the river, then of the houses and the city as a whole:

> Ne'er saw I, never felt, a calm so deep.
> The river glideth at his own sweet will:
> Dear God! the very houses seem asleep;
> And all that mighty heart is lying still!
>
> (11-14)

This transfer from person to personification is the point at which the poem becomes "touching." A curious, even contradictory personification (the City wearing bare beauty like a garment) falls away, and an altogether different kind of visionary metaphor appears. That new personification absorbs the poet, who is now only one locus of being, so that the line between person and personification is erased, or personification becomes what it should be. It is a moment Coleridge would have identified with the workings of Imagination rather than Fancy, and concerning which, as at the end of chapter 12 of *Biographia Literaria*, he might have quoted Jeremy Taylor: "He to whom all things are one, who draweth all things to one, and seeth all things in one, may enjoy true peace and rest of spirit."

It cannot be said that this sabbath vision reposes the will entirely but it does distinguish between the world as will and as representation. The "Dear God!" at the poem's climax not only recapitulates casually the paradox of intimacy and might, but reproduces as a verbal flow, as a spontaneous utterance, the "sweet will" attributed to the river. The cornerstone of Wordsworth's poetics, of his subtle style, is not to reject but to justify the personification of nature by grounding it once more in this excursive and animating language of the heart.

V

"Open unto the fields, and to the sky" so extends the horizon of visibility that it evokes a state "which knows not any line where being ends." The technique again is subtle: things "lie Open," and the qualifying "unto" intimates not only a horizontal direction (open as far as the sight can reach, even to the sky) but also a metadescriptive or mythical direction (open *to* the fields, and so undoing the boundary between city and country, yet also *up to* the sky in a vertical, ascensional manner). In "Tintern Abbey" a secluded rural scene connects with "the quiet of the sky"; here the city itself exceptionally points upward, as if it belonged to that region, more earthy or substantial than that sky, more firm than the firmament. Wordsworth will write in a sonnet of 1806:

> Nor will I praise a cloud, however bright,
> Disparaging Man's gifts, and proper food.
> Grove, isle, with every shape of sky-built dome,
> Though clad in colours beautiful and pure,
> Find in the heart of man no natural home:
> The immortal Mind craves objects that endure....

The emphasis, in the Westminster Bridge sonnet, should be on its initial word: "Earth." The thematic contrast, at least the emergent one, is between earth and sky rather than between Edenic countryside and smoky city. The image of the city, when industry begins to alienate it as a natural home or enduring object, is represented as a site of organic human power ("all that mighty heart") and saved from the temptation of visionary fantasies, skiey adventures. Wordsworth writes against his own foreboding, against nature's diminishing hold on the imagination during a revolutionary era of industry and war. This poem, consequently, as much an epitaph as a descriptive sonnet, is a faithful sign of the times. As a poetic marker, as an inscription, the sonnet can neither insist on itself by artificially heightening an effect of nature, nor not insist on itself as a memorial trace—for such impressions may be all of nature a future generation will know. The poet's reticence is considerable. He does not allow us to upset the wavering balance of his design by interpreting the tranquillity of this naturalized city as a dying rather than as a vital sign. A "good-bye" may ultimately have to be said to earth itself, to that world "which is the world of all of us," but here it is in the form of a blessing, not a viaticum, and a silent intuition, not an oracle. Yet the line, the border, between these states is as indeterminate and extensible as the prospect of the city itself, lying open in the way it lies open.

The act of description, in Wordsworth, tends to "compose" a precarious relation between signs and sensibility, between what befalls—accidents, incidents—and imaginative character—the active or prophetic mind, and perhaps the poetical character as such. Rarely has the very process of composition been regarded so intensely as a divination ("Another omen there!" Yeats writes, but far more comfortably). Wordsworth weighs every thought, every feeling; and the balance in which they are weighed is the poem, his composition of signs that, like absences ("smokeless") or uncertain presences ("wreaths of smoke"), may not be passed by.

Keats objected to the "palpable design" of some of Wordsworth's lyrics, accusing the poet of not remaining long enough in a state of "negative capability." It would be fairer to say that Wordsworth was literally worn out by "dim sadness and blind thoughts" that encompassed his perception of nature and made him cling to every auspicious hint that might counter them, even "one soft impulse saved from vacancy." This movement into vacancy, this dying of nature to the mind, is the condition he confronts; he would like to read it as a dying into the mind, a providential process related to the growth of a poet's mind ("internalization" we might now say), but he cannot neglect other, untoward readings. One is that nature is dying indeed, in the sense that the industrial revolution, or the era of which it is a symptom—an era racked by other turmoil also—is despoiling nature and destroying natural rhythms, so that by prophetic extension the human sensitivity to nature as a benevolent and calming force (a sensitivity which had barely developed in the century before Wordsworth) will soon be but a memory. Wordsworth, the poet of nature, is he already an Ancient of Days? The other fearful thought is simply that of mortality: a growing anxiety that his penchant toward repose and tranquility is a leaning, however premature, toward the grave.

> How strange, that all
> The terrors, pains, and early miseries,
> Regrets, vexations, lassitudes interfused
> Within my mind, should e'er have borne a part,
> And that a needful part, in making up
> The calm existence that is mine when I
> Am worthy of myself! Praise to the end!
>
> (1850 *Prelude* I, 344-50)

Even this "Praise to the end!" is not a simple benediction. It may be saying: I laud the end (calm of spirit, an assured identity) which those strange and adverse means have produced. It may also be saying: may I have the strength to praise what has happened to me, as I am doing now, to the very end—the end of my days. But if this second meaning is admitted, the word "end" in "Praise to the end!" anticipates death, and so praise of nature's role in the poet's psychic development becomes a praise of the death-principle, lending further precision to Freud's startling epigram: "The aim of life is death."

The careful reader cannot fail to catch the complex tenor of Wordsworth's utterances, especially when his theme is praise or complacency. It is often in these moments, foreign to a more modern sensibility, that Wordsworth is most elusive and most original. "Praise to the end!" seems to impose an optimistic turn on experiences that are dark or perplexing. I would agree that the optimism is sometimes stuck on; but I would also argue that it arises from an extraordinary resilience having to do with the *reading of signs*: with events that impinge like omens, sometimes even bad omens, yet are converted, explicitly or implicitly, into blessings.

VI

In the Westminster Bridge sonnet I have dealt with a tenuous and fortunate incident. It is time to adduce more dramatic examples. One is close to a literal curse and focuses on the shock words can give. When the young poet traveled to London at the age of 18 or 19, he heard, as he tells us in the *Prelude*,

> and for the first time in my life,
> The voice of woman utter blasphemy—
> Saw woman as she is, to open shame
> Abandoned, and the pride of public vice;
> I shuddered, for a barrier seemed at once
> Thrown in, that from humanity divorced
> Humanity, splitting the race of man
> In twain, yet leaving the same outward form
>
> (1850 *Prelude* VII, 384-91)

This "first time"—it comes surprisingly late—produces a double image: a separation from simplicity, a "splitting" like a psychic wound. ("This is, and is not *Cressid*," Shakespeare's Troilus cries when he has ocular proof of Cressida's infidelity. And Wordsworth in effect: this is, and is not, woman). Yet there is no wound except in the consciousness of the poet, since "the same outward form" remains. His "shudder" is therefore like a mimicry of what should be rather than what is: the *poet* intuits a visible wound; he wants the outward form changed to harmonize with inner reality. What is terrible is not simply the conjunction of "voice of woman" and "blasphemy" but that *the internal cause of this conjunction is not clearly marked*, not overt. The darkness is not made manifest except by a seeing through the ear.

Yet that there is no visible mark ultimately shelters the eye. Wordsworth may be afflicted with the thought that appearances betray, that the evidence of sight is deficient, and even when not deficient, unable to overcome (as was the case with Alypius in Augustine's *Confessions*) the power that images of shame ("open shame. . . pride of public vice") exert. Primarily, however, Wordsworth's anxiety focuses on the absence of correspondence between what is seen and what is heard. The fact that the human form is relatively immune to internal shock or change does more than disable sight: it saves it from the breach opened by words.

Let me follow more closely this movement toward immunity in Wordsworth. In the seventh book of *The Prelude* he describes another shock on a later visit to London, when he spotted a blind beggar in the midst of a crowd. It comes while he is distracted, even oppressed by the thought that his mind, in this over-crowding, cannot grasp what it sees: "The face of every one / That passes by me is a mystery." Again, he does not wish simply to pass by or be passed by, dull of soul.

> lost
> Amid the moving pageant, I was smitten
> Abruptly, with the view (a sight not rare)
> Of a blind Beggar, who, with upright face,
> Stood, propped against a wall, upon his chest
> Wearing a written paper, to explain
> His story, whence he came, and who he was.
> Caught by the spectacle my mind turned round
> As with the might of waters; an apt type
> This label seemed of the utmost we can know,
> Both of ourselves and of the universe;
> And, on the shape of that unmoving man,
> His steadfast face and sightless eyes, I gazed,
> As if admonished from another world.
>
> (1850 *Prelude* VII, 636-49)

This too, is a picture of "open shame." But the values of the "spectacle" are very different. Eye and voice are both sheltered here, so that the shock comes not from a radical disparity of sight and sound, of voice and human form, but from the character of the signpost or marker, which intimates a state of quasi-divine impassibility—nothing is left to be wounded. Life is reduced to a marker, a living stele with its inscription. This is, indeed, a sight that lies "beyond / The reach of common indication" (1850 *Prelude* VII, 635-36).

The absence of wounds is relative, of course. The poet's eyes are still vulnerable (he is "smitten") even if blindness makes the form of the beggar seem steadfast: the "written paper" is still like a voice in effect, even if as mute as the beggar is blind. The desire for immunity is stronger than the achieved immunity. Perhaps the subtlest distancing of shock comes in the very description of the effect of the beggar on Wordsworth. "My mind turned round" describes a reversal, a recognition strong enough to be traumatic, but it is naturalized by being deprived of specific direction and being subtly associated with the earth's own motion, the wheeling or rolling of the seasons prominent in Wordsworth's consciousness. What does the mind turn to, or turn back to? There are no signs here as a road, however crooked, might supply. "Indication" merges with the "dark, inscrutable workmanship" of natural process (1850 *Prelude* I, 341ff.).

This movement beyond markings or the desire for them, even beyond anything "exposed," I have discussed elsewhere, and linked to the wishful possession of a psyche "From all internal injury exempt."[4] The desire for an invulnerable or immortal state of being, as Freud realized in *Beyond the Pleasure Principle*, is hard to tell from the desire for inertia and even death. Seeking immunity, the psyche transfigures the wounded part. We approach here such a transfiguration. Wordsworth's stated moral concerns the simplicity or limit of what we can know of the "mystery" behind the human face, but that moral is conveyed through eyes that are baffled, smitten, occluded. To turn the catatonic image of a blind beggar, propped up like a stick, into a symbol of impassive, quasi-divine, invulnerable being, reveals, on the poet's side, a euphemism so extraordinary that we can risk the contagion of the episode, and call it blind as well as tacit. Wordsworth in his way stages as remarkable an act of blessing, saved from the jaws of its opposite, as when Job's wife is made to say to her suffering husband, "Bless God, and die" rather than "Curse God, and die."

Notes

Notes

2. A Touching Compulsion

1. *Prelude* II, 234-40. All references to *The Prelude* are to the version of 1850. On "intercourse of touch" see also *Prelude* II, 265-68.

2. On the concept of reality testing, see Freud, "Negation" (1925) in *The Complete Psychological Works* (Standard Edition), 19, 235-39 and the further references indicated there. Freud's "Verneinung" includes both negation as a *judgment* ("She is not there" or "It's not my mother") and negation as *denial* (the refusal to accept the reality-principle, or "Nature" as Wordsworth mythifies it). See also Freud's "Metaphysical Supplement to the Theory of Dreams" (1916) and J. Laplanche and J.B. Pontalis, *The Language of Psychoanalysis*, sv. "reality-testing."

3. Milton, *Samson Agonistes*, line 80; and cf. my *The Unmediated Vision* (New York, 1966), pp. 127ff. My remark on ears as less ghostly than eyes has to be modified by an analysis that would examine the link between poetry and "hearing voices" (see section IV of this essay). The visual stationing achieved in fiction or dreams may already be a way of giving voices that cannot be purged a "local habitation and a name." Despite Wordsworth's explicit statements, it may be the tyranny of the ghostly ear which poetry or nature seeks to counteract.

4. On the relation of visual desire to scientific construction including geometry, and the theory of light waves, and perhaps imaginative logic generally, there are a large number of texts, from Valéry's early essay on Leonardo da Vinci to Jacques Lacan's studies on "Speculation." In Wordsworth there is considerable ambivalence, of course, concerning the "geometric" habit of mind. See especially *Prelude* II, 203ff.

5. Cf. Ferdinand de Saussure's concept of the anagram developed in the notebooks presented by Jean Starobinski, *Les mots sous les mots* (Paris, 1970). The remarks I adjoin on mourning are influenced, of course, by Freud's essay "Mourning and Melancholia" (1917).

3. Inscriptions and Romantic Nature Poetry

1. *The Letters of Charles Lamb*, ed. E.V. Lucas, 2 vols. (London, 1935), 1:112. It is pleasing

to speculate that Wordsworth's verses (together with the boiling milk) may have been partially respon-
sible for "This Lime-Tree Bower." The central emblem in both poems is a retreat, a tree prison; and
Coleridge's mind, though meditating in solitude, follows a path contrary to that of the recluse by
attaching love of nature to the development of the social sense.

2. Though the "on" in Warton's title is only vestigially locative, and the poem could be placed
among such different genres of the eighteenth century as effusion, impromptu, and even ode, the poet's
situation (his sense of locality and spirit of place, and the fact that he responds to a work of art) relates
his poem to the inscription. The term *inscription*, of course, simply translates *epigram*. Warton wrote
an explicitly titled "Inscription in a Hermitage at Ansley-Hall, in Warwickshire" (composed 1758;
published 1777) and published in 1753 an inscription for a Grotto translated from the Greek Anthology. For other inscriptions, see the section under the title (and also under "Epigrammata") in
Richard Mant's edition of *The Poetical Works of Thomas Warton* (Oxford, 1802).

3. See R. Dodsley, "A Description of The Leasowes" (1764), affixed to the second volume
of Shenstone's *Works in Verse and Prose*.

4. The lemma seems to have been an explanatory comment added to the epigram during the
process of editing but which Renaissance fashion elaborated into a title. For the fashion, see H.H.
Hudson, *The Epigram in the English Renaissance* (Princeton, 1947), pp. 11-13.

5. The "left on" in Wordsworth's title, though generally equivalent to "written on," links his
poem also to the votive epigram which might be left under a picture, on a hearse, etc.—I have found
no study of the titling of poems. Lengthiness of title as well as the emerging significance of place and
date might also have been influenced by the journalistic broadside ballad which tended toward concrete and elaborate titles. One of them is parodied in Sir Walter Scott's *The Antiquary*: "Strange and
Wonderful News from Chipping-Norton, in the County of Oxon, of certain dreadful apparitions which
were seen in the air on the 26th of July 1610, at half an hour after nine o'clock at noon." Cf. "Verses
found under a Yew-Tree at Penshurst, July 18, 1791. By a Country Blacksmith" (from *Gentleman's
Magazine*) or "Written Sept. 1791, during a remarkable thunder storm, in which the moon was perfectly clear, while the tempest gathered in various directions near the earth" (Charlotte Smith, *Elegiac
Sonnets*, no. 59).

6. On this distinction, see n. 21 below.

7. *Zerstreute Anmerkungen über das Epigramm*, first published in *Vermischte Schriften* (Berlin,
1771). I use the translation in Hudson, *Epigram*, pp. 9-10.

8. Wordsworth, "Upon Epitaphs" (first essay). See *The Prose Works of William Wordsworth*,
ed. A.B. Grosart, 3 vols. (London, 1876), 2:32. E. Bernhardt-Kabisch in "Wordsworth: The
Monumental Poet" has discerned how profoundly epitaphs influenced Wordsworth's sensibility and
poetry (*Philological Quarterly* 44 (1965): 503-18).

9. This is not altered by the fact that a fashion for funeral urns and commemorative benches
prevailed in the second half of the century: see Dodsley. "A Description of The Leasowes," and J.
Delille's *Les Jardins* (1780), chant 4.

10. For general information about the Greek Anthology, I am mainly indebted to J.W. Mackail,
Select Epigrams from the Greek Anthology (New York, 1906), and the two invaluable books of James
Hutton: *The Greek Anthology in Italy to the Year 1800* (Ithaca, N.Y., 1935) and *The Greek Anthology
in France. . . to the Year 1800* (Ithaca, N.Y., 1946). Though the Anthology has individual parts devoted
to epitaphs and dedications respectively, it will become clear that, as Mackail observes in his introduction, "the earlier epigram [i.e., the Greek as distinguished from the Greco-Roman] falls almost
entirely under these two heads."

11. In English literature the naively paganizing strain is displaced by the hermit poem with its
Christian simplicities, but Wordsworth's lyrics on Matthew here and there touch on the spirit of the
older tradition. The sonnet, which was strongly related to the votive epigram and which allowed simple
personal (and first-person) sentiment, is too large a subject to be broached here. See, however, a significant remark in Coleridge's introduction to his sonnets in the 2nd (1797) edition of *Poems on Various*

Subjects: "Perhaps, if the Sonnet were comprized in less than fourteen lines, it would become a serious epigram.... The greater part of Warton's Sonnets are severe and masterly likenesses of the style of the Greek *epigrammata*."

12.   Jean Hagstrum in *The Sister Arts* (Chicago, 1958) covers—and recovers—this tradition as it extends from Dryden to Gray and clarifies its sources in earlier literature. I adopt his use of the term *iconic*. For Anna Seward's inscriptions, see *The Poetical Register and Repository of Fugitive Poetry for 1801*, pp. 177-80, 180-81.

13.   Quoted by Victor Lange, *Die Lyrik und ihr Publikum in England des 18. Jahrhunderts* (Weimar, 1935), p. 60.

14.   *Gentleman's Magazine* 78 (1808): 728, 924, 1020. T. Warton's "Inscription in a Hermitage" has been mentioned. Two more examples of interest are Mrs. West's "Inscription," *Gentleman's Magazine* 61 (1791): 68, and an anonymous "Ballad" in the *Poetical Register for 1802*, pp. 254-55. To the hermit poems, a devotional poetry in disguise, Wordsworth adds his "Inscriptions supposed to be found in and near a Hermit's Cell" (1818). They revert to the eighteenth-century quatrain style, though this is chastened, as the persona of the Hermit required, to hymnlike simplicity. Wordsworth practiced the conventional kind of inscription throughout his career: among his juvenilia are two versions of an inscription for a wayside bench which were never printed under his name, though one was published pseudonymously. His interest in Sir G. Beaumont's garden at Coleorton produces several further instances, and when he thinks he may have to leave Rydal Mount he composes an inscription to be placed in its grounds. The 1815 edition of his collected poems contains a section explicitly titled "Inscriptions." As late as 1830, remembering the old exhortation "Woodman, spare that tree," he writes some unusually playful verses on a stone saved from the builder's hand.

15.   W.L. Bowles, "Inscription," *The Poetical Works of William Lisle Bowles*, ed. Rev. G. Gilfillan, 2 vols. (Edinburgh, 1855); 1:155-56. The poem signs off: "Bremhil Garden, Sept. 1808." Bowles published a set of "Inscriptive Pieces" as early as 1801, distinguishing them from "Inscriptions" because of their more personal, impressionistic character; and his "Coombe Ellen," a blankverse poem "written in Radnorshire, September, 1798," shows more patently than "Tintern Abbey" a formal indebtedness to inscriptive poetry. See Bowles, *Poems* (London and Bath, 1801), 2:15-27, 87ff. On the influence of the early Bowles, see M.H. Abrams, "Structure and Style in the Greater Romantic Lyric," in *From Sensibility to Romanticism*, ed. F.W. Hilles and H. Bloom (New York, 1965), pp. 539-44.

16.   "On a Cave, From the Greek of Anyta, A Lesbian Poetess," in Thomas Warton the Elder, *Poems on Several Occasions* (1748).

17.   The middle of Bowles's poem, quoted above, reverts to the allegorizing which vitiates so many songs and descriptive pieces of the eighteenth and early nineteenth century. For a nondidactic allegorical song, see Shelley's "The Two Spirits: An Allegory" (1820). But the song, as a genre, has its own development and is not the subject of this essay.

18.   "For a Cavern that overlooks the River Avon" (written at Bristol, 1796). I have quoted the version in the *Poems* of 1797.

19.   *The Complete Poetical Works of S.T. Coleridge*, ed. E.H. Coleridge, 2 vols. (Oxford, 1912), 1:381-82. The capitalization of Twilight and Coolness shows how close the allegorical habit is, and how finely subdued.

20.   Hudson's *The Epigram in the English Renaissance* was left unfinished and covers but a small chronological area. Mr. Hutton was kind enough to communicate a list of authors indebted to the Greek Anthology, but the range, quality, and epoch of its possible influence would need a study as thorough as his own previous works. Much knowledge of Greek can be taken for granted (see the two books of M.L. Clarke: *Classical Education in Britain*, and *Greek Studies in England 1700-1830*); the Greek influence, moreover, was mediated by the best Latin writers in such poems as Horace's *Odes*—3.13 (to the Blandusian fountain) and 3.18 (address to Faunus), both of which spring from the votive epigram—and in Virgil's *Eclogues*, through which the blend of elegiac and pastoral poetry

first reached England. It is interesting that one book of English versions of the Anthology (only three small volumes of translation have come to my hand in the period under discussion, but this might be explained by the custom of rendering the Greek into Latin rather than English) was published in 1791 for the use of Winchester School of which Joseph Warton was headmaster, and that his brother Thomas was the first to publish in England an edition of selections from the Palatine ms. (*Anthologiæ Graecæ a C. Cephala Conditæ* [1766]). See also, for an example of the use of inscriptions in a popular novel, *Paul and Virginia*, tr. from B. de Saint-Pierre's French by H.M. Williams (1st ed. 1795), p. 86.

21.   On the difference between the Alexandrian (and earlier) epigram and the Augustan type, see Hudson, *Epigram*, pp. 6-9; Mackail, *Select Epigrams*, pp. 4-5; Hutton, *Greek Anthology in Italy*, pp. 55-56; and [R. Bland and J.H. Merivale,] *Translations chiefly from the Greek Anthology* (London, 1806), p. vii. Hutton states that "we preferably think of the Greek epigram as . . . the brief elegy, written before and during the Alexandrian age"; and Bland and Merivale say that "the small poems which claim the greatest attention, are those which are written as memorials of the dead, as tokens of regard for living beauty or virtue, or as passing observations and brief sketches of human life." Charles Batteux, interestingly enough, thinks the distinction between the two types of epigrams is one between the (earlier) *inscription* and the (later) *epigram*: "Plus on remonte vers l'antiquité, plus on trouve de simplicité dans les Epigrammes. . . . dans les commencements. . . L'Epigramme se confondait avec l'Inscription qui est simple par essence. Il suffisait alors que l'Epigramme fût courte, d'un sens clair & juste. Peu-à-peu on y a mis plus d'art & de finesse, & on a songé à en aiguiser la pointe" ("Traité de l'Epigramme et de l'Inscription," *Principes de la littérature* [Paris, 1774]). T. Warton's *Inscriptionum Romanorum Metricarum Delectus* (1758) tried to single out the simplest Roman inscriptions— so much so, in fact, that Shenstone writes they are too simple even for his taste. See *The Letters of William Shenstone*, ed. M. Williams (Oxford, 1939), p. 496.

22.   *Poems on Several Occasions* (1748). The exact date of the translations is unknown: the *Poems* are published posthumously by Joseph Warton.

23.   Three Shenstone poems under the title "Rural Inscriptions" were included in Dodsley's Collection of 1755. They are antique and simple only vis-à-vis the French-Italian tradition and cannot compare with Akenside's, which are genuine distillations of the mood and various types of the Greek votive epigram. Akenside seems almost to have written them against or in rivalry with Shenstone. All of the latter's inscriptions are given in Dodsley in his "A Description of The Leasowes."

24.   Southey acknowledges Akenside as follows in a prefatory note to *Poems* (1797): "The Inscriptions will be found to differ from the Greek simplicity of Akenside's in the point that generally concludes them." (But what Southey calls "point," Chaucer would have called "sentence.") In the 1837 edition of his poems Southey also mentions the later influence of Chiabrera, whose epitaphs had made a vivid impression on Wordsworth and Coleridge (see Wordsworth's "Essays upon Epitaphs" and his translations from Chiabrera). The Italian poet may himself be strongly indebted to the Greek Anthology. Coleridge's early imitation of Akenside was published, according to his editor, in the *Morning Chronicle* for September 23, 1794 (*Poetical Works* 1:69-70) and has nothing Akensidean about it. The theme is treated in rhyme and with the sentimentality of the contemporary pastoral ballad.

25.   I assert this with more conviction that I feel. There are, however, very few blank-verse lyrics which are not (1) translations or close imitations of the classics, (2) paraphrases of the Scriptures, or (3) borderline cases in which didactic and lyrical blend as in Thomson's influential didactic-descriptive *Seasons*. (Though not a short poem, it can easily be divided into short episodes.) Cf. the relevant chapters in the second volume of G. Saintsbury's *History of English Prosody* (New York, 1961); H.A. Beers, *A History of English Romanticism in the Eighteenth Century* (New York, 1899), chap. 4; and H.G. de Maar, *A History of Modern English Romanticism* (Oxford, 1924), vol. 1, chap. 8.

26.   Hudson, *Epigram*, p. 9.

27.   The two factors are probably related, since the Greek epitaph was the primitive form through

which nature poetry developed, but I keep them distinct to suggest the peculiar English interest in local poetry. Topographical antiquarian articles in, for example, *Gentleman's Magazine*, as well as numerous guidebooks, blend the interest in locality with interest in inscriptions and make the traveler a familiar figure of English landscape.

28.   *Poetical Works of William Wordsworth*, ed. E. de Selincourt, 5 vols. (Oxford, 1940-49), II, 2nd ed. (1952): 433. *Idyllium* was a conventional term for the kind of poetry represented by the idylls of Theocritus. Wordsworth esteemed Theocritus as a poet faithful to spirit of place and the simple, permanent manners (ethos) of his time. See his letter of February 7, 1799 to Coleridge, *Early Letters of William and Dorothy Wordsworth*, ed. E. de Selincourt (Oxford, 1935), pp. 221-22.

29.   "The Contemporaneity of the *Lyrical Ballads*," *PMLA* 69 (1954): 486-522.

30.   One sign of the change from indication to evocation in nature poetry is that consciousness of place and of the moment of composition are stronger. But before Wordsworth this shows itself mainly in the titles, which remain, as they must, an indicative device. It is significant that a late commentator claims that Warton's "Inscription in a Hermitage at Ansley-Hall, in Warwickshire" was composed "upon the spot, with all the objects around him, and on the spur of the moment." See *Gentleman's Magazine* 85 (1815): 387-88.

31.   Cf. Northrop Frye, "Toward Defining an Age of Sensibility," in *Fables of Identity* (New York, 1963). Frye overstates the degree to which, with the 1800 *Lyrical Ballads,* recollection in tranquillity took over from the Age of Sensibility's "concentration on the primitive process of writing" and "oracular process of composition." But his thesis is basically very sound and exciting. The 1800 *Lyrical Ballads* contain overtly identifiable inscriptions and also the "Poems on the Naming of Places" in which naming is a joyfully spontaneous act that almost escapes elegiac implications. About Wordsworth's primitivism compared to that of the poets of the Age of Sensibility, see below, esp. note 36.

32.   This fundamental attitude of reading the (epitaphic) characters of nature joins "The Ruined Cottage" (1797-98) to Bks. Vff. of *The Excursion*, composed more than ten years later, in which the village Pastor resuscitates his parishioners in a series of "living epitaphs."

33.   From the third sonnet of Wordsworth's *The River Duddon* (1820).

34.   "Epitomized biography" is Wordsworth's own phrase (Grosart, *Prose Works of Wordsworth*, 2:69). "The excellence belonging to the Greek inscriptions in honor of the dead," we read in the preface to [Bland and Merivale] *Translations chiefly from the Greek Anthology*, "consists in the happy introduction of their names and peculiar characters or occupations."

35.   [Bland and Merivale] *Translations chiefly from the Greek Anthology*, p. 30. I have slightly modified this still frigid version: cf. Mackail, *Select Epigrams*, p. 203. For Theocritus' wayside inscription, see *The Greek Bucolic Poets*, trans. J.M. Edmonds (London and New York, 1928), p. 367.

36.   The return to the archaic is found in most poets of the Age of Sensibility and in Wordsworth's own "Vale of Esthwaite." We may have to decide that there are two, interrelated kinds of greatness: one represented primarily by Wordsworth (the directest "poet of human heart"): the other by the tradition going from Collins to Blake and which Coleridge elected for his "Ancient Mariner."

37.   I adapt this to the Lucy poems from "She was a Phantom of delight." Lucy is a laric figure, if we admit that the fire she tends can burn in nature as well as in the home—that, in fact, nature and home are one to her. Compare Lucy as she appears in "I travelled among unknown men" with Louisa who "loves her fire, her cottage-home; / Yet o'er the moorland will she roam" ("Louisa" was also composed ca. 1801).

38.   One can think of "A slumber did my spirit seal" (called "a sublime epitaph" by Coleridge) as an epigram or brief elegy (see Hutton, *Greek Anthology in Italy*, p. 55). The sense of early and sudden death, the balance between personal lament and subdued hope in the living earth, and the casting of lament in the form of an epitomized action, are as if perfected from the Greek.

39.   Selincourt, *Poetical Works of William Wordsworth*, IV, 451-54. See also the 1800 *Lyrical Ballads*, and *Poetical Works*, IV, 68-73.

40. Rimbaud is probably the greatest exception to this general statement. French developments are especially complex: they begin with Chénier, whose favorite book was Brunck's edition of the Greek Anthology, and begin a second time with Lamartine and Hugo. But the older classicism was still so strong that a third insurrection, that of Rimbaud, was needed.

41. See *Collected Letters of Samuel Taylor Coleridge*, ed. E.L. Griggs, 2 vols. (Oxford, 1956), 1:450-53, and Selincourt, *The Early Letters of William and Dorothy Wordsworth*, pp. 203-11.

42. Wordsworth's split structure is curiously akin to the inscription's ecphrasis, in which the mute object, or its interpreter, addresses us. (The Beggar is such a mute object.)

43. The proper literary context was first pointed out by Leo Spitzer in *Comparative Literature* 7 (1955): 203-25, and was also noted by Hagstrum, *Sister Arts*, pp. 22-23. Both Spitzer and Hagstrum refer to a wealth of secondary literature showing the prevalence of art epigrams and their closeness to sepulchral epigrams.

4. False Themes and Gentle Minds

1. *On the Prospect of Peace* (1712, dated 1713).

2, *The Pleasures of Imagination*, 1st ed. (1741), Bk. 2.

3. A. Berquin, "Discours sur la Romance," in *Romances* (1776).

4. Written in 1749; published in 1799 in the *Transactions* of the Royal Society of Edinburgh.

5. *Ode on the Popular Superstitions*, xii.

6. E. Panofsky's study of Dürer's *Melencolia I* has pointed to one source of the modern idea of Genius in the Renaissance concept of "generous melancholy." See Klibansky, Panofsky, and Saxl, *Saturn and Melancholy* (New York, 1964), chap. 2, and also pp. 28ff. on *Il Penseroso*.

7. Emil Staiger, "Zu Bürgers 'Lenore,' vom literarischen Spiel zum Bekenntnis," *Stilwandel* (Zurich, 1963).

8. *Letters of Anna Seward, Written between the Years 1784 and 1807*, 6 vols. (Edinburgh, 1811), 4:231. The letter is from the year 1796, which saw five separate translations of *Lenore* published. See Alois Brandl, "Lenore in England" in Erich Schmidt, *Charakteristiken* (Berlin, 1902), pp. 235-38; also F.W. Stokoe, *German Influence in the English Romantic Period* (Cambridge, 1926).

9. "Von Ähnlichkeit der Mittlern Englischen und Deutschen Dichtkunst" (*Deutsches Museum*). How fast things were moving toward a recovery of the Romance heritage is evidenced by the fact that Goethe's *Urfaust* dates from 1775 and Wieland's *Oberon* ("the first long romantic poem of modern Europe," says W.W. Beyer in his *The Enchanted Forest*) was published in 1780.

10. "Aus Daniel Wunderlichs Buch" (*Deutsches Museum*, 1776). Bürger probably knew something of Percy's *Reliques*, although he did not study them till 1777. See Staiger, *Stilwandel*, p. 90; and Erich Schmidt, *Charackteristiken*, pp. 93-94.

11. The theme of the spectral horseman is most vivid, of course, in *Lenore*: on the folklore (popular) as distinct from the mythic (learned) basis, see Scott, *Ballads and Lyrical Pieces* (1806), introductory note to his translation of Bürger's poem. On the hunter lured into visionary experience cf. Malory's *Morte Darthur*, 1. 19-20; and D.C. Allen, *Image and Meaning* (Baltimore, 1960), pp. 99-101.

12. In Chaucer's *Pardoner's Tale*, where Death leads the hunt for Death, the Christian elements blend with, rather than overpower, such figures from Romance as the Old Man whose mode of being contrasts so movingly with the unreflecting action of the rioters.

13. Some remarks by Wordsworth on "character" versus "incidents" can be found in a letter to Coleridge on Bürger (Wordsworth read him in Germany during the winter of 1798-99). See *The Collected Letters of S.T. Coleridge*, ed. E.L. Griggs, 4 vols. (Oxford, 1956, 1959), 1 (1956): 565-66.

14. E.R. Curtius, *European Literature and the Latin Middle Ages* (London, 1953), chap. 6, "The Goddess Natura."

15.   Cf. also Coleridge's *Ancient Mariner*, with its obliquer use of the hunt theme, but overt moral: "He prayeth best who loveth best / All things both great and small."

5. Wordsworth and Goethe

1.   The quotations that follow are from "Über Ossian und die Lieder alter Völker," in *Von Deutscher Art und Kunst* (Hamburg, 1773). I have translated freely.

2.   Herder is referring, at one and the same time, to a mental experience and to his actual journey from Riga to France in 1769.

3.   J.P. Eckermann, *Gespräche mit Goethe* (1823-32).

4.   *Northern Antiquities...*, by Bishop Percy. New Edition, revised throughout, and considerably enlarged...by I.A. Blackwell (London, 1847), p. 243. I have been unable to trace these sentences to Mallet's original French edition (1755-56) or to Percy's original version (1770). The history of the *German* translations of Mallet is somewhat unclear: a section was translated into Danish in 1756, and the complete work was put into German in 1765-69 as *Geschichte von Dänemark*. Mit einer Vorrede von Gottfried Schütze. 3 bde. (Rostock, Griefswald bei A.F. Röse). The first part of this translation was reviewed by Herder in the *Königsbergsche Gelehrten und Politischen Zeitung* of 12 August 1765. "Es kann dies Buch eine Rüstkammer eines neuen Deutschen Genies seyn, das sich auf den Flügeln der Celtischen Einbildungskraft in neue Wolken erhebt und Gedichte schaffet, die uns angemessner wären, als die Mythologie der Römer." (I am grateful to Beth Gaskins for pointing out Herder's review.)

5.   The North/South or Celtic/Classic (etc.) dichotomy appears in standard form in Percy's preface to this volume, which was delayed till 1763. Percy singles out an exceptional feature of the ancient Danes: "It will be thought a paradox, that the same people, whose furious ravage destroyed the last poor remains of expiring genius among the Romans, should cherish it [poetry] with all possible care among their own countrymen: yet so it was. At least this was the case among the ancient Danes."

6.   "Though founded on a Danish tradition, this Ballad was originally written in German, and is the production of the celebrated Goethe, author of Werter, etc." (Lewis's note). Lewis was collecting materials for his "hobgoblin repast" as early as 1798; he had been to Weimar and seen Goethe in 1792; and he inserted translations of the "Erl-king's Daughter" and Goethe's "Erl-king" into the fourth edition (1798) of *The Monk*. Both of these poems had appeared in *The Monthly Mirror* for October 1796. Chapter 8 of the third volume of the original edition (1796) of *The Monk* already included "The Water-king—A Danish Ballad."

7.   Cf. "The Two April Mornings," also composed at this time, in which Emma's singing comes at a specific moment and is followed by death. The disconcerting contrast of numerals in "Nine summers" (the age at which Emma sang and died), "Six feet in earth," and even "Two April Mornings," seems to subvert the concept of "timely utterance" on which *lyrical* or *natural* poetry depends.

8.   See Appendix 1 for the full text of "The Danish Boy."

9.   E. de Selincourt, ed., *The Poetical Works of William Wordsworth*, 2nd ed. (Oxford, 1952), II, 493. That Wordsworth could be inspired to write as late as 1842 "The Norman Boy" (and its sequel) shows how deep the imaginative scene of a legendary child in a border-region or dreary Wild lay in him. This "Southern" (yet English) version of "The Danish Boy" has its own charm and climaxes in the vision of a "Chapel Oak" which seems to reconcile the orders of Nature, Religion, and Poetry (human artifice.)

10.   If one were to analyze the verbal style minutely, one would find in it a shifty series of self-weakening affirmations, corresponding to the decremental or declining plot-series in "We Are Seven" or "The Last of the Flock." Compare also the subversive interplay in "The Danish Boy" between "is" and "seems" or the reversal of the weak "there" ("There is") in "There sits he..."

11.   See esp. "The Ruined Cottage" (1798), later revised as *The Excursion*, Bk. I; also *The*

Excursion, Bks. VI-VII, entitled "The Churchyard among the Mountains," where the "silence" of the "characters" is of course the death of persons with universal or at least "type" features.

12. The kinship theme in these ballads or stories is remarkable. "With a brother's love / I blessed her" restitutes a broken "bond of brotherhood" the pedlar had noticed at the beginning.

13. See Appendix 2 for the text of "Der Erlkönig."

14. Friederich Gundolf, *Goethe* (Berlin, 1925), p. 507.

15. De Selincourt, *Poetical Works* II, 511.

16. Emil Staiger suggests that "anmutig" should be understood as "anmutend" (*Goethe* [Zürich, 1952], I, 342). The repeated rime "Wind" / "Kind" helps us travel back to childhood where such sensations had a durée which did not need the artifical support of poetry or story; it may even clarify the nature of the particular sensation by suggesting that this wind, like the child affected by it, is of more than natural origin. "Der Wind, der Wind, das Himmlische Kind." Goethe's comment on "Der Fischer," cited above, comes from remarks on the ballad in *Über Kunst und Altertum* (dritten Bandes erstes Heft, 1821).

17. What we know of Goethe's *Singspiel* suggests that its theme was that of the Lost Girl (Dortchen, who recites "The Erl-King"), and that its main theatrical effect was to have been that of an outdoors illumination provided by the torchlight of the search party. The theme of the Lost Girl (cf. the Lucy poems) is at least indirectly related to the Persephone myth and so to an Orphic katabasis.

18. Eckermann, *Gespräche mit Goethe* (1823-32).

19. "Dies Werden der Wissenschaft überhaupt oder des Wissens ist es, was diese Phänomenologie des Geistes darstellt. Das Wissen, wie es zuerst ist, oder der unmittelbare Geist ist das Geistlose, das sinnliche Bewusstein. Um zum eigentlichen Wissen zu werden, oder das Element der Wissenschaft, das ihr reiner Begriff selbst ist, zu erzeugen, hat es durch einen langen Weg sich hindurch zuarbeiten.— Dieses Werden, wie es in seinem Inhalte und den Gestalten, die sich in ihm zeigen, sich aufstellen wird, wird nicht das sein, was man zunächst unter einer Anleitung des unwissenschaftlichen Bewusstseins zur Wissenschaft sich vorstellt; auch etwas anderes, als die Begründung der Wissenschaft;—so ohnehin als die Begeisterung, die wie aus der Pistole mit dem absoluten Wissen unmittelbar anfängt und mit anderen Standpunkten dadurch schon fertig is, dass sie keine Notiz davon zu nehmen erklärt" (Hegel, "Vorrede," *Die Phänomenologie des Geistes* [1807]).

20. "Everything is hateful to me that intends only to instruct without at the same time increasing or directly stimulating my creative powers," are the words of Goethe with which Nietzsche introduces his *Vom Nutzen und Nachtheil der Historie für das Leben* (1874).

21. Moneta's accusation against Keats, or the figure of the Poet, in *The Fall of Hyperion: A Dream* (composed in 1819).

22. The notion of the "characteristic" (raised by Goethe as early as his "Von Deutscher Baukunst" included in Herder's *Von Deutscher Art und Kunst*) is, of course, a very complex one, especially in conjunction with nationalistic music-metaphysics that involved Rousseau, Gluck, Diderot, and others.

23. It is no accident that Richard Onorato's psychoanalytic study of Wordsworth is entitled *The Character of the Poet* (Princeton, 1971). On the concept of character in traditional poetics, and its relation to Wordsworth, see also Robert Langbaum, *The Poetry of Experience* (New York, 1957); and Herbert Lindenberger, *On Wordsworth's Prelude* (Princeton, 1963), pp. 15-40.

24. Goethe's Helena, is, it seems to me, the culmination of all these frigid ghostly beauties.

6. Blessing the Torrent

1. *The Poetical Works of William Wordsworth*, ed. E. de Selincourt and Helen Darbishire (Oxford: Clarendon, 1946) III, 43. The "1824" in the title is not found till 1836.

2. See 1850 *Prelude* VII, 643-44, the encounter with the blind beggar in London.

3. *The Letters of William and Dorothy Wordsworth: The Later Years*, ed. E. de Selincourt (Oxford: Clarendon, 1939) I, 155.

4. "Composed among the Ruins of a Castle in North Wales" and "To the Lady E.B. and the Hon. Miss P." *The Poetical Works of William Wordsworth*, III, 42-43.

5. See "Nuns fret not at their convent's narrow room" (published 1807) and 1805 *Prelude* VI, 553. A further interesting use of "narrow room," referring this time to "ancient Manners," occurs in prefatory stanzas that were addressed to his brother and that accompanied the River Duddon sonnets: "Remnants of love whose modest Sense / Thus into narrow room withdraws." See, for perhaps the first use of the phrase, *The Early Letters of William and Dorothy Wordsworth* (1787-1805), ed. E. de Selincourt (Oxford: Clarendon, 1935), p. 312.

6. The allusions are to the Greek mountain chain of Pindus, sacred to the Muses, and to the Greek War of Independence, where Byron had lost his life the year before. Since, moreover, the analogy of poetic inspiration to a stream is very old (Horace uses it of Pindar, e.g.), Wordsworth may be insinuating a question about the dignity of the vernacular muse (cf. "I seek the birthplace of a native stream," in the first of the River Duddon sonnets). This nativity quest is related to the Alpheus myth: here simply a feeling, not a myth, that wherever poetry appears it is the same river that has surfaced after running underground to reach its desired place.

7. I refer to the combined *topoi* of asking a god or angel his name and of finding it inexpressible. A third *topos*, more appropriate to this natural setting, is the address to an unknown god or spirit, or one variously named. As in Thomas Gray's "Alcaic Ode" (1741), inscribed in the Album of the Grande Chartreuse Monastery: "O Tu, severi religio loci, / Quocunque gaudes nomine (non leve / Nativa nam certe fluenta / Numen habet, veteresque silvas...)." Basically the form is that of the *hymnos kletikos* invoking a deity by name—here, asking for the name. Adjuration and apostrophe are classified by Longinus as sublime figures in his famous discussion of them: *Peri Hypsous*, Secs. 16 and 18.

8. First published as *Fourteen Sonnets, Elegiac and Descriptive*, in 1789. I am indebted to Walter Schindler for this reference.

9. "All streights, and none but streights, are wayes to them." John Donne, "Hymne to God my God, in my sicknesse." It is not certain that the scene from the chasm is precisely that described in 1805 *Prelude* VI, 553-72 though there does seem to be some conflation of the Ravine of Gondo and Viamala. But compared to that description in the *Prelude* the sonnet stresses the "peace" without the "tumult." "Woods, above woods" leaves a different impression from "the immeasurable height / Of woods decaying, never to be decayed" or "winds thwarting winds"; it may even recall Milton's depiction of the approach to Eden as "Shade above shade, a woody Theatre" (*Paradise Lost* IV, 141).

10. "Essays on Epitaphs" (1810) in *The Prose Works of William Wordsworth*, ed. W.J.B. Owen and J.W. Smyser (Oxford: Clarendon, 1974), II, 51. Naming a torrent created by the confluence of two streams (the one in Wales was fed by the Funack and the Rydol) is, in the light of this passage, a special instance of the problematics of location—of mapping by means of time, place, or word. Haunting confusions that unsettle the "repose" of the travelers—that disturb the stable location (identity) of place or time—also characterize the episodes following closely on the Simplon Pass experience (see 1805 *Prelude* VI, 617-54). Such expressions as "The sister streams of Life and Death" (1850 *Prelude* VI, 439; cf. *Descriptive Sketches*, 1, 72), referring to the "Guiers vif" and "Guiers mort" that mingle as one torrent, should also be noted. It is appropriate to conclude by returning to Wales and the "chasm" through which innumerable "waters, torrents, streams" roar with "one voice" (1805 *Prelude* XIII, 56-65).

11. *The Poetical Works of William Wordsworth*, III, 47. The Quillinans were living on the banks of the Rothay when their daughter was born in late 1821. The first Mrs. Quillinan died in May

1822. Wordsworth consented to Dora's marriage with Edward Quillinan in 1841. On naming, cf. Coleridge's christening his second child "Derwent."

12. "Passed away": literally of the Duddon entering the Irish Sea, the "Deep / Where mightiest rivers into powerless sleep / Sink," as Sonnet 32 says eloquently. For the ominous and apocalyptic meaning, see my *Wordsworth's Poetry* (1964; rpt. New Haven: Yale Univ. Press, 1971), p. 336.

13. "Poets, young or old," is also not unambiguous: it could mean poets in their youth and their old age or poets of olden times (Spenser, Drayton, etc.) and of the present day.

14. See "The Ruined Cottage," 499-500.

15. See 1805 *Prelude* V, 12 and MS variant of the Snowdon vision quoted by de Selincourt in his edition of *The Prelude* (2nd ed., rev. Helen Darbishire, Oxford: Clarendon, 1959), p. 622.

16. In bare summary: there can be an instability of the signified (is "How art thou named?" addressed to a god, river, or . . . ?), but there is no express instability of the signifier, as in James Joyce's "riverrun" of words. In Wordsworth the instability of the signifying phrase remains deeply implicit and can only be brought out by the echo effect Kenneth Burke calls "joycing." So "dread chasm / dead chasm" or even "dread chasm / d(r)ead calm." The conjunction of stable sign and unstable referent has a more uncanny effect (an effect, actually, hovering between homelessness and *unheimlichkeit*) than Joyce's pattern, which tends toward unstable sign and stable (if multiple) referent. The extraordinary thing in the case of "Viamala" is that both the name (sign) and the region denoted by it (referent) become unstable: the name "crosses" literal and figurative significations, and the region expands to cover various chasm experiences, each characterized by a chiasmic structure of narrowing and opening, constrictive and compensatory features.

17. It is likely that Wordsworth was thinking in *Descriptive Sketches*, 207-14, of the name "Devil's Bridge," though what is actually described is a wooden covered bridge and not the famous stone bridge of that name in the Viamala region. Dorothy Wordsworth's journal of the 1820 trip describes another Devil's Bridge, that in the Schöllenen gorge of the St. Gotthard pass, of which William Turner made a fine watercolor after his 1802 visit. (See *Turner in Switzerland* by Andrew Wilton [Zurich, 1976], pp. 60-63.)

> Ere long, winding to the right, we come into the narrow pass, till then unseen. The Devil's bridge is before us, and the cataract beyond, raging between the crags. From that point, the river tumbles down, in a succession of cataracts, to the glen which we had left behind . . . . The bridge, a single arch, light in appearance compared with the rocks above it, is built of grey granite which sparkles through an overgrowing of lichens, of the richest orange hue, that has crept over its walls and over the neighboring rocks. Three young kids were standing in perfect peacefulness, on a crag close to the bridge and the impassioned torrent, a living image of silence itself, in the midst of a deafening and dizzy tumult! . . . we enter under an arch hewn out of the rock, and pass through a long vaulted way, the roof continually dripping. This passage is imperfectly lighted in the middle by a hole hewn out in the side of the rock which lets in the sound of the river. I looked not through it, but made towards the outlet at the end, through which also the *light* is seen and nothing else. But all at once ere we are fairly out of this gloomy passage, the green, smooth and spacious Vale of Urseren. . . .
>
> (*Journals of Dorothy Wordsworth*, ed.
> E. de Selincourt [London, 1959], II, 186)

Some pages later she refers to her brother's previous journey. "The vale of Missox [is] on our left into which my Brother and Jones descended from the head of Como in their way to Urseren, crossing the Spluga, and taking the Via Mala in the Country of the Grisons" (p. 198). The Viamala of the St. Gotthard Pass region is clearly not the Simplon Pass region, yet there may have been a conflation of various "gloomy passage" experiences. In his well-known article on "Wordsworth and the Simplon Pass" Max Wildi points out that the chasm through which Wordsworth and Jones passed narrows at one point to a gap that "was impassable in earlier centuries, like the Schöllenen gorge at the Devil's

Bridge on the Gotthard route" (*English Studies*, 40 [1959], 229). Helena Maria Williams had written that "the only architecture which I thought admirable, were the performance of the Devil over the abysses of St. Gothard, and the tremendous chasms of the Via Mala" (*A Tour in Switzerland* [London, 1798], II, 35). As to "Devil's Bridge," the name, as we read in *The Penny Magazine* of the "Society for the Diffusion of Useful Knowledge" (No. 216, Aug. 1835), "is very generally applied to bridges placed in difficult and hazardous places, the popular ignorance of old times easily getting over the difficulty of their construction by attributing them to the evil one. There are many devil's bridges along the Alps, in Savoy, Switzerland, the Tyrol and the Grisons." D.V. Erdman has kindly drawn my attention to a topographical tract published in London, 1796, by George Cumberland, with the title *An Attempt to Describe HAFOD, and the Neighboring Scenes about the Bridge over the FUNACK, Commonly Called the DEVIL'S BRIDGE etc.* It refers to the same bridge that the *Penny Magazine* goes on to describe vividly. Cumberland intersperses his account with allusions to Milton, and stresses (like the *Penny Magazine*) that the Welsh waterfall is as grand as anything found in the Alps. He evokes the "incredibly stupendous chasm of intervolving valleys, clothed to their misty top with wood of—'Thickest covert, interwoven shade, a verdant wall,'" and how the torrent "pours headlong and impetuous. . .leaping from rock to rock, with fury, *literally* 'lash[ing] the mountain's sides'. . .and flashing at last into a fan-like form. . .[it falls] rattling among the loose stones of the Devil's Hole; where, to all appearance, it shoots into a gulph beneath," etc. This is also the Devil's Bridge and torrent Wordsworth visited, although placed by him in "North" Wales. Other descriptions of it can be found in B.H. Malkin, *The Scenery, Antiquities, and Biography, of South Wales, from Materials Collected during Two Excursions in The Year 1803* (London, 1804), pp. 364-68, and George Borrow, *Wild Wales* (1862), Chs: lxxii-lxxiv. As to "Devil's Hole," it reminds us of the "Verlorene Loch" in the Alps, so closely associated with Viamala.

> Beyond Thusis the valley takes a sudden rise of 984 feet, and through this the Hinter Rhine flows in a gorge nearly two miles long. Only skilled mountaineers were able to use the way near the river, and the main path led over the mountains. The remains of this "via strata" are still visible. This was called the "good road," and the valley path used by the chamois-hunters "the bad road." and the whole ravine, which could scarcely be used at all, was called the "Verlorene Loch."
>
> (F. Umlauft, *The Alps* [London, 1889], p. 144)

For a dramatic description of the same region, see Friederike Brun, *Tagebuch einer Reise durch die östlich südliche und italienische Schweitz, Ausgearbeitet in den Jahren 1798 und 1799* (Copenhagen, 1800), pp. 69-78. Hölderlin's "Der Rhein," from which my first epigraph is taken, seems conscious of similar reports or descriptions.

    18.   See 1850 *Prelude* XIII, 64, and the sonnet "To a Friend, Composed on the Road Leading to Ardres, August 7th, 1802." On the significance, vacillating between apocalyptic and edenic, of water (especially water-sound) imagery in Wordsworth, see my *The Unmediated Vision* (New Haven: Yale Univ. Press, 1954), pp. 29-35, 41-44.

7. Words, Wish, Worth

    1.   See pp. 116-119 below for the entire text of the poem, preceded by a bibliographical note. References to lines in the poem appear in parentheses.

    2.   But see my discussion of "voice" in Heidegger, pp. 111-112.

8. Diction and Defense

    1.   For the entire poem, see E. de Selincourt and H. Darbishire, eds., *The Poetical Works of William Wordsworth* (Oxford: Clarendon, 1947), Vol. 4, 92-94.

2. *The Tragedies of Sophocles*, trans. R. Potter (London: 1788), pp. 177-78.

3. For a full consideration of the poem's development, see Chapter 7 this volume, "Words, Wish, Worth."

4. "Iteration" means journeying as well as repetition, on the basis of the Latin *iter*. "Mournful iteration" has, in any case, a double referent, in that it alludes both to the internal, structural phrasing, "A little onward...a little further on," and to the temporal or historical echo of Oedipus' words by Milton's Samson. In what follows I do not mention all the Shakespearean echoes: the "brink precipitous," for example, can recall the imaginary cliff near Dover which in *King Lear*, act 4, plays a central role in the survival of Gloucester. He comes on stage "poorly led" (scene 1, line 9) and asks an Edgar, who is disguised and speaks with "altered voice" (scene 6, line 7), to lead him up a cliff "from whence / I shall no leading need" (scene 1, line 78). Edgar pretends to do his bidding and persuades his father, by a fanciful description of the supposed precipice, that he has jumped down and survived. Cf. also *Hamlet* I, iv, 69.

5. Lear's pathetic mimicry of the sentinel's role (Edgar replies "Sweet Marjoram," Lear says "Pass," then comes "Gloucester's "I know that voice") also links words to defenses via the notion of password.

6. Ophelia, too, when she becomes mad, knows "There's tricks i' th' world," and her "speech is nothing" (IV, v, 5ff.) even if "This nothing's more than matter" (IV, v, 177).

9. Use and Abuse of Structural Analysis

1. "Interpretation and Descriptive Poetry," *New Literary History*, 4 (1973), 229-57. All my quotations from Riffaterre are from this essay and will not be footnoted further.

2. For a fuller understanding of Riffaterre, the reader is referred to his *Essais de Stylistique Structurale* (Paris, 1971), and an article focusing on the question of literary history, "The Stylistic Approach to Literary History," *New Literary History*, 2 (1970), 39-55. Needless to say Riffaterre's structuralism is one of many types; but I try to emphasize what he has in common with structural method generally. He stands close, on the one hand, to Leo Spitzer's historically oriented stylistics, and, on the other hand, to the structural semantics of A.J. Greimas. His approach is also important for raising the issue of the "perceptibility" of structure, or what reading (reader) model we ideally posit when interpreting a text.

3. "The voices come in a continuous stream, a continuous revelation. Through them rise recognitions of immortality and, simultaneously, a repose in the moral and creative will, since they suggest both the final peace and the final judgment which is God's alone.... The fundamental relation may be described as one between light and sound, light and revelation." *The Unmediated Vision* (New Haven, 1954), pp. 42-43.

4. Cf. *The Unmediated Vision*, p. 22, and *Wordsworth's Poetry, 1787-1814* (New Haven, 1964), p. 182. In "Expostulation and Reply" (1798) the poet affirms explicitly that "there are Powers / Which of themselves our minds impress."

5. Mary Moorman is so struck by this "first sign of a change in Wordsworth's handling of natural themes—the introduction of mythical or allegorical figures into the natural landscape" that she associates "Yew-Trees" with "Laodamia" (1814) and Wordsworth's intensified interest in the classics. See *William Wordsworth: The Later Years* (Oxford, 1965), pp. 273-74.

6. See the Appendix for two poems of this kind. Cf. also Cowper's "Yardley Oak" (1791) for a significant allusion to the oracle tree. On trees in Wordsworth, see Jonathan Wordsworth, *The Music of Humanity* (New York, 1969), pp. 118-20; and on the genius loci concept, my *Beyond Formalism* (New Haven, 1970), pp. 212ff., and 311ff.

7. See Wordsworth's "Mutability" in *Ecclesiastical Sonnets* (1822) and "A slumber did my spirit seal" (1800).

8. 1850 *Prelude* XIV, 126-27. The affinity of *Aeneid* VI, 276ff., was pointed out by Moorman, p. 273.

9. "Ode on the Power of Sound" (1828, 1835). Cf. Hartman, *The Fate of Reading* (Chicago, 1975), pp. 289ff.

10. 1850 *Prelude* II, 309.

11. It begins "Pass not the [? Place] unvisited—Ye will say / That Mona's Druid Oaks composed a Fane / Less awful than this grove. . . ." Ernest de Selincourt, ed., *The Poetical Works of William Wordsworth*, (Oxford, 1952), vol. II, p. 210.

12. Cf. *Wordsworth's Poetry*, p. 122.

13. 1850 *Prelude* XIII, 290-91.

14. For "pining" see the analysis in Brooks and Warren, *Understanding Poetry* 3rd ed. (New York, 1960), p. 276.

15. Cf. the "Conclusion" to *Ecclesiastical Sonnets*, "Why sleeps the future."

16. 1850 *Prelude* VI, 480-81; XIII, 327; V, 595-99; XIV, 71-73.

17. *The Notebooks of S.T. Coleridge*, ed. Kathleen Coburn (New York, 1961), II (Text), Entry 2453; copyright © 1961 by Bollingen Foundation, rpt. by permission of Princeton University Press.

18. "The Nightingale. A Conversation Poem." First published in *Lyrical Ballads* (1798).

19. I have quoted the poem as revised for the second edition (1800) of *Lyrical Ballads*.

20. Cf. James A.W. Heffernan, *Wordsworth's Theory of Poetry* (Ithaca, 1969), pp. 134-35.

21. "Christabel" is also a night poem but where the obverse danger to streaminess, of not being able to move on (toward dawn or awakening), and so again being a prisoner of the dark, is represented.

22. *Biographia Literaria* (1818), opening of Ch. 10. Cf. also Entry 4244 in the *Notebooks*, III (Text): "The interpenetration of the absolute opposites (which could not *be*, & yet be absolute *opposites*, if they were not the manifestation of *one*), & the perfecting synthetic Third, = Depth, = Gravitation = Galvanism = Chemical Combination—! And these are all the reflected Image of 'I' boundless because I; 'I' bounded because of self-intuitive, & self-intuitive because 'I'—thence I in itself, & the Not-I or Thing itself—& all restored again to its Unity in the Imagination or Eisenoplasy."

23. I borrow the pun from Coleridge's *The Destiny of Nations* (1796), line 100.

24. *Notebooks of S.T. Coleridge*, II (Text), Entries 2623f. Reproduced with permission.

25. On that involvement see Thomas McFarland, *Coleridge and the Pantheist Tradition* (Oxford, 1969).

26. 1850 *Prelude* I, 341-44.

27. *Notebooks of S.T. Coleridge*, III (Text), Entry 4243. The date is uncertain but probably ca. 1815. The words kept in Greek, *Australis* and *Axiologus*, refer, respectively, to Southey and Wordsworth. The latter is also alluded to as "Septentrionismou," i.e., of the North (cf. South-ey).

28. "Ode: Intimations of Immortality" (composed 1802-04), stanza 11.

29. Thomas Gray, "Alcaic Ode" (composed 1741). It became well known and was often translated after Mason published it in 1775.

30. Coleridge, "Dejection Ode" (1802).

31. Keats, *The Fall of Hyperion*, I, 167-69. The debate goes back, of course, to that between the active and the contemplative life; but with Thomson's publication of *The Castle of Indolence* (1748), the role of pastoral and (Spenserian) romance enters this debate in a new way. Wordsworth's not entirely happy consciousness concerning "rest" emerges naively in his poem on "Gipsies" (1807) and more basically in his Introduction to the *Prelude*, I (1850), 1-105.

32. This date is disputed. Wordsworth's Fenwick note assigns the poem to 1803, but Mark Reed, in *Wordsworth: The Chronology of the Middle Years* (Cambridge, Mass., 1975), finds no evidence of its composition before Sept. 1804. See his "General Chronological List," item 123 and note; also his main "Chronology," item 107. It is possible that the Lorton yew verses were composed ca. 1804, and the rest between 1811 and late 1814. Even if a portion of the poem postdates 1803, much

depends, as in *The Prelude*, on the poet's self-image, or how he placed himself retrospectively while composing. The 1803 date assigned by Wordsworth may reflect the remembered poetic consciousness of ca. 1803.

33. "Ode: Intimations of Immortality," stanza 3. Is there in the sound shape of "cataracts" a scramble association with "Characters," as in "Characters of the great Apocalypse," *Prelude* (1850) VI, 638?

34. "Home at Grasmere" (composed between 1800 and 1806).

35. "Ode: Intimations of Immortality," stanza 3. The preceding paragraph should suggest that Wordsworth's emphasis on memory is countervailing rather than regressive: an attempt to save "contemporaneity" from futuristic fears and philosophies.

36. Cowper, "Yardley Oak."

10. Timely Utterance

1. "The Immortality Ode," reprinted in *The Liberal Imagination* (1948).

2. That we are reluctant to develop the resonances of a critic's prose, even a critic as deliberate as Trilling, does not mean they are not felt. Ironically, Trilling's answer, when it does come (in the fourth section of his essay) is one that leads to a displacement from one phrase or word-complex to another, and so enlightens without disburdening the poem.

3. "Surprised by joy,—impatient as the wind," (1815).

4. Cf. in the second stanza of "A slumber did my spirit seal" the verse "Rolled round in earth's diurnal course." An image of *gravitation* elides or displaces that of the *grave*; and the tacit verbal pun is reenforced by the fact that "di*ur*nal" is followed by "course," a word that sounds like the archaic poetic pronunciation of "corpse." (I owe "course-corpse" to Jay Farness.) Could one show, in Wordsworth, a convergence of nature's eliding (subliming) of the corpse, and poetry's eliding (subliming) of the referent?

5. See Trilling, *The Liberal Imagination* (New York, 1953), p. 130.

6. I agree with Paul de Man ("The Dead-End of Formalist Criticism," *Blindness and Insight*, 2nd ed., 1983) in his understanding of pastoral as much more than convention or genre. "There is no doubt that the pastoral theme is, in fact, the only poetic theme, that it is poetry itself." De Man's insight comes by way of a critique of Empson and the doctrine of "reconciliation," a critique that limits the rigorous and principled criticism initiated by Richards.

7. The placement of "unknown" causes an ambiguity. It could refer to the bond or to its character vis-à-vis the receiver. "An unknown bond was given—to me, who was unaware (unknowing) of it at the time." The "unknown" points to what is knowable yet difficult to locate as conscious knowledge at a single spot in time. Its place in the verse-line is self-displacing.

11. The Poetics of Prophecy

1. Ordinary language, like ordinary incident, does indeed become very condensed and tricky here. "Thither I repaired," writes Wordsworth of the crag (l.296), and again, toward the end, "to which I oft repaired" (l.325), referring to the voluntary, sometimes involuntary, return of memory to the haunting scene. This "repaired" means simply "to go," the "re-" functioning as an intensifying particle. But in the second use of the word, the "re-" inclines the word toward its original sense of "return," or more specifically, "return to one's native country," *repatriare*. So that the first "repaired" may already contain proleptically the sense of returning to the father's house: climbing the crag is the first step in a conscious yet unconscious desire to overgo time and repatriate oneself, return home, to the father. The relation of "repair" to its etymological source is as tacit as unconscious process; so it may simply be a sport of language that when Wordsworth introduces the notion of "spots

of time'' a hundred or so lines before this, he also uses the word, though in its other root meaning of "restore," from *reparare*:

> There are in our existence spots of time,
> That with distinct pre-eminence retain
> A renovating virtue, whence, depressed
> By false opinion and contentious thought,
> Or aught of heavier or more deadly weight,
> In trivial occupations, and the round
> Of ordinary intercourse, our minds
> Are nourished and invisibly repaired:
>
> (1850 *Prelude* XII, 208-15)

Though the young Wordsworth repairs to that which should nourish and repair (his father's house), he finds on the crag houseless or homeless phenomena, which hint at a stationary and endless patience. Whether "repair" may also have echoed in Wordsworth's mind as the re-pairing of man and nature (ll.298-302, which call hawthorn and sheep his "companions," as well as "kindred" [l.324], suggest his integration into a nonhuman family at the very point that the human one seems to fall away) must be left as moot as the foregoing speculations. The latter may suggest, however, not only the overdetermination of Wordsworth's deceptively translucent diction, but the consistency of his wish to join together what has been parted.

12. Elation in Hegel and Wordsworth

1. Paragraph numbering is that of *Phenomenology of Spirit*, translated by A.V. Miller (Clarendon, Oxford, 1977). For the translation I have also consulted J.B. Baillie's *The Phenomenology of Mind* (2nd ed., London and New York, 1949).

2. Cf. Paul de Man, "Landscape in Wordsworth and Yeats," *In Defense of Reading*, eds. R. Brower and R. Poirier.

3. See "On Significance in Music," in *Philosophy in A New Key* (Cambridge, Mass., 1942), ch. 8.

4. See *Articulate Energy* (London, 1952), ch. 2.

5. "The Bridle of Pegasus," in *Coleridge on Imagination* (New York, 1935), ch. 9.

6. See *Lords of Limit* (London, 1984).

7. They differ from the massive architecture of ancient funeral monuments and animate or replace even the grace of Greek statuary. "The perfect element in which inwardness is just as external as externality is inward is once again speech" (726). This, at least, is the ideal.

8. Letter to Carlyle, 12 March 1835.

9. *The Psychology of Elation* (New York, 1950).

10. Edited by H.G. Hotho in 1835; now available as *Aesthetics: Lectures on Fine Art*, tr. T.M. Knox, 2 vols. (Oxford, Clarendon Press, 1975). The passage in question is found on pp. 480-81.

13. Wordsworth before Heidegger

1. See *Sein und Zeit* (first edition, 1927) as reprinted by the Max Niemeyer Verlag, Tübingen, 1963. For the English version, see *Being and Time*, translated by John Macquarrie and Edward Robinson (Harper and Rowe: New York and Evanston, 1962).

2. The most important book on this subject is Hans Blumenberg's *Die Legitimität der Neuzeit*, first published by Suhrkamp (Frankfurt am Main) in 1966, but revised and lengthened as *Der Prozess der theoretischen Neugierde* in 1973 and again in 1974.

3. *An Introduction to Metaphysics*, tr. Ralph Manheim (Yale University Press, New Haven, 1974). I occasionally modify this translation. For the German version, see *Einführung in die Metaphysik* (Niemeyer: Tübingen, 1953).

4. Cf. Walter Benjamin, on "The Task of the Translator" (1923) in *Illuminations*, tr. Harry Zohn (Harcourt, Brace and World: New York, 1968), which quotes Pannwitz: "Our translations, even the best ones, proceed from a wrong premise. They want to turn Hindi, Greek, English into German instead of turning German into Hindi, Greek, English" (p. 80). Parallel thoughts are expressed by Franz Rosenzweig in the 1920s, when he asks the translator of (especially) Scripture "not to adapt the foreign tongue to German, but German to the foreign tongue." In *Franz Rosenzweig: His Life and Thought*, presented by Nahum N. Glatzer (Schocken: New York, 1953, 1961²), pp. 252ff.

5. See the opening pages of *An Introduction to Metaphysics*. The question of the possibility of metaphysics was renewed by Kant in his *Prolegomena to Any Future Metaphysics* (1783). It was on Kant that Heidegger worked immediately following *Being and Time*; and an interesting though very general account of his dispute with Cassirer about Kant during a conference at Davos in 1929 is found in Hendrick J. Pos, "Recollections of Ernst Cassirer," *The Philosophy of Ernst Cassirer*, ed. P.A. Schilpp (The Library of Living Philosophers, Evanston, 1949), pp. 66-69. Such subjects as the "influence of the inner linguistic form of Greek" on "the construction of metaphysical concepts" which also interested Cassirer (Pos, p. 71) constitute another parallel. For a concise and open view of Heidegger's use of and concern with language, see George Steiner, *Martin Heidegger* (The Viking Press: New York, 1978).

6. My text throughout is that of the Ode's first publication in *Poems in Two Volumes* (1807), as given in the reprint edited by Helen Darbishire (Oxford: Clarendon, 1952²).

7. On the quiet use of paradox and pun, cf. Cleanth Brooks, *The Well-Wrought Urn: Studies in the Structure of Poetry* (Harcourt Brace and World: New York, 1947), ch. 7: "Wordsworth and the Paradox of the Imagination."

8. The vision of the moon on Snowdon, in the last book of Wordsworth's autobiographical *The Prelude*, presents the "naked" orb as "the emblem of a mind / That feeds upon infinity, that broods / Over the dark abyss, intent to hear / Its voices issuing forth to silent light." In Coleridge's "The Rime of the Ancyent Mariner," published in Wordsworth's and Coleridge's *Lyrical Ballads* of 1798, a spectral voice projects the obverse image: " 'Still as a Slave before his Lord, / The Ocean hath no blast: / His great bright eye most silently / Up to the moon is cast—.' "

14. The Unremarkable Poet

1. I do not know whether it has been noticed, but something in the enumeration "Ships, towers, domes, theatres, and temples" may call to mind Prospero's famous lines (*The Tempest*, IV.iv) on the vanished rural masque. He foretells a similar vanishing to the more substantial "pageant" of earth: "And, like the baseless fabric of this vision, / The cloud-capt towers, the gorgeous palaces, / The solemn temples, the great globe itself, / Yea, all which it inherit, shall dissolve." It would be too tenuous an exercise to compare Shakespeare's "baseless" and Wordsworth's "smokeless"; but the fair show seen from Westminster Bridge is viewed by the poet as Earth's own "majestic vision" (*The Tempest*, IV.iii) that promises to stand more firmly than Prospero's enactment of his "present fancies."

2. Time-switching is felt even on the simplest biographical level. There is evidence that the poem was composed (or started) on the way to France at the end of July; by 3 September Wordsworth was back in London and must have recrossed the bridge, so that there may be a conflation (or mental retraveling) as so often in his poetry. For another conflation, also involving bridges and morning, see my "Blessing the Torrent," Chapter 6 of this book.

3. See especially the section "The Poem as Response" in Michael Riffaterre's still valuable essay called "Describing Poetic Structures: Two Approaches to Baudelaire's *Les chats*," in *Structuralism*, ed. Jacques Ehrmann (New York: Anchor Books, 1970).

4. "A Touching Compulsion," Chapter 2 of this book.

Index

Index

Theory and History of Literature

Geoffrey H. Hartman is Karl Young Professor of English and Comparative Literature at Yale University. His *Wordsworth's Poetry*, winner of the 1965 Christian Gauss Award, will be reissued by Harvard University Press this year. His other books include *The Unmediated Vision*; *Beyond Formalism*; *The Fate of Reading*; *Criticism in the Wilderness: The Study of Literature Today*; *Saving the Text: Literature/Derrida/Philosophy*; and *Easy Pieces*. Hartman also served as editor of *Bitburg in Moral and Political Perspective* a collection of essays that grew out of Ronald Reagan's visit, in May 1985, to a World War II cemetery in Bitburg, West Germany. Hartman numbers among his lectureships the Gauss Seminar at Princeton University and the Clark Lectures at Trinity College, Cambridge.

Donald G. Marshall is professor of English at the University of Iowa. Marshall's principal work is in literary theory and its history. He is editor of *Literature as Philosophy: Philosophy as Literature*, to be published by the University of Iowa Press in 1987; his essays and reviews have appeared in *Partisan Review, boundary 2, Diacritics,* and other journals.